The Cartel System of States

The Cartel System of States

An Economic Theory of International Politics

AVIDIT ACHARYA
ALEXANDER LEE

OXFORD
UNIVERSITY PRESS

OXFORD
UNIVERSITY PRESS

Oxford University Press is a department of the University of Oxford.
It furthers the University's objective of excellence in research, scholarship,
and education by publishing worldwide. Oxford is a registered trade mark of
Oxford University Press in the UK and certain other countries.

Published in the United States of America by Oxford University Press
198 Madison Avenue, New York, NY 10016, United States of America.

Library of Congress Cataloging-in-Publication Data

Names: Acharya, Avidit, author. | Lee, Alexander (Alexander Mark), author.
Title: The cartel system of states : an economic theory of international
politics / Avidit Acharya, Alexander Lee.
Description: New York, NY : Oxford University Press, 2023. |
Includes bibliographical references and index.
Identifiers: LCCN 2022041781 | ISBN 9780197632260 (hardback) |
ISBN 9780197632277 (paperback) | ISBN 9780197632291 (epub)
Subjects: LCSH: Boundaries—Economic aspects. | Territory,
National—Economic aspects. | International relations—Economic aspects.
| Sovereignty. | State, The.
Classification: LCC JC323 .A35 2023 | DDC 320.1/2—dc23/eng/20221024
LC record available at https://lccn.loc.gov/2022041781

1 3 5 7 9 8 6 4 2

Marquis, Canada

For Katie, my love
A.A.

For my teachers, Mrs. Walker, Mr. Toy and Jim Scott
A.L.

Contents

List of Figures and Images

List of Figures

List of Images

Acknowledgments

Parts of this book and our paper titled "Economic Foundations of the Territorial State System" on which some of it is based, were presented to audiences at Stanford, NYU, the University of Rochester, the Barcelona GSE summer forum, UC-Irvine, UCSD, Yale, and APSA. We are grateful to all of the participants for their valuable feedback.*

This project was originally conceived while one of the authors was a post doctoral fellow at Stanford's Center on Democracy, Development and the Rule of Law. We thank Steve Stedman, Larry Diamond, and the other fellows for their advice during this period.

Some individuals deserve special thanks. Two individuals in particular provided special inspiration for this project. Steve Krasner's work on sovereignty has been an inspiration to both of us. It was his comments about the Macartney mission that led us to think more carefully about the expansion of the European cartel to the rest of the world. Jim Scott's works on the motivations and actions of states in domestic politics inspired us more than a decade ago to think about ways in which his ideas could be extended to international relations. We are grateful to these two individuals for their support and encouragement over the years.

Jim Fearon and Ken Schultz gave us numerous helpful comments on many aspects of the book. But one that stands out and deserves mention is an idea that led to our discussion of African borders in Chapter 4.

Conversations and correspondences with Alexandre Debs influenced our view on the role of interstate conflict in our argument, and along with suggestions by Jim Fearon led us to include a critique of offense-defense balance theory, which is popular among IR realists. We are also grateful to Barry Weingast for his advice on how to situate our contribution and relate it to the standard way of thinking in IR.

Comments from David Stasavage were also very helpful. One question that he asked us was how our theory of the state system as an exploitative cartel could survive past the advent of democracy when power was devolved

* The paper, Acharya and Lee (2018), appeared in the *American Journal of Political Science*, and its online appendix from which some material is drawn here is available in the working paper version, available at: http://stanford.edu/~avidit/statesystem.pdf.

to the broader citizenry. A related issue came up in a brief but instructive email exchange with Robert Keohane. Their comments and questions led us to substantially revise and reframe the argument about democracy that we make in Chapter 5.

Didac Queralt raised questions about who the term "ruler" represents in our theory, and where these rulers come from. His questions led us to add comments and clarifications on this throughout the manuscript, especially in Chapters 2, 5, and 7.

Jordan Branch suggested that our model of space could also have non-territorial interpretations, which informs our discussion in the final chapter of the book on the evolution of the state system in the last century. In particular, what we are explaining in this book is not territoriality per se, but market division. His comments led to major improvements in Chapter 2. We have also learned a lot from reading his work on related topics.

Melissa Lee got us to think about how our model would work in weak state settings. In fact, her comments have impacted every chapter of the book. She helped us navigate some related literatures in international relations that we were previously unfamiliar with. Her own work on governance and governance capacity has influenced our thinking on the topic.

David Carter and Hein Goemans both interrogated the boundaries of our arguments, especially those related to international border fixity and change. Comments from them were very helpful in improving Chapters 2, 3, and 6. Both of us are lucky to have had the privilege of having Hein as a fantastically supportive colleague at different times.

Tom Romer reminded us that international institutions like the United Nations have not always worked to deter the entry of new states into the state system; during the period of decolonization, for example, these institutions worked to welcome many new countries into the state system. He urged us to think carefully about the role of these institutions.

Ken Scheve gave us detailed comments on every part of the book. He has been a remarkably supportive colleague. His comments encouraged us to think more carefully about the role that international institutions play in our argument. It is not clear that we have adequately addressed his critiques on these topics, but we have tried to acknowledge them throughout the manuscript, and our work has improved as a result.

Gary Cox asked us a question regarding the portability of our model of borders to the feudal world in which kings would use boundaries to aid in selling fiefs. We thought about this question (and the portability of our model to other settings) for a long time. Although we do not address it in the book, his question led us to some alternative interpretations of our model, some of which are alluded to in Chapter 2.

Steve Haber reminded us that although we emphasize the European origins of the cartel system, there are many non-European precedents as well. Comments from him also led us to separate two claims that were mixed up in the early drafts as well as our published paper—that cartel theory provides a useful lens with which we can view the state system as it exists today, and that the state system originated historically as a cartel. One does not have to believe the second claim to appreciate the first.

Conversations with David Laitin were helpful in improving our discussion of nationalism, not as an alternative explanation for the state system, but as a phenomenon that helps stabilize borders even if states did not invest in the creation of national identities for this purpose.

Conversations with Judy Goldstein influenced our ideas in Chapter 7 in which we delve into issues in modern international political economy. Judy has been a very supportive colleague while providing frank and incisive criticisms of our work.

In a conversation over drinks, Jon Elster challenged one of us to define the term "sovereignty." Completely disarmed by the question, we revisited the way we were previously using the term, and decided to use it more carefully and more sparingly than we had been.

Paul Sniderman's comments on how to frame our contribution were particularly helpful. In fact, they led us to completely rewrite our introduction, focusing more on our main points and getting to them more efficiently.

The junior faculty group at the University of Rochester is a remarkable group of young intellectuals that has expanded our thinking on many topics, and provided a constant spur to work harder and more theoretically. We are especially grateful to Scott Abramson, Jack Paine, and Bethany Lacina. In addition, our senior colleagues at Rochester also provided encouragement on this project. Besides Hein, we are especially grateful to Randy Stone, Gretchen Helmke, and John Duggan. Research is easier when such colleagues make the other parts of the academic endeavor easier.

Many conversations with our colleagues and friends helped us realize that this was not going to be a traditional international relations book, nor was it going to be a comparative politics book. After getting tenure in our respective departments, we happily abandoned any ambition that it would be either, and fully embraced the political economy approach that we take.

We are also grateful to three fantastic graduate students—Christina Toen-shoff, Zuhad Hai, and Denis Tchaouchev—who not only provided expert research assistance, but also contributed many useful comments and criticisms and helped us navigate the many literatures that the book touches on, some of which we were unfamiliar with and learned from them.

We also thank five reviewers of the book manuscript for their comments, and the anonymous reviewers who gave us feedback on our paper. We are especially grateful to Lisa Blaydes, Mark Dincecco, Andrew Coe, Vicky Fouka, and Francisco Garfias for giving us comments on the paper that have influenced this book as well.

We are grateful to the Stanford political science department for sponsoring our book conference and to the staff, especially Eliana Vasquez for her help in organizing the event, and Joy Li for helping us secure permissions to reproduce several of the images that appear in the book. We also thank the staff of the University of Rochester Political Science department, especially AnneMarie Tyll, for their administrative support. We thank Katy Robinson for compiling the comments that we received at our book conference, and for her participation and contributions as well. We thank Bill Kte'pi for editing the manuscript, and we thank our editor Dave McBride at Oxford for being a patient and reliable partner through the whole process.

Finally, we are grateful to our families.

Avi is grateful to his parents, Jayaraj and Usha, and brother, Achal, for their love and support. He is especially grateful to his loving wife, Katie, who has been in his corner for so long, and who encouraged him to power through and finish the project even during the dark days of the Covid lockdown when childcare was unavailable. He also thanks his father-in-law, Claude, for helping with the kids during that time, and for taking an interest in the project. He looks forward to the day that his two boys, Devin and Theo, will read the book and find out for themselves what Baba was doing at his computer all that time.

Alex is grateful to Mark, Therese, Matt, Rebecca, and Nathan. The state system may be interesting, but family is what makes life worth living.

A.A.
Palo Alto, CA

A.L.
Rochester, NY

1

Introduction

A View from the US-Canada Border

Neche, North Dakota (population 371), and Gretna, Manitoba (population 541), are two towns that lie on opposite sides of the US-Canada border. Gretna was settled in the mid-19th century after the 1818 Anglo-American Convention established the 49th parallel as the US-Canada border in much of the region west of the Great Lakes. Neche was laid out a couple decades later.

The two communities are very similar, and they are in fact each other's nearest neighbors. Residents frequently cross the border, for example to buy gas in Neche or eat out at Nora's Diner in Gretna. At the same time, however, the border between these two communities corresponds to a sharp change in political authority that has profound consequences. The residents of Gretna are Canadian residents; are subject to Canadian laws; pay their taxes to the various tiers of Canadian government; and enjoy access to Canadian public services such as Canadian government healthcare. The residents of Neche, on the other hand, are residents of the United States; are subject to American laws; pay their taxes to the various tiers of American government; and enjoy American public infrastructure and services, such as American roads and highways, public schools and universities.

That the international border between places like Gretna and Neche is so meaningful is a fact of modern political life—one that many of us have come to take for granted even when it is the cause of remarkable inconveniences. Consider another example of a town on the US-Canada border: Point Roberts, Washington, which lies on the southernmost tip of the Tsawwassen Peninsula, just across the Strait of Georgia from mainland Washington. Residents of this enclave must cross the US-Canada border twice when traveling to other parts of the United States. Because of this, they do much of their shopping for goods and services in Canada. But they cannot do all of their commerce in Canada, for some important Canadian services are not available to them. The town has no hospital, doctor, or

The Cartel System of States: An Economic Theory of International Politics. Avidit Acharya and Alexander Lee, Oxford University Press. © Oxford University Press 2023. DOI:10.1093/oso/9780197632277.003.0001

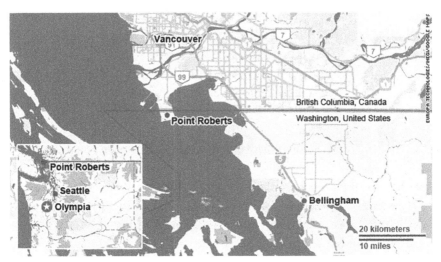

Point Roberts, Washington, is a small American enclave. Its residents must cross the US border twice to access important services in the nearest American city of Bellingham, Washington, even though these services are provided in Vancouver, British Columbia, which is much closer. Why do they have to put up with these inconveniences?

dentist, and American insurers do not pay for coverage by Canadian health care providers. In cases of emergency, the residents of Point Roberts have to get care in Bellingham, Washington, even though Vancouver is much closer.

Enclaves like Point Roberts exist around the world. They are curious to us, but not just because of the interesting events that led to their creation. Equally important is the degree to which they highlight how borders often conflict with the interests of the people who live near them. As citizens of a thriving democracy, the inconveniences experienced by the residents of Point Roberts are not as great as they would be in other examples from developing countries (the last remaining *chitmahal* of Bangladesh in India, for example), and perhaps most of them could easily choose to move elsewhere if they wanted. But the continued existence of an enclave like this on the US-Canada border is still a curiosity. If the residents of Point Roberts could access all of the services available in Vancouver but not in their small community, life would certainly be more convenient for them.

In modern times, international borders reflect discontinuous changes in political authority, no matter what the inconveniences and inefficiencies are for the individuals that are separated by them.

The Questions

Borders are one of the most tangible features of the international state system—a system that exists now almost universally. What explains this fact? Why are the citizens of neighboring regions that happen to lie across an international border often subject to very different governance systems? These questions are the subject of this book.

To put these questions in perspective, consider the fact that in much of human history, borders did not carry the same degree of political significance that they do today. Borders have existed since antiquity, but the tremendous social and economic implications for life in the neighboring regions that they separate are relatively new, associated with the rise of modern territorial states. Western Europe in the medieval and early modern periods, for example, did not have territorial states in the modern sense of this term. A few ambitious polities, such as the papacy and the Holy Roman Empire, claimed universal (or at least undefined) dominion, while the rulers of numerous smaller units—city-states, duchies, baronies—contented themselves with less than absolute political authority.

The borders between these units were correspondingly fuzzy, with personal loyalty and feudal obedience being more important than territorial division. Unlike the residents of today's Gretna and Neche, skillful elites like the Valois dukes of Burgundy who lived in borderlands between two larger polities played their neighbors off against each other to great benefit.*

All of this changed over the last half millennium. By the time the League of Nations was formed in 1920, both the big empires and small feudal polities had disappeared in Europe, either evolving into or being absorbed into the modern territorial states that claimed absolute internal control and freedom from external influence, and which recognized one another as possessing these traits. Most borders were formally demarcated on the ground and recognized by the relevant states. Universal claims were abandoned as either farcical or dangerous. Stephen Krasner (1993, 261) puts it succinctly: "the clearest storyline of the last thousand years is the extruding out of universal alternatives to the sovereign state."

---

* Outside of Europe, Tokugawa Japan and Mughal India similarly contained hundreds of lordships and cities that exercised autonomous political authority, raising taxes and waging war, much as modern states do. At the same time, these units acknowledged some degree of authority held by higher-level political authorities, perhaps paying them some tribute, sending contingents to their wars, and allowing appeals to their courts.

As more and more borders became formally demarcated, a state system emerged that sought to guarantee the traits of modern statehood to those of the world's polities that came to be recognized by their peers as states. This system continued to develop from the early modern period through the 20th century as new states emerged. By the end of the period of decolonization, the European conception of statehood and territoriality had spread to virtually the entire world. The limits of the newly created states were defined by borders of unprecedented salience. And while the intervention of more powerful states in less powerful ones continues to this day, these interventions have become increasingly cloaked in an elaborate regard for the political independence of even the most powerless states.

How do we understand the modern state system as it exists and continues to develop? What purpose does it serve? And what effect does it have on the lives of people—the individuals that it governs?

Another way to provide perspective on these questions is to consider some hypothetical alternatives to the current state system. Imagine, for a moment, a world in which the residents of towns like Neche and Gretna that we mentioned above could decide for themselves if they wanted to pay a portion of their taxes to the Canadian government to buy in to Canadian health care while also paying taxes to the US government to enjoy access to American public services, such as the ability to enjoy in-state tuition in nearby public colleges. We could even ask this question of cities, towns, and communities that are not border communities. Why can't public services be bought piecemeal, on an *à la carte* basis, with governments competing with one another to provide higher quality services at the lowest cost, in some marketplace for government services? Even if governments demand that all of their services be purchased together, or that there are synergies from having all services provided by a single government, why are most citizens not allowed to choose which bundle they will purchase instead of being assigned to a government based on birth or residence? If the basic rules of economics apply, this competition would be good for citizens since governments would be compelled to provide more and better services at lower costs, or else be driven out of the market. Why haven't citizens living in two bordering democracies voted to implement such a competitive market system in the provision of governance?

We argue that the defining feature of the modern territorial state system is the local, bounded, monopoly that states have in governing their citizens. States refuse to violate each other's monopolies even when they could do so easily. Even attempts to seize territory by force have become rarer over time. We examine what makes this system stable, when and how it emerged, how it spread, how it has been challenged, what led it to be so resilient over time, and how might it evolve in the future.

The State System as an Economic Cartel

The territorial state system represents an economic cartel. It is an agreement among states to divide what we call the *market for governance* in ways that reduce competition and deter entry, at the expense of their citizens. The system exists because early states were governed by rulers that were farsighted and self-interested, always seeking to maximize their power over their citizens and enrich themselves.

While many of us—especially those of us who live in democracies where citizens enjoy a high quality of life and hold their leaders accountable—do not think of states in such exploitative terms, the vast majority of states in human history were founded and designed to serve the interests of their rulers at the expense of their citizens. The modern French state, for example, originated in the efforts of King Philip Augustus to consolidate power over the territories that would become France, and his descendants ruled exploitatively over their subjects until the French Revolution. So, although power is sometimes distributed in a more egalitarian manner today (a point to which we will return below) we will proceed for the moment with the historically accurate assumption that most states were built to serve the interests of a relatively small ruling class.

In our cartel theory, the term *governance* refers to a package of services that states provide to their citizens. The most basic of these are protection and dispute resolution, but states can also provide a wide range of modern public services and infrastructure, such as education, health care, and scientific research. Because these services have value, there is a demand for them, whether they are provided by the state, by other actors, or not provided at all. Since there is both a demand for these services and a supply, we say that there is a market for governance. This is the loose sense in which we use the term *market*.

A key premise of our theory is that the market for governance has the potential to be competitive. Communities or powerful individuals facing taxes that they consider too high relative to the benefits they receive may instead join another polity. Individuals that are placed between two states can potentially pit them against each other, demanding more services or less taxation in return for their allegiance. The tax rates paid by individuals for these services are regulated by the availability of alternative states or providers, and the costs that those providers face in delivering the services. Individuals in a competitive governance market will pay a price for services that is only a small markup above the costs of the competing states, with the more efficient states offering the most competitive prices. Individuals in noncompetitive markets, however, pay a monopoly price, which can be substantially greater than the cost of providing the services. This is a feature that the governance market shares with other markets. Citizens in a town with a single hardware store, for instance, will pay more for their nails than those of a town with multiple, competitive hardware stores.

The cost of providing governance for each state varies spatially. Each state possesses a zone, often (but not always) around the capital, where its ability to extract resources and apply coercive force is very high. The farther away from this zone the state attempts to expand, the longer communications become, the farther armies have to travel, and the more unfamiliar local society becomes to officials. All of these features raise the costs of providing governance relative to the taxes that can be extracted from these peripheral areas. Hawaii is more costly for the United States government to administer and defend than Pennsylvania, and the Amazon is more costly for Brazil to govern than Minas Gerais.

The increase of cost with distance is not necessarily linear. Topography can have a crucial impact on the spread of state administration, with flat settled areas easy to administer than rougher terrain that may be closer. Culture and language also affect the costs of governing. It is cheaper to govern individuals who share the same culture and language as the administrators of the state, and express a loyalty to the state through their sense of national identity.

Taking this variation in costs into account, as we move from the center of one state, we may be moving towards the center of another. This will have an effect on the taxes that the state would collect under a competitive system, since its residents living near the border have an outside option. By threatening, even if only implicitly, to switch their allegiance to a rival polity, these border residents may be able to extract concessions, usually in the form of lower taxes, increased services, or increased local autonomy. Put in economic terms, competition in the governance market is accompanied by lower prices and higher levels of services. In colonial India, for example, the British Raj was the main provider of governance and thus had broad discretion in setting tax rates. On the North-West Frontier, however, where the colonial government was competing with the Afghan government, the state not only did not collect land taxes but also furnished the local khans with generous subsidies.

The desire to eliminate unstable, unprofitable border zones has been an important motivation in the creation of the state system. The system is a product of cooperation among rulers against their citizens, where rulers divide the governance market among themselves and agree to not provide governance outside their borders. Since each state is now a local monopolist in the provision of governance, individuals must pay them the monopoly price, leading to higher tax burdens.

In our theory, the individual is the actor who receives governance. However, in most historical cases only relatively powerful individuals, such as medieval counts and African chieftains, played a political role and engaged in the types of calculations we discuss. These local elites provided whatever government occurred in the ungoverned space between larger states, and bargained with their larger neighbors. In modern times, it is not just individual citizens who are the relevant actors but also businesses and corporations, both national and multi-national. When we say that competition in the governance market favors individuals, it is worth emphasizing that the individuals in question are often only the powerful, who are able to arrogate the gains to competition to themselves.

The state system that we describe resembles an economic cartel in many respects. Just as Archer Daniels Midland and its Japanese and Korean competitors distributed the global market in lysine among themselves in the 1990s, or Osram, General Electric, Associated Electrical Industries, and Philips divided the global market in lightbulbs in the 1920s, contemporary states divide among themselves the right to tax and govern the world. This coordination could occur in large multilateral meetings like the Congress of Vienna or the Treaty of Versailles which deliberately redrew the boundaries of much of the world to allocate and reallocate shares of the governance market to different states. But more typically, it occurred in bilateral treaties between neighbors that adhere to a loose set of international norms. By limiting competition, the members of the cartel can charge their citizens much higher prices (taxes) than they would be able to otherwise.

What makes the cartel system stable? Unlike most modern economic cartels, the state system is untroubled by the legal anti-trust restrictions on collusion that exist in many countries. However, very much like economic cartels, the state system is haunted by the specter of cheating—the fear that one player will attempt to steal the market share of others. The territorial division that is characteristic of the contemporary state system is a means for reducing this type of cheating. Violations of the norm of noncompetition are easier to police when they are unambiguous and visible. The mutually agreed, demarcated territorial border serves as a marker of political division between one taxing monopoly and another. While a medieval border violation may be difficult to separate from the legitimate exercise of political authority, any state that tries to govern outside of its internationally recognized borders today is clearly violating the norms of the system. These violations do occur in practice, but they are often very indirect.

It is this mutual recognition of territorial sovereignty that sets states apart from other political units, rather than the efficiency of their institutions. In fact, some states, such as many in contemporary Africa, are so institutionally weak that they are unable to provide much in the way of state services, or to extract much in the way of taxes. These efficiency problems might doom these states in a perfectly competitive system—they may be replaced by new states or gobbled up by their neighbors, possibly with the cooperation of some of their own citizens. But, instead, the state system guarantees them a share of the market, much as economic cartels can also guarantee the survival of inefficient producers. Even failed states that are unable to provide a minimal amount of state services outside their capitals are considered the formal equals of more competent states.

Cooperation between states can be made self-enforcing with the help of strategies that punish deviating states for violations of the cooperative norm. While a state might gain revenues by collecting taxes from its neighbors' citizens, this would lead to a loss of future revenue, as then the cheating state would have to reduce taxes in the face of competition for the allegiance of its own border residents. However, it may still be in a state's interests to seek to alter the border in its favor. To reduce such attempts, the state system has developed a complicated set of norms that discourage the unilateral initiation of conflict and annexation of territory.

There is another important way in which borders have become more stable. Since most, though not all, states nationalize their citizens (through public education, state media, etc.) many individuals are socialized to be loyal to a particular state, and prefer its governance to any other. In the context of cartel theory, this means that today even substantial financial concessions would not convince the citizens of many states to switch governments; indeed, many of them are prepared to die rather than accept doing so. Borders, even the most seemingly arbitrary ones, can over time come to correspond to steep changes in governance costs. This extreme and self-reinforcing brand loyalty, which we call nationalism, is an important difference between economic and governance cartels. It is a key to both the latter's exceptional stability and why competitive alternatives to the system are so rarely considered, even in theory.

How does cartel theory help explain the puzzle of discontinuous political changes that take place at international borders? The residents of Neche or Gretna or Point Roberts cannot buy government service across the border because the governments of the United States and Canada have mutually agreed that they cannot do this. As long as this agreement between the states is in effect, both governments can then provide levels of taxation and services that are unconstrained by the threat of competition. This benefits states at the expense of citizens. This is the argument that we lay out and develop in this book.

The Origins and Growth of the Cartel

Cartel theory helps us understand the origins of the territorial state system in early modern Europe, its spread to the rest of the world, and its development through the centuries. Both in the field of history and in political science, quite a bit of ink has been spilled theorizing about the origins of this system. We argue in Chapter 3 that it developed in Europe as rulers sought to exert control over the peripheral areas of their growing states, where their influence came into contact with the influence of other rulers. In Chapter 4 we discuss the spread of the cartel system to the rest of the world through colonialism and other Western influences.

In pre-modern times, states had difficulty projecting their power over great distances, due to the fact that governance costs were sharply increasing in distance away from the state's administrative centers. News and orders could travel no faster than a man on horseback, literacy was limited, and military technology and bureaucratic institutions were primitive. Vast amounts of territory in pre-modern Europe were not governed by any of the bureaucracies of the larger polities. Consequently, the central governing institutions of one large ruler hardly came into contact with that of another.

These lands, controlled by local elites (the feudal nobility), lay in the marginal spaces between the administrative centers of the largest polities.

It was not until the invention of gunpowder and improvements in military and bureaucratic organization that took place gradually starting in the late medieval period that the high costs of governing began to decline. Rulers started being able to exert control over territory farther away from their capitals with greater ease and sophistication, and developed organized administrative practices to do so. At the same time, the profitability of long-distance trade made these faraway places valuable to colonizers and conquerors. Rulers came to appreciate being able to tax commerce in distant regions that would previously have been unprofitable.

The true boundaries of states thus shifted outward. More and more people were incorporated as citizens of these growing states. Areas that were previously ungoverned by the central administration of a ruler growing in power disappeared as the true boundaries of one growing state came in contact with the true boundaries of another. Eventually, there reached a point where these rulers could not incorporate one another into their growing polities, and therefore could not increase their influence further without becoming competitors in the market for governance in the regions in which their influence overlapped. This competition threatened the profits they could earn from governing these places, and they started to devise plans to avoid their losses. They signed border treaties, developed bilateral agreements to respect each other's rights to govern within their borders, exchanged ambassadors to facilitate communication, and entered into multilateral agreements involving many players.

The non-European world before the 19th century had many similarities to medieval Europe, with a few powerful polities that claimed broad dominion (e.g., Qing China and the Mali Empire) that were separated from each other by vast stretches of space inhabited by small political units of "barbarians." As in Europe, these empires considered it unprofitable to even attempt to govern in distant areas. However, in the 19th century, the natural evolution of governance systems of these parts of the world was disrupted with the conquests of European powers.

Europe imposed its own state system on the rest of the world largely by force. In some polities that were not colonized, such as China and Japan, rulers were intimidated into adopting the evolved practices of the European state system, such as mutual recognition of sovereignty and the exchange of ambassadors. In most of Africa, South and Southeast Asia, and the New World, by contrast, Europeans divided and controlled territory themselves.

The process of colonial map drawing was made easier by the actors involved abiding by the rules of the system at home, and in some cases by the replacement of native populations with Europeans who were already familiar with such a system. For these reasons, colonial state-building exercises such as the Congress of Berlin were in many ways a purer demonstration of the logic of the cartel theory than the bilateral agreements that fixed the borders between European polities. A small group of leaders of the most powerful states divided the rights to govern Africa among themselves, and did so with sharp lines on a map. They negotiated with an eye to their own profit and internal balance of power and no concern for the interests of the native populations. Despite the artificiality of colonial boundaries, so many of them have remained stable, with the new rulers who control post-independence capitals seeing the advantages that their status as rulers of modern states gives them over other political actors within their borders.

In economic cartels, firms usually set out at a precise moment in time to create the cartel. Anti-trust prosecutors can sometimes even point to a specific meeting or unearth the secret communications that led to the start of collusion. The state system, on the other hand, was created by people who may have had no intention of creating a new global order, and who might well have been ideologically opposed to the state system as it exists today.* Rather, over several centuries, statesmen simply sought to shape bilateral relations with other states in ways that benefited them mutually, at the expense of local elites in the frontier zone. Even in the 19th century, when the triumph of territorially bounded states over alternative political arrangements seemed complete, the state system was less a conscious, intentional arrangement than a complex agglomeration of bilateral relationships. Yet as these bilateral arrangements became more sophisticated and widespread, they generated a set of norms that became widely accepted. It is precisely these norms that represent what we mean by the state system.

The Development of the Cartel over Time

If the state system represents simply a set of norms, how is it so stable? Norms tend to change over long periods of time, especially in the face of a changing environment, and often in unpredictable ways. The cartel system too has

---

* In fact, this is why attempts to identify a single point of origin, such as the Peace of Westphalia, have failed. We say more about this at the end of Chapter 2.

faced some major, potentially destabilizing challenges over the course of its history. But it has dealt with these challenges with remarkable success. In Chapter 5 we discuss three of these challenges, and in Chapter 6 we discuss two factors that have enabled the cartel to overcome these challenges. We summarize these as follows.

Conflict. An important threat faced by the cartel has been the challenge of interstate conflict, which represents the possibility that more efficient and more powerful states will steal the governance market share of less capable ones. But the cartel has handled this challenge with notable success. Even the two great wars of the last century did not unravel the system, and following the end of World War II interstate wars have become even more uncommon. How has the cartel survived the destruction of interstate conflict? How has it made interstate war as rare as it is?

We can draw a loose analogy between interstate conflict and the challenges that economic cartels face in managing price wars between their members, or fights to control market share ("turf"). Wars can be understood within the cartel system as ways of credibly communicating changes in relative market power. As the strength and efficiency of one supplier improves, it is natural for it to seek a greater share of the market. But at the same time, it is difficult for others to know whether the claims of that provider are based on real improvements in efficiency or strength. If a state is willing to go to war over a piece of territory only if these improvements are real (and state efficiency is associated with success in war) then war serves as a mechanism that credibly resolves the dispute. In this model, once the war is over, the cartel members return to cooperation. They continue to recognize each other's sovereignty, or at least the limits of their own claims. Just as it is possible for oligopolists to return to collusion after their relationship is briefly destabilized by a price war, so too is it possible for states to return to cooperation after a period of conflict. In cartel theory, brief periods of war are not at all inconsistent with long spells of cooperation.

Entry Deterrence. Another important challenge faced by the cartel is the threat of entry into the governance market by opportunistic actors seeking to establish new states. The threat of entry is certainly a real threat—the number of countries in the world has grown over time, especially in key periods such as the period of decolonization and the end of the Cold War. But the number of states today is still much smaller than the number of areas whose elites would like to establish their own states. How has the cartel virtually eliminated both territorial war and unilateral entry (i.e., entry without the consent of the existing cartel members)?

We discuss entry deterrence by building on the idea that an important objective of any successful cartel is to suppress the emergence of new market entrants, an act that may require coordination among its existing members. Throughout history, groups that have attempted to challenge existing cartel members have been labeled as rebels, pirates, or terrorists. They have been cut off from international assistance and have occasionally been the targets of coercion. In some notable instances, the efforts of these opportunistic market entrants have succeeded; but in a great number of cases, they have failed. The Rif State in Morocco, the Confederate States of America, and the Biafran secession in Nigeria are examples of moderately successful states that failed to gain de jure recognition from existing cartel members. Somaliland is a polity that has remained unrecognized for nearly three decades despite developing many state institutions. Even regimes that control all of a state's recognized territory, like Afghanistan's Taliban today, could be denied recognition if other states consider them unreliable participants in the governance cartel.

At the same time, there have been some critical moments in history when incumbent states actively welcomed the entry of new states into the world system rather than deterred their entry. Belgium, Algeria, and Ukraine are examples of successful new states that were able to win recognition from the existing cartel and claim a share of the governance market. Cartel theory attributes their success to an alignment of interests between the entrants and the most powerful states, who led the cartel's response on behalf of the smaller and weaker cartel members. Belgian independence was favored by Britain; the dissolution of colonial empires was actively encouraged by the newly powerful United States and Soviet Union; and the dismemberment of the Soviet Union following the end of the Cold War was actively supported by the lone superpower at the time, the United States, along with its Western European allies. In all of these cases, the great powers that led the cartel believed that they could more easily exercise influence over the smaller new states than the larger old ones. The point is that the cartel is typically powerful enough to decide who has the right to enter, and will allow entry if it suits the interests of its most powerful members.*

---

* This is part of the argument Coggins (2014) makes.

Democracy. Over the course of the 20th century, the number of democracies grew, and established democracies greatly expanded voting rights. This growth in democracy, however, points to a puzzle: If the cartel is an exploitative system that serves the interests of states and their rulers at the expense of their citizens, why wasn't the system undermined following the advent of democracy? Wouldn't citizens vote to replace the governance monopolies that they face with a system in which there is more competition in the governance market—if competition benefits them?

At least in the early days, the expansion of democracy certainly did not undermine the cartel system, which became ever more stable in the 20th century. To explain this fact, we offer a simple model whose logic proceeds in three steps. First, we point out that the cartel helps rulers exploit their citizens, and this is true whether the "ruler" is an autocrat or the pivotal voter (or powerful special interest group) in a democracy. Second, we note that incrementally increasing competition in the governance market typically benefits only a minority of citizens at each step. Third, we draw on standard political economy models that assume that democracies redistribute what they collect from taxes back to the populace, in the form of transfers, social insurance, and public services that benefit the citizenry. If opening up the governance market to foreign competition reduces what the state can collect from a minority of citizens, then under balanced-budget redistribution, it necessarily harms the interests of the majority of net receivers. As a consequence, the majority of citizens may oppose incremental increases in competition in the governance market.

This argument hinges on the assumption that opening up competition in the governance market would have to take place in incremental steps. This assumption is motivated by the fact that the main development that has increased competition in the governance market in the last half century— namely, the lowering of trade barriers between states—has in fact proceeded incrementally. To increase competition in the governance market in any other way would carry significant transition costs, and result in massive and uncertain changes in how power is divided within and across societies. This uncertainty is a powerful force that can lead to inertia, as is often argued in theories of institutional stability and path dependence.[1]

It was mainly the industrialized democracies of the West that led the effort to open up competition in the governance market following World War II by promoting globalization and free trade. While these policies create winners and losers, the most powerful political interests in an industrial democracy (producers with lobbying power or the majority of consumers) typically benefit from this enhanced competition in the governance market. By contrast, support for free labor mobility has been comparatively weaker as most of these countries still heavily regulate immigration. This is not surprising since it is natural for voters to seek the kind of competition in the governance market that enhances their own consumer surplus, not that of other populations seeking to migrate into their societies.* The more general point is that voters and special interest groups in a democracy (as well as powerful interests in an autocracy) may support or oppose increasing competition in the governance market depending on whether these increases in competition benefit or harm them.

International Institutions. Over the last five centuries, world politics and the world economy became increasingly complex, fueled by developments such as the Age of Discovery and the Industrial Revolution. As a result, the management of the cartel also became more complicated over time. In response, states started to develop international institutions to clarify the norms of the cartel, and to enable them to adapt to the concomitant changes in technology, culture, and economics. In the 19th century, they held ad hoc international conferences like the Congress of Vienna to manage relations between them and to clarify and propagate the norms of the cartel. In the 20th century, they tried to institutionalize many of these norms, or at least supplement them, with the creation of formal bodies like the United Nations (UN) and the World Trade Organization (WTO). The principal objective of these bodies was to improve coordination between cartel members through codified rules of engagement. There are obvious parallels to economic cartels such as the Organization of the Petroleum Exporting Countries (OPEC), which has a permanent secretariat to facilitate coordination.**

We take up the question of how to understand the role of international institutions in enhancing the stability of the state system. We argue that their primary goal is not to suppress conflict, but to help the cartel leaders coordinate their collective interest in the governance market when such a collective interest exists. In some cases, this may coincide with suppressing aggression by one state upon another, as when the United States, through a series of UN

---

* Peters (2017) makes this argument.
** But since these organizations do not have the same degree of coercive power that the rulers of states exert upon their citizens, it is most accurate to think of the state system as continuing to represent a set of self-enforcing norms.

Security Council resolutions, organized a coalition of 35 nations in 1991 to prevent the Iraqi takeover of Kuwait. In other cases, it may mean ignoring unilateral land grabs such as the Russian takeover of Crimea. In some cases, it may mean fighting entry into the governance market on behalf of existing cartel members, as with the UN's refusal to admit Taiwan as a full member in its own right. In other cases, it may mean welcoming new providers into the governance market, as when South Sudan was recognized as a state and granted UN membership in 2011. International institutions help the most powerful cartel members coordinate action on issues of common interest when such a common interest exists.

International institutions also serve an important function by simply clarifying the norms of the system even if they do not have the power to enforce them. The WTO provides a good example. It clarifies exactly what a member state can expect to happen if it breaks the rules governing trade. More generally, the WTO helps stabilize the norms of the cartel by clarifying what happens when those norms are broken, even if it is ultimately up to the member states themselves to carry out any punishments.

Nationalism. The creation and strengthening of national identities has helped the cartel overcome the challenges of war and democracy in important ways, even though it is not obvious that national identities were created to serve this purpose. An important byproduct of nationalism has been the creation of steep changes in governance costs that coincide with the borders between states—steep changes that have stabilized the borders between them. Nationalism simultaneously lowers the cost of governing one's own population while raising the costs of governing other populations, thereby generating sharp differences in governance costs at interstate boundaries. These sharp differences shield neighboring states from the risk that small changes in the cost of governance could shift the efficient boundary between them dramatically to one side or the other.

The logic is as follows. If it is too expensive for a state with expansionist ambitions to govern a neighboring population relative to what it can earn from providing governance to that territory, then it is less tempted to initiate a conflict to try to conquer that territory. On the flip side, if it is cheap for a state to govern its own population, then it is more willing to defend its right to do so against an aggressor state. Nationalism creates precisely these conditions. It makes it expensive to govern other populations, and cheaper to govern one's own population. Cartel theory provides an economic rationale behind this argument by casting it in terms of the costs and benefits of claiming a greater share of the governance market.

In addition, nationalism also works against the temptation for democracies to open up the governance market to competition from foreign providers. If national attachments are so intense that the costs to rival states of governing the citizens of other countries are higher than the value that can be extracted from them, then opening the governance market to more competition will not benefit anyone, even in a democracy. Nationalism makes citizens of democracies loyal to their own monopolist provider however extractive that provider may be. This is very similar to the kind of brand loyalty that enables producers of economic goods and services to extract a larger share of the consumer surplus.

This logic helps explain why increased competition in the governance market arising out of globalization has benefited mainly those who are willing to forgo national attachments to take advantage of foreign opportunities, including economic migrants who are willing to change their nationalities to find better work opportunities or avoid paying taxes.* In fact, some of the biggest beneficiaries have been corporations that register themselves in tax havens around the world to lower their tax burden. While nationalism makes individuals loyal to their states, unwilling to be governed by other states, corporations are typically not subject to these sentiments.**

The Cartel Today

In recent decades, the state system has faced new challenges created by technological developments, globalization, and the uneven success of states in providing governance, as well as a myriad of other challenges. We elaborate upon these in the final chapter of the book.

Globalization. Today's governance market is more than a market for control of physical territory. Competition in this market now takes place in the

---

* To deter such behavior in the US, Senators Chuck Schumer (D-NY) and Bob Casey (D-PA) introduced the Ex-PATRIOT Act (S. 3205), which would levy a 30 % capital gains tax on individuals who had renounced US citizenship, with evaders barred from re-entering the country.
** To quote Rodrik (1997, 70): "owners of internationally mobile factors become disengaged from their local communities and disinterested in their development and prosperity." Stiglitz (2002, 40) is more blunt: "firms threatened to leave the country unless taxes were lower: there was no patriotism among these multinationals."

complex and abstract space of economic policies that regulate international commerce and the world economy. Technological improvements that have resulted in better communication, cheaper transportation costs, and greater financial mobility have complicated a state's task of exercising control over its share of the governance market. On the one hand, these technologies are available to governments to track the movement of people, money, and goods in and out of their borders. On the other hand, human migration, trade, and financial competition have all increased, tempting many states to break the collusive cartel agreement in creative and often subtle ways. Several developed economies have welcomed high-skill workers from developing countries, and many rich countries, from the oil-exporters of the Middle East to the emerging economies of Southeast Asia, have brought in foreign unskilled workers, who are willing to accept low wages. All countries, especially the fast-growing economies of Asia, have worked hard to attract greater foreign direct investment. Many small countries like Andorra, Mauritius, Lichtenstein, and Monaco have offered favorable tax rates to entice wealthy individuals and corporations to relocate their businesses. Even the small stream of revenue that these low taxes generate can contribute significantly to the funds required to run their small governments.

These trends have changed the way the cartel operates. They have generated countervailing pressures against the cartel's original intent to limit competition in the governance market. Nevertheless, the choice to soften borders has clearly been a political choice made as part of a coordinated strategy to reap the benefits of globalization. Because of this, it is probably more appropriate to think of the cartel's objective in today's interconnected world economy as seeking to control and manage competition in the market for governance rather than to limit it in all instances.

As a result of these trends, new political challenges have emerged. Incremental increases in competition in the governance market through free trade policies may have increased the overall pie, but they have also created distinct groups of economic winners and losers. In many cases, governments have found it difficult to identify these groups in the short run, complicating the development of policies to quickly compensate the losers by redistributing some of the gains from the winners.[2] This in turn has made it harder for governments to further increase political support for greater international openness. Part of the challenge has been that for any two distinct policies that regulate competition in the governance market in different ways, the sets of supporters of the policy may differ significantly. An individual who supports one policy that enhances competition in the governance market may oppose another one that does the same, if the individual stands to benefit from the first policy but lose from the second. This can lead individuals to oppose broad policies even when they include some components that they can identify as clearly benefiting them.

These factors have led many voters to oppose increasing competition in the governance market even if their countries are well positioned to take advantage of the economic gains from globalization. In Europe and the United States, this opposition has come in the form of a new kind of populist nationalism. Donald Trump's election as president of the United States, Britain's exit from the European Union, and the rise of parties like the Rassemblement National (previously the Front National) in France are some examples. These movements have drawn the support of citizens who want the cartel to operate as it did historically. Some of the citizens who support these movements see themselves as benefiting from closed borders and the suppression of competition in the governance market because they believe that the closing of borders helps them materially or prevents them from being harmed, in expectation. Even when greater competition in the governance market leads to efficiency, these voters don't perceive themselves as sharing in those benefits. Others support these movements out of nationalist emotional attachment. Yet others are driven by economic concerns, seeing interstate competition in governance as a destructive race-to-the-bottom in social provision. Whatever their reasons, the goal of these voters has been to exclude external labor, goods, and influences on state policy.

Uneven Governance Quality. Another political challenge has to do with the fact that some states have failed to provide even the most basic forms of governance to their citizens, such as security. For many citizens of poor countries, the value of governance they receive is lower than the costs they pay to receive it, especially if we measure these costs as including not just the direct taxes they pay to the state but also the opportunity costs of not being able to earn a higher return on their labor were they to move to a more functional state. Inequalities in state strength and the ability of states to govern have always existed, but in a world in which the costs of migration are smaller than they have ever been, citizens are also on the move, quite as much as corporations seeking better tax and regulatory environments. Even when they do not relocate personally, they may move their wealth to safer jurisdictions abroad, further draining resources from inefficient states and potentially amplifying any existing disparities in governance ability.

An important question that emerges from these observations is whether the cartel system can withstand the uneven distribution of governance quality that we see around the world, as migration costs continue to decline. In the opening paragraphs of this book we talked about the US-Canada border. But on this point, it is the US-Mexico border that is more pertinent.* Even though governance in Mexico has steadily improved over the years, the number of Mexican immigrants in the United States surged in the 1990s and early 2000s and has leveled off after the Great Recession. On the other hand, the number of immigrants from other Central American countries such as El Salvador, Guatemala, and Honduras—many sof whom arrive by crossing the US-Mexico border—has continued to rise.[3] Out-migration from countries with poor governance creates a vicious reinforcing cycle: people leave these places to escape crime and insecurity, but when this happens their voices are lost and the political power of those who oppose terrorism, organized crime, and drug and human trafficking diminishes while the power of the criminals grows. This leads even more people to leave, exacerbating the power difference. Such countries can then become the breeding ground for actors who challenge the norms (and in the case of the Islamic State, the very premise) of the state system, resulting in major negative externalities on the rest of the world.

Other Challenges. In addition to globalization and state failure, there are also many other new challenges to the cartel in recent decades: nuclear proliferation, global climate change, and cyber-warfare, to name a few—all consequences of developments that allow actions within one state's borders to create negative externalities for other states. Effective solutions to these problems require interstate coordination in the face of temptations to pursue private interests at the expense of cartel stability. We discuss some of these challenges in further detail in the final chapter, and comment on how the cartel might evolve with time to address them.

---

* The inequality in governance quality across this border is notable. The residents of El Paso, Texas, for instance, receive much better protection from murder, assault, and theft than those of the neighboring Mexican city of Juarez, not to mention a better set of roads, schools, and hospitals. Because they are born on the wrong side of the border, residents of Juarez live seven fewer years and earn an old age pension of approximately 17% of the size of an El Paso resident (Social Security Administration, 2015).

A New Theory of International Politics

Our goal in this book is to offer a new theory of international political economy based on the competitive political economy of governance. The cartel theory that we develop in subsequent chapters provides a new basis for understanding a wide range of phenomena in international politics—the drawing of borders, the control of capital flows and human migration across these borders, the role of national identity in international politics, and the cooperation of states through international institutions on persistent political issues such as trade, terrorism, state failure, and climate change.

In our model, states are competitors in a market for governance, in which they provide governance to citizens and citizens pay taxes to the states that govern them. The system of states in the world, we argue, is a collusive arrangement held together by a set of norms under which states segment the market for governance and exercise monopoly power to tax and govern within their shares of the market, free of competition from other states.

States have managed to reach a high degree of consensus and cooperation in dividing the market. Outside of Antarctica, nearly every square inch of land in the world belongs to a state, and the fraction of land that is claimed by more than one state is less than 1.6%.[4] This means that almost nowhere in the world do two or more states openly compete to provide governance to the same citizens. While much of international relations theory is fixated on understanding the sources of conflict between states, we are interested, on the other hand, in understanding this remarkable degree of cooperation between them. This cooperation is so deep and widespread that it easily escapes our notice, leading us to often focus on violations of the cooperative norm rather than on the norm itself.

This new understanding of the state system raises a number of questions. Why do states sometimes fight each other? Why do they so often return to cooperation after the war is over? Why is it so difficult to create new states without the consent of existing states? How will states approach the emergent problems of the 21st century associated with globalization, in which corporations and citizens exploit the lower costs of movement across borders to (at least partially) reestablish interstate competition in the governance market? The struggle, currently ongoing, between this renewed competitive dynamic and the formidable set of institutions, norms, and incentives woven into the current system of territorially bounded states will determine both the system's future stability and the internal politics of its members.

2

The Cartel Model

The Market for Governance

At the center of our theory is the concept of *governance*. By this we mean an evolving package of centrally provided services that states have supplied to their citizens from the late medieval period to the present.

But what exactly is this evolving package of services? Frederick Lane (1979) and Charles Tilly (1985) argued that the early states of medieval Europe did little beyond providing basic protection to their citizens. They, in fact, described medieval states as "protection rackets," under which rulers supply protection to their citizens against the threat of violence and exploitation from themselves.[1] More recently, Kai Konrad and Stergios Skaperdas (2012) have argued that by establishing monopolies of violence, these early states also provided valuable protection from other local bandits or distant robbers, thereby reducing economic insecurity overall. According to their work, states competed in a "market for protection," which is closely related to our concept of the market for governance.

Modern states, on the other hand, are complex organizations that serve a variety of functions, reflecting the fact that they grew in their complexity over time and developed new forms of governance in response to changing needs. For example, with the rise of long distance trade in late medieval and early modern Europe, the demand for governed economic exchange grew, and states found it in their interest to provide some level of dispute resolution and commercial regulation, in addition to protection—services that had previously been provided privately by local actors.[2]

Eventually, the development of industrial manufacturing economies created further demand for an even wider array of additional government services and public infrastructure. In England (the first country to industrialize), this included the development of public sewage systems and water lines, the establishment of universal primary public education, and the creation of policies regulating labor conditions and labor-management relations, among other things. The most advanced states today provide an

The Cartel System of States: An Economic Theory of International Politics. Avidit Acharya and Alexander Lee, Oxford University Press. © Oxford University Press 2023. DOI:10.1093/oso/9780197632277.003.0002

even greater array of services, such as environmental protection and scientific research. In the United States some of the largest funders of scientific research are government agencies that include the Department of Defense, the National Institutes of Health, and the National Science Foundation. The exact mix of services that make up governance can vary based upon the needs and preferences of the citizens and their rulers. The United States government does not offer health insurance to most of its working age citizens, while most other developed countries do. Other countries, however, do not fund scientific research and global defense and security to the same extent as America does. For this reason, access to even relatively homogenous goods such as COVID-19 vaccines varied considerably across even developed countries when these vaccines were first introduced.

The evolution of governance is analogous to the way in which technological innovations have improved the quality and bundle of services provided in many smaller markets. Cars today are much more advanced than their predecessors a hundred years ago, and include features such as heaters, radios, gas gauges, automatic transmissions, and anti-lock brakes that were either unavailable or available only as optional extras to the wealthy in the 1910s. As with governance, these extra features gradually became standard, and they remain less common in poor countries than in rich ones. And, as with governance, the expansion of such features—even when different manufacturers provide different mixes of them—has not changed the competitive nature of the car industry, or eliminated the possibility for producer collusion.

So to summarize, it is the evolving package of state-provided services beginning from protection all the way to public health care and scientific research that we refer to as governance. Our model views states as the suppliers of governance in a market where there is a demand for such a package of services. States are potential competitors in the governance market.* The revenues that they collect for the provision of these services are their taxes. If the market for governance were competitive, then individuals facing tax demands that they consider too high relative to the benefits they receive could instead join another state, by moving. But the modern state

---

* As many works in comparative politics point out, states also have competitors in the governance market besides other states. These include private actors such as the Mafia, insurgent groups, associations of merchants, or local elites (Migdal 1988; Milgrom, North, and Weingast 1990). The fact that states compete against these entities as well is orthogonal to our argument, though we will address this fact in Chapter 5 where we consider the deterrence of opportunistic entry into the cartel system.

system attempts to put real limits on the extent to which citizens can shop for better deals. In the rest of the chapter, we present a model that helps us explain the causes and consequences of this fact.

A Simple Model

Our model is centered on the geography of the governance market but also abstracts away from it in a number of ways to get to our main points quickly and parsimoniously. Many of our assumptions will appear to make the model seem far from reality. We will first lay out and analyze the model, and then return to these assumptions at the end of the chapter, commenting on which can be relaxed and which can be reinterpreted in a way that enhances the model's realism.

The terrain of our model is one-dimensional, with two rulers called A and B located at the endpoints of a line segment depicted in Fig. 1. The space between the rulers is inhabited by a set of individuals. The actual distribution of these individuals across this terrain is not important for the points we are going to make. Some areas may be sparsely inhabited while others may be dense urban centers. For simplicity, we will assume that the individuals are spread out uniformly. One can think of these individuals as citizens or as chieftains, bishops, local lords, and other types of small-scale authorities who exercise power within a given area.

Each ruler provides governance and collects revenue in the form of taxes. The costs to each ruler of providing governance are c_A and c_B respectively. Consistent with the figure, we assume that these costs increase with distance from the ruler's location. The substantive basis of this assumption is the fact that most states possess an administrative center, often (though not always) the zone around the capital, where its ability to extract resources and apply coercive force is very high. The farther away from its administrative center the state attempts to expand, the longer communications become, the farther armies have to travel, and the more unfamiliar local society becomes to officials. All of these raise the costs of providing governance. The Roman Empire, for example, found the administration of Britain more costly and less profitable than the administration of northern Italy. Similarly, the Mughals found the administration of the Deccan plateau more costly and less profitable than the administration of the North Indian plain.*

---

* Boulding (1962, 262) famously referred to the decline of a state's ability to project military power over distance as the "loss of strength gradient."

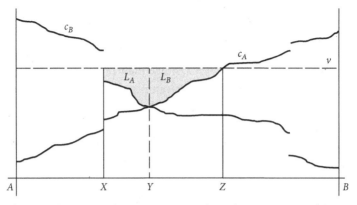

Fig. 1 The one-dimensional governance market. There are two states A and B whose centers of administration are at the endpoints of an interval. The two states govern a population that is spread out between these points. A's cost of governing is c_A and B's is c_B. v is the value of governing, which is constant across space and the same for both states. States will not want to govern in regions where their cost exceeds the value of governing, that is in the region east of Z for state A and in the region west of X for state B. But in the zone between X and Z the two states are potential competitors in the governance market. The outcome of this competition will be that A will govern to the west of the point Y and B to the east, and competition will depresses the value of governing by L_A for state A and L_B for state B.

In addition, as the figure depicts, the costs of governance may increase with distance in a nonlinear and discontinuous fashion. Geographic breaks such as rivers and mountains that are difficult to traverse can result in such abrupt changes in the costs of governing. Physical infrastructure and the human geography of an area can also shape these costs. For example, areas with settled agriculture may be more "legible" to states, to use James Scott's (1998) terminology, than hunter-gatherer societies, or nomads.

We assume that governance provides some value to society, and we fix this at $v > 0$. The assumption that this value is constant across citizens in space is another abstraction, and we do not require it to make our basic points.* A ruler is able to extract a profit from providing governance only in places where the value of governance exceeds the cost of providing it. In fact, the maximum revenue that a ruler can extract from governing a specific location is v. In practice, v can be thought of as the point at which additional marginal taxation would become self-defeating, leading citizens to revolt,

---

* We will investigate the consequences of relaxing this assumption in Chapter 7.

exit the formal economy, or engage in costly schemes of tax-avoidance. In an economic cartel, this is the reservation price: the highest price at which customers would rather pay the inflated price than go without the good.

We assume that rulers seek to maximize their revenues net of costs; thus, they are profit maximizing. The maximum profit that a ruler can extract from governing a part of the interval is therefore given by the area that lies between v and the ruler's cost curve—c_A for ruler A and c_B for ruler B.

Figure 1 shows three basic assumptions of our model. The first is that there is a point in space Y to the west of which ruler A's cost of providing governance is lower than that of ruler B, and vice versa to the east of this point. If this assumption does not hold, then one ruler's cost of providing governance will be lower than the other's throughout the interval, and in this case it would be hard to justify why the higher-cost ruler is even active in the governance market.

A second assumption is that each ruler has a set of individuals for whom the cost of providing governance does not exceed the value of governance. For ruler A these are the individuals west of Z. For ruler B they are the individuals east of X. If this is not the case for either ruler, then that ruler would not be interested in building a state in the first place.

The third assumption is that X is to the west of Z so that for citizens between these two points in space, the two rulers could be competitors in governance provision. Ruler B cannot provide governance profitably to individuals residing to the west of X: his cost of providing the service is greater than the revenue he can collect for it. The same is true for ruler A and the individuals to the east of Z. But for individuals between X and Z either ruler could profit from governing these individuals, and this makes them potential competitors. If X were to the east of Z then there would be no region in which the rulers compete in the governance market, and in fact the region between these two points would be an ungoverned buffer area between the two rulers' states. This case arises when there are high governance costs and the value of governance is low. (See Fig. 4 in Chapter 3.)

Competition in the Governance Market

In prior work, we studied a game theoretic version of this model where we assumed that the rulers are Bertrand (1883) competitors who compete in the governance market by setting location-specific taxes—the price that individuals who reside at that location pay for governance.*

In the core areas of each ruler, rulers squeeze their citizens as hard as they can. Ruler A collects v in taxes from all individuals to west of X while B does the same to the east of Z. This is because to the west of X ruler B cannot compete with A in the governance market since B's cost of providing governance exceeds the maximum amount that can be extracted. Ruler A is effectively a monopolist in this region's governance market, and is therefore able to extract the maximum amount in revenue. The same is true for ruler B to the west of Z. Rulers thus are able to tax their citizens an amount just below the amount that would cause them to leave or exit the economy.

For individuals between X and Z, the familiar results of price competition apply. The lower-cost ruler serves the market at a price that equals that of the higher-cost ruler. This means that ruler A is the governance provider to the west of Y. The revenue that this ruler collects from an individual between X and Y equals the value that c_B takes at the location of that individual. Similarly, B is the governance provider to the east of Y and the revenue that he collects from each individual between Y and Z is the value that c_A takes at the individual's location. Thus, Y serves as the border between A's state and B's state. Citizens choose the best deal in terms of lower taxes for the same level of services, and are served by the lower-cost provider—the locally more efficient state.

Consequently, the rulers' profits fall short of their monopoly profits. Under joint profit maximization, ruler A would extract the monopoly price v from *all* individuals west of Y and ruler B would extract this price from all individuals east of this point. The shortfall in A's profit under competition relative to the monopoly level is the area L_A shaded in Fig. 1. Ruler B's shortfall is the area L_B. These shortfalls in profit are the result of competition, as individuals in the zone of competition between X and Z have credible outside options to accepting to be governed by their ruler. In particular, elites in the region between X and Z will always have fewer taxes and more privileges than those in the core, since they have the option to be governed by the rival ruler, who is willing and able to govern them. As Douglass North (1981, 27) writes:

---

* In that analysis, we imposed the following mild condition: no ruler ever taxes any individual an amount lower than his cost of providing governance to the individual.

The ruler always has rivals: competing states, or potential rulers within his own state.... The closer the substitutes, the fewer degrees of freedom the ruler possesses, and the greater the percentage of incremental income that will be retained by the constituents.

In what follows, we will interpret these shortfalls in profit broadly, and figuratively, as the privileges that peripheral elites and other individuals can win from central governments by playing them off against their neighbors. By threatening, even if only implicitly, to switch their allegiance to a rival polity, residents in the zone of competition between X and Z who live near the border can extract concessions from their rulers. Thus, when we connect our model to specific cases, we will operationalize these concessions either as lower taxes or as the individuals being able to enjoy greater privileges that translate to them earning more, or keeping more of their earnings. The net effect of this is the same as that of lower taxes: border residents are wealthier and more autonomous than they would otherwise be, at the expense of the ruler.

Collusion in the Governance Market

The shortfall in profits that competition brings is a nuisance for the rulers. Is there a way for them to collude at the expense of their citizens?

In a repeated interaction, the rulers could improve their profits by setting up a cooperative agreement to not interfere in each other's states—a sovereignty norm. In one such agreement, the rulers divide the governance market at the border Y and stay out of the market for each other's citizens. Territorial sovereignty thus emerges as a cartel agreement between rulers: ruler A promises not to compete to provide governance to individuals east of Y and ruler B promises not to compete to provide governance west of this point. With each ruler staying out of the other's market, each is able to act as a monopolist and recover his profit shortfall.

Many economic cartels operate in exactly this fashion, dividing up the exclusive right to sell to customers on a monopoly basis. The Great Lightbulb cartel (also known as the Phoebus cartel), for example, granted much of the world to its members as exclusive territory, in which the other parties were obligated not to sell. As in our model, the cartel members generally received the territories that were nearest to them geographically: General

Electric received North America, Cuba, and the West Indies, while the French Compagnie General received France, Greece, and joint rights in Bulgaria, Romania, Yugoslavia, and Turkey.[3] Similarly, the Mafia-controlled cartel that dominated the commercial trash business in New York in the late 20th century divided customers ("stops") among its members, and banned competition among them.[4] Customers were tied to their trash hauler for life, unless they were willing to pay a hefty fee to their existing hauler for the privilege of switching to a different service provider.

For such an agreement to work, however, the cartel members should not succumb to the temptation to break their promises and try to steal customers on their neighbor's side of the border. In most cartel agreements, there is no external enforcer that can determine and punish rule breaking. The agreement must be self-enforcing. And this is true also for the international state system.

Since the rulers in our model are engaged in the same interaction repeatedly over time, the requisite incentives for self-enforcement can be put in place provided that the rulers are sufficiently future-oriented to value the continuation of the cartel over the short-term gains from cheating.[5] Consider, for example, the usual specification of a cartel agreement: So long as the rulers have kept their ends of the bargain, they will continue to cooperate, but as soon as one of them breaks his promise, they become competitors again in the border region, with each suffering his profit losses from competition. If the rulers find it sufficiently important to not suffer these profit losses in the future, they will abide by the sovereignty norm. Neither ruler will want to violate the border at Y by providing governance on the other side, for fear of ruining the relationship once and for all.*

In our previous analysis, we showed that if the common weight that rulers put on future profits is larger than the share of each ruler's profit shortfall, then the rulers will be able to maintain collusion at the expense of their citizens, per the cartel agreement described above.** This condition states that the losses from competition cannot be too lopsided. If they are, then one of the shares becomes large, making it harder to satisfy the condition that the weight of future profits is greater than both of the shares. Consequently, the

---

* The strategies that we use to support cooperation between rulers are the usual trigger strategies that have been used in repeated games, and serve as the basis of cooperation in many of the classical neo-liberal theories of international relations (e.g., Keohane 2005). In our analysis, we assumed that the individuals between A and B optimize statically (i.e., myopically) and that deviations by them are ignored by all players.

** Specifically, the discount factor has to be larger than both $L_A/(L_A + L_B)$ and $L_B/(L_A + L_B)$.

cartel agreement emerges when the rulers have similar amounts to lose from competition in the governance market.

The Assumptions of the Model

The Terrain

Our model assumes a one-dimensional terrain in which citizens are distributed uniformly.

By now, however, it should be evident that this assumption plays no substantial role in our story. Even if the terrain were two-dimensional, we could posit that rulers would compete to provide governance in border areas; and if this competition is costly to them, the impetus to collude at the expense of their citizens would still be present.

If individuals (or economic production) are not uniformly distributed, then governing some areas may be more valuable or more costly. The cost functions may not rise gradually, and the value of governance may not be fixed, but if the rulers stand to lose from competition over a region in the governance market, then again they would gain from colluding against their citizens. Models more realistic (and complex) in this regard can be written, but as far as the core points go, the basic message of our analysis would remain unchanged.

Similarly, while our model envisages states as blocks divided by a single border, there is no reason why non-contiguous territorial units would be inconsistent with state collusion in the governance market. If the costs of providing governance are oddly shaped, they could lead to an area where ruler *A* is the more efficient provider being surrounded by areas where ruler *B* is the more efficient provider, perhaps because of superior familiarity with the local population. There are many examples of such exclaves: Alaska is not connected to the rest of the United States by land, Nakhchivan is not connected to the rest of Azerbaijan, and for 24 years East and West Pakistan were separated by a thousand miles of the country's main adversary, India.* Most states in the world are contiguous, however, because cost functions

---

* The eventual split of the two parts of Pakistan under Indian pressure, however, illustrates the practical difficulties of maintaining control over non-contiguous territories in competition with a nearer neighbor.

were typically not oddly shaped: at the time that borders were drawn, they were likely to be increasing in distance from the state's core.

The interpretation of our terrain, on the other hand, is a more interesting issue. We have opted for a geographic interpretation, but there is nothing in the model that requires boundaries to be set in geographic space rather than some other space. For example, we could suppose instead that the interval simply represents an ordering of individuals according to how cheap it is for a ruler to govern them. This could be for cultural or linguistic regions: those who are placed closer to A speak the language of A's administrators, and are hence easier for A to govern and harder for B. While such an ordering is likely to coincide in many instances with geography, there is no guarantee of this.* Sovereignty would then be established over people rather than territory, as in pre-colonial Africa, where as Jeffrey Herbst (2014) argued, labor was scarcer than land, at least in comparison to Europe.[6]

Since it takes spatial delineation as given, our model does not explain why boundaries were set in geographic space rather than other spaces. This is a question that has been the subject of much prior scholarship, but which we will leave mostly unaddressed.[7] That said, we do note that establishing authority over people rather than territory would be suboptimal when it is hard to monitor the movements of people, and when most taxable value is in immobile assets such as land. Individuals can pick up and leave, but this would be irrelevant to the rulers if it is the land that has value, and can be repopulated with new people to cultivate it. This was indeed the case in the predominantly agrarian Europe of the late medieval and early modern periods. In fact, prior to industrialization, land was the main source of income, and remained a major income source until the last century. Other sites of economic value, such as mines and rivers, were similarly tied to specific locations.

Nevertheless, it is interesting to note that as taxable value has shifted over time from land to mobile physical assets, and now to human capital—and as technological progress has further lowered transportation costs—rulers have sought to exercise control over their citizens through innovations such as border controls, visa requirements, and tax treaties. American citizens and permanent residents are required to pay US taxes even if they live abroad.

---

* For an example of this logic Pakistan's founder Muhammad Ali Jinnah made the case that the areas of East and West Pakistan should be governed by the same state because the common religion of the two regions' majorities trumped other considerations.

This suggests that in modern times, the division of control in the governance market can be, and is, extended over both territory and people. We will have more to say about this in Chapter 7.

Citizens, Rulers, and Their Objectives

The idea of there being stationary rulers taxing stationary citizens in order to maximize their earnings may seem like we are limiting the scope of our model to exclude much of the modern world.

But, in fact, the assumption that the actors are stationary can be interpreted broadly enough to cover most interesting cases. As we mentioned above, on the ruler side, the assumption that the locations of A and B are fixed captures the idea that all states have administrative centers where they can govern cheaply and as we move away from these centers the costs of governing increase. Some large states have multiple centers, corresponding to major cities that host the national government administrative offices. The location that we label A in the figure is meant to represent the administrative center that is relevant to ruler A's relationship to B, rather than the literal physical location of the state's ruler, or even the state's capital.

The assumption that citizens are stationary is somewhat more consequential, but also has a flexible interpretation. As we suggested above, our model provides a reasonable approximation of reality if individuals cannot easily migrate to change their governance provider, or the costs of moving are sufficiently high that they will not do so. Even when migration is possible, if the main sources of revenue for rulers are (relatively) immobile capital assets such as land, then the model continues to serve as a reasonable approximation, since the value of a location lies in the income that can be generated from these immobile assets. Individuals may roam freely, but rulers sell governance to those working in a particular location, whoever they may be, and the value of governance is tied to the location rather than to the individual.

If, on the other hand, taxable value can be moved at low cost, whether that is citizens themselves moving, or them moving their businesses and taxable assets to foreign lands, then it may seem that there would be more competition in the governance market than there actually is. Rather than build in the assumption that the individuals and businesses are themselves mobile, another way to think about this case is to consider it as corresponding to the situation where the cost of governing is pretty much flat in distance. Every individual or business is capable of being governed by every ruler, and there is vigorous competition in the governance market.

The Apple corporation, for example, registered a significant portion of its business in Ireland by simply moving money on paper in search of favorable corporate policies. Following a tax crackdown just a few years ago, it discovered a new home for its profits in the English Channel island of Jersey, which does not tax corporate income. For many American companies and wealthy individuals, the islands of Bermuda and Grand Cayman serve similar roles. The OECD estimated in 2015 that tax competition in the world governance market cost governments around the world as much as $240 billion a year, which is probably an underestimate given that not all tax avoidance attempts are detectable.

This kind of tax avoidance is a reflection of intense competition in the governance market, which results in the tax revenues of all states being lower than their monopoly level. The case in which all individuals can enjoy such competition is the one in which both rulers' cost functions in Fig. 1 remain below v, either because the value of governance is high or governing is cheap. Importantly, this is a case that is easily covered by our model. In fact, it is a case that really highlights our core point that there is the potential for intense competition in the governance market. The question then is: just how do states collude when moving people and money is so cheap? This is again where international treaties and border protections come in, and we will take up this question in later chapters. But the point, for now, is that while it may seem that the assumption of fixed locations is restrictive, it is far less restrictive than it appears.

Finally, who exactly are the rulers? If they are unitary actors, such as monarchs, then by referring to rulers are we implicitly excluding democratic republics and other complex polities that are governed by large groups and coalitions of interests? The answer depends on whether there is, for the purpose of our analysis, any meaningful distinction between the objectives of states that are governed by unitary rulers and these other states that are governed by many actors. In our model, the ruler is simply a stand-in for the state's objective to minimize the loss from competition in the market for governance. The fact that the US and Ireland, despite being democratic republics, have governments that seem to care that their citizens and businesses are taking advantage of legal loopholes to reduce their tax burden suggests that, at least behaviorally, not much is lost by using the term "ruler" even for democratic polities. We will return to this issue in greater depth in Chapter 5, where we embed a standard model of democratic political economy into the model that we have described here.

Coercion in the Governance Market

One may wonder why we are we assuming that there is a voluntary transaction that takes place between rulers and citizens if in real life the rulers simply set their taxes and the citizens are compelled to pay, regardless of the scope and size of services offered. Certainly, this kind of coercion is an important— perhaps even a defining—aspect of statehood. If taxation were voluntary, citizens would be tempted to free ride. In the context of our model, the coercive nature of taxation would seem to violate our assumption that the costs and value of governance are exogenous, and that there exist levels of these costs for which it would be unprofitable to govern.

However, citizens are not entirely without recourse to high taxation or low services. Individuals facing tax demands that they consider unreasonable, like Scott's (2014) Southeast Asian peasants, may withdraw from the formal sector or from production entirely. If property rights are not protected, transportation is slow and expensive, and taxation is high, why should anybody engage in more than subsistence economic production and extortion? And if nobody is engaging in economic production above the subsistence level, what is left to tax, even at confiscatory rates? Moreover, citizens always have the option to invest in expensive tax avoidance, and often do to take advantage of the high costs that governments encounter trying to fund very high levels of internal coercion.* Seventeenth-century Spain, among many other societies, discovered that there is a point at which increased attempts to extract revenue can, even in the short run, lower revenue collection.[8] This economic exit constraint serves as an alternative interpretation of the maximum value of governance to rulers—the value of the expropriation rate beyond which citizens will not produce.

Citizens can also do a little coercion of their own, by revolting against government demands they see as excessive. By themselves, these efforts may not often succeed, due to the asymmetries of coercive power involved. But a

---

* One can think of weak states in the developing world as being those that have revealed an unwillingness or inability to pay these high enforcement costs.

revolt in alliance with an external power is another matter. The allegiance of local elites with their knowledge and resources could easily tip the balance between two large powers. Many switches of territory take the form of an invading outsider allying with dissatisfied locals. Bengalis living in East Pakistan in 1971, for example, welcomed the invading Indians as their allies against the West Pakistanis. The borderlands of medieval Europe saw even more contested patterns of allegiance, with locals using the possibility of allying with an external enemy as a negotiating strategy.

All this is to say that there are practical limits on how much a ruler can extract from his citizens, and even coercion by the ruler is not without limits. More to the point, a model in which the relationship between rulers and citizens is a more coercive one but in which coercion has its limits may seem qualitatively very different from the open market for governance that we have stylized. But this is a superficial difference. The practical implications of these two approaches—as far as the collusion of rulers against their citizens is concerned—are broadly the same. In a different interpretation of our model, v is not the value of governance at which citizens stop paying but the point at which they become not worth exploiting, while the cost functions correspond to the difficulty that rulers face in projecting coercive power. Our formalization, precisely because of its abstraction, clarifies the practical equivalence between these two interpretations.

Coordination

We have assumed that the rulers can find a way to cooperate even though it is possible that they fail to do so and keep competing forever. In the language of game theory, our game has multiple equilibria that involve varying levels of cooperation.

But even if rulers do find ways to cooperate, why should they maintain the boundary Y if there are collusive agreements that could be maintained at other boundaries as well, to the east or to the west of Y? In fact, if L_A and L_B are very unequal, then there may be a boundary other than Y which would be mutually profitable for both parties.

Our answer is that even though there are other boundaries at which the rulers could cooperate, Y is the one and only boundary at which they maximize their joint profits. For this reason, we think that Y would be focal if cooperation can be sustained there, and if no previous boundary existed.[9] But the caveat to this claim leads to an important question that we address in detail in Chapter 5. If the costs of governing change, and the joint profit-maximizing boundary shifts, will rulers consider the new joint profit-maximizing boundary to be focal, or will the old historical boundary be focal (supposing that full-scale cooperation continues to be self-enforcing under the historical boundary)? There is good reason to think that historical boundaries may be the more focal ones. If there is confusion, however, then one side's attempts to nullify and change the historical boundary may lead to conflict between the two states.

More generally, any inability to coordinate on a boundary may lead to conflict. Thus, despite being inherently a theory of cooperation between states, our model is also able to accommodate the fact that interstate conflict too has been an undeniable fact of political life.

In any case, returning to the question of which of many boundaries the rulers are likely to set, we recognize that our model admits multiple self-enforcing agreements, and so we make very limited comparative statics claims on the boundaries that rulers set. For any such claim, the usual caveat holds that in a long-run repeated interaction with farsighted players, a range of different agreements can be self-enforcing.

From Two Rulers to Many

In the model we have laid out, any competition or cooperation between states that takes place is bilateral. Are we then saying that the territorial state system merely represents a stitched-together collection of bilateral agreements between states, each relationship independent of another?

While we developed our key ideas in a parsimonious setting with two states, it is possible to extend our arguments to the case of many states. We demonstrate how this could work by considering the case of three states, depicted in Fig. 2. In the figure, the states correspond to locations A, B, and C. A's state is the territory between X and Y. C's state is to the west of X and B's state is to the east of Y.

In the scheme that we call *independent cooperation*, A cooperates with B independently of C, and with C independently of B. That is, even if A violates the border Y with B, this does not affect A's relationship with C; and, similarly, violations of border X with C do not affect A's relationship with B either. In this setting of multiple relationships, independent cooperation

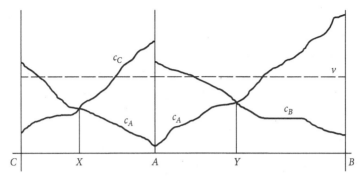

Fig. 2 If there are three states A, B, and C then A's relationship with B could depend on its relationship with C, and vice versa.

refers to idea that the state system is merely a collection of bilateral relationships stitched together.

In a different mode of cooperation that we call *interdependent cooperation*, A's relationship with each of the other two rulers cannot be separated from his relationship with the other. If, for example, all three rulers are cooperating to maximize their joint profits at the boundaries X and Y and A defects on B, then that could also harm A's relationship with C. It could be that A is seen as untrustworthy. It could alternatively be that C and B are in an alliance together, and that they too have a relationship under which they are cooperating to discipline A. Either way, interdependent cooperation refers to the idea that the state system is not merely a collection of separable bilateral relationships; it is a complex multilateral agreement between states. Even if it is not possible for two states, say A and C, to fully extract the benefits of cooperation in a self-enforcing agreement when their relationship is independent of B, it may be possible for them to do so when their relationship involves B.

This kind of interdependent cooperation may explain the existence of small weak states. For example, consider Germany's intention to annex Belgium during World War I. Rulers recognized that this would also affect Germany's relationship with Britain. Indeed, Britain would now be directly across the Channel from Germany—a much stronger nation than Belgium and which by the very act of invading Belgium had shown contempt for the sovereignty norm. For this reason, Britain had guaranteed Belgium neutrality throughout the 19th century and entered World War I principally to honor that guarantee. Similarly, a large international coalition combined to keep Iraq from annexing Kuwait during the first Gulf War, concerned both about the violation of sovereignty norms and the effect on oil markets. The Monroe Doctrine, by which the United States deterred European powers from interfering in (let alone annexing) Western Hemisphere countries, is an even more far-reaching example of the threat of third-party enforcement being enough to keep predatory states at bay. In Chapters 5 and 6, we will discuss some indirect evidence for this claim, showing how international institutions such as the Organization for African Unity and the United Nations seek to make the relationships between states increasingly interdependent.

Closely Related Ideas

The basic premises of our cartel theory are not completely new. Several of the component ideas in our model draw on the work of some of the most influential thinkers. In particular, our model draws inspiration from:

- The work of Lane (1979), Tilly (1985), and others in comparative politics that views states as monopolies of violence. From this, it is a short step to extend their arguments to understand the state system as an oligopoly of violence.
- The work of Margaret Levi (1989) that views rulers as revenue maximizing. From this, it is a short step to ask how multiple rulers manage their collective revenue-maximizing project together when their interests collide.
- The work of North (1981) that highlights how competition between rulers can advantage citizens at a cost to their rulers. From this, it is a short step to ask how rulers might seek to avoid this competition that is costly to them.
- The work of Robert Keohane (2005) and other neo-liberal scholars who argue that farsighted states can cooperate with each other even in the absence of international institutions. From this, it is a short step to ask how their cooperation could be put to use against the citizens that so many rulers in human history have tried so hard to exploit.

Besides these, the theories that are most closely connected to ours are the political economy theories of the state and state system. One particularly related theory is that of Alberto Alesina and Enrico Spolaore (1997), in which borders are determined by factors that shape how tax revenue is collected and redistributed back to citizens. But there are important qualitative differences between our work and theirs. In their baseline model, borders (and hence the size and configuration of states) are the outcome of a majoritarian voting process—an assumption that appears to run counter to historical development of states, as the development of territorial states preceded the advent of democracy by at least a couple centuries.* Alesina and Spolaore do develop an extension of their argument in their Chapter 5 that is more in line with our cartel theory. In that chapter, they assume that borders will be drawn to maximize the joint revenue of the world's "Leviathans."[10] However, they do not provide a foundation for this outcome, while we argue that it arises as the consequence of states seeking to minimize the losses they suffer from competing with one another in the market for governance.

We also build on the work of David Friedman (1977), who develops a theory of borders based on rulers maximizing tax revenue net of collection costs. As in our model, territory in his model is allocated to maximize joint profit; but, unlike our model, this outcome is not based on cooperation between rulers in a cartel. Friedman's argument is most closely related to work in comparative politics that asks questions about the development of states while neglecting the fact that as states grow they come into contact with, and hence must develop relations with, other states. A theory of the optimal size and shape of states must necessarily deal with the consequences of this contact, which is inherently a question of international relations.

In other related prior work, Kenneth Schultz and Hein Goemans (2014) propose a model of conquest in which the net value of territory for some types of rulers is negative after a point in geographical space. This consequently limits the claims that one ruler will make on territory held by another. Our theory can be seen as providing a foundation for their key assumption, since the net value of territory for a ruler in the model that we develop is also negative after a point. Since this foundation is based on the economic relationship between rulers and citizens, cartel theory takes the domestic political economy of states as an important factor in

---

* In our model, states are oligopolists that collude against their citizens, which is more in line with the tradition in comparative politics mentioned above, as well as the work of Olson (2000) that views states and rulers in more exploitative terms (e.g., protection rackets or stationary bandits that benefit from creating monopolies of violence). Nevertheless, in Chapter 5 we extend our argument to account for how the advent of democracy affected the rationale for the state system. We do so by developing an extension of our argument that is more in line with the perspective of Alesina and Spolaore.

understanding the state system. Our view is that the political economy of the relationship between rulers and citizens is an important factor in understanding world politics and therefore should not be neglected by any theory of the international state system.

Finally, in concurrent work Samuel Barkin (2021) develops a very closely related philosophical theory of sovereignty as the outcome of a cartel arrangement. The focus of his work is different, however, as it is primarily interested in the norms of sovereignty, which are viewed as analogous to property rights. Barkin does not discuss why this particular set of norms is self-enforcing, and how it is supported in a market of potentially competitive providers. Still, our theories share much in common and complement each other both normatively and positively.

Other Theories

We are not the first to ask questions about how to understand the territorial state system, nor are we the first to give answers. But many of the most prominent existing theories of the origins and functioning of the state system fall short of answering the precise questions that motivate us. Some prior work has focused on explaining the origins of the state system without explaining what makes it persist. Other contributions focus on how rulers and states have used the existing state system to organize politics and the provision of governance. Yet other work focuses on understanding how the system structures relations between rulers, neglecting the relations that citizens have with multiple rulers. We now review three sets of the most prominent theories, as follows.[11]

Theories of Ideological Change

The first explanations of the territorial state system were theories of ideology and ideological change. The oldest and perhaps most influential among these is the *Westphalia hypothesis*: the idea that the Peace of Westphalia (1648) engendered the norm of territorial sovereignty, marking a critical juncture in the development of the modern state system.[12] Andreas Osiander (2001) and Krasner (1993), along with other skeptics, have challenged the Westphalia hypothesis, arguing that the treaty only dealt with the affairs of the Holy

Roman Empire, and even in that case did little more than codify existing practice.[13]

However, the proposition that the roots of the territorial state system are based on some ideological development that took place in early modern Europe is still influential, despite the fact that there is no consensus on which ideas were the most important. John Ruggie (1993, 157) writes, for example, that "the mental equipment that people drew upon in imagining and symbolizing forms of political community itself underwent fundamental change." Daniel Philpott (2001, 4) echoes this view, claiming that "revolutions in sovereignty result from prior revolutions in ideas about justice and political authority." Other authors point to other moments, events, or periods that they claim were critical in promoting the construction and spread of the ideas and norms of sovereignty. Daniel Nexon (2009), for example, discusses the role of the Reformation in changing the ideological basis of European politics in a way that made the composite polities that were common in the early 16th century obsolete. Osiander (1994, 281) argues that the French Revolution represented the most important watershed in the context of a gradual long-term evolution of political ideas that led to the development of "a shared, rather elaborate code of structural and procedural legitimacy."[14]

At the same time, some authors have expressed skepticism about the primacy of ideas, suggesting that state building altered political theory rather than the other way around. Krasner is among the skeptics, arguing that ideas were simply "legitimating rationales" that rulers could draw on to provide justification to actions that they undertook primarily in their material self-interest. He writes (1993, 257):

> Initially, the ideas were just hooks to justify actions that were motivated by considerations of wealth and power, not by visions of justice and truth. European leaders were fortunate in having many hooks because of the diversity and richness of European intellectual traditions.

Evaluating the causal impact of ideas is difficult. We do not deny that the ideas that succeeded and spread were not just shaped by material interests, but also had an influence on the way rulers construed their interests. But if new principles were the primary drivers of change, rulers should also have an incentive to adhere to these principles; that is, those principles should be self-enforcing. Otherwise it becomes difficult to explain why the stability of a system built upon these principles would not gradually be undermined by rulers realizing their interests in violating them. Herein lies the missing element of these ideological theories—one that cartel theory provides.

Modern Realist Theories

The medieval and early modern periods in Europe were periods of rapid change in the capabilities of states to finance war, which has been the focus of much of international relations scholarship.[15] Within this literature, one of the most prominent models that emphasizes the role of conflict in making the state system is the realist model of the "offense-defense balance" proposed by Robert Jervis (1978) and elaborated by others.[16]

The standard realist account goes as follows. Growth in the capacity of states to make war and conquer territory led powerful rulers with better military and administrative organization to grow in size by progressively conquering their neighbors. This process continued so long as offensive capabilities were advantaged, but eventually there came a point at which the remaining powers, now significant in size, confronted each other with none being able to wipe out another. By this point, a shift had occurred that made it easier to defend territory than to conquer it: the offense-defense balance shifted from favoring offense to favoring defense. At the time of this shift, states stopped growing their borders, and arrived at an equilibrium. States were then compelled to recognize each other's borders because there was no other choice.[17]

The key shortcoming of this model is that it is not clear why there is no other choice. In the model, states are treated as whole, unable to conquer territory incrementally. But one ruler need not be able to wipe out another to still be willing and able to conquer small portions of a rival's territory. The modern bargaining theories of war take this shortcoming into account and suggest a modification to the story in which rulers cut a deal at their current boundaries to not attack each other for fear of destroying the relationship: if they have agreed on a boundary but one tries to conquer new territory, then that may lead the other to want to do the same in the future, which will be costly to both in the long run.*

---

* Even with this modification, however, the model does not adequately explain why a strong power would cooperate with a weaker neighbor.

As an explanation for the emergence of the state system from the early modern period to the 20th century, however, the mutual cost-reduction argument has a difficult time explaining some key facts. If the state system originated in the 17th century as a device to limit conflict, the immediate returns to rulers were extraordinarily poor. For instance, in the 167 years from 1648 to 1815, France was at war with another European power for 89 years, Britain for 84, and Spain for 110. Wars persisted well into the 20th century, which saw some of the most devastating conflicts in human history and sacrifices in the form of high rates of casualties and taxation for all social groups.[18]

More importantly, the realist account does not explain why states do not provide governance to their citizens in competitive fashion and respect each other's boundaries in non-military spheres such as taxation. Citizens play no role in most bargaining theories of conflict, even though issues about how to govern one's citizens occupy the lion's share of any ruler's thinking. Existing theory has treated this internal governance problem as completely separable from the problems that arise in international relations, such as the problem of interstate conflict. But these problems cannot be separated. More specifically, explaining the absence of conflict (a goal of realist theory) is not the same as explaining the incentives for cooperation. To explain interstate cooperation, what is needed is a richer theory that incorporates the economic and political relationship between states and their citizens.

Spruyt's Theory of Institutional Selection

Realist theory also does not deal with the question of what advantaged the territorial state against the other institutional forms that were prominent in early modern Europe. Hendrik Spruyt addresses this question head-on by proposing what is essentially a Darwinian theory of state institutions that (like the realist theories) is also rooted in the importance of conflict.

Spruyt argues that a gap emerged in the capabilities of different kinds of political units to succeed politically, and this gap was tied to the economic and technological changes taking place in Europe during the period of state-building. In Spruyt's model, the modern territorial state had "institutionally superior arrangements" relative to city leagues, city-states, and large empires, particularly in its ability to wage war. Spruyt holds that changes in the internal structure of states altered the state system as "sovereign states selected out and delegitimized actors who did not fit a system of territorially demarcated and internally hierarchical authorities" (1996, 28). Combined with the superior resources of the sovereign state, over time this process would lead to non-territorial polities being selected out through "mimicry and exit" (1996, 171). Thus, Spruyt offers what might be interpreted as a natural selection theory of the state system, leading to "the victory of the sovereign state" (1996, 154).

One shortcoming of Spruyt's story is that it is not clear why improvements in the economics of coercion or taxation, even uneven ones, must lead to a territorial state system of the kind we now have. In fact, improvements in military and administrative capacity are compatible with both claims of universal empire and the practice of mixed sovereignty. Outside of Europe, the introduction of early modern military innovations such as gunpowder was not accompanied by the development of a sovereignty norm, but rather by big empires getting even bigger.[19]

Spruyt's theory, like the standard realist account, also does not consider the political economy of the relationship between rulers and citizens. Peace is not incompatible with a system in which states allow their citizens to freely access public services from whomever they choose, paying portions of their taxes to whomever charges the more reasonable price for the service that is provided. By focusing on conflict and war, these theories neglect the way in which the relationship between rulers and their citizens affects the relationships between rulers.

To answer the questions that motivate us, what we need is not a theory in which cooperation between states serves to avoid or reduce the costs of war, but one in which cooperation can increase the benefits of peace.

Two Claims

We have set out in this chapter the central claims of our theory of the state system, and the assumptions on which they are built. We have laid out these claims through a simple model in which two rulers compete over the right to govern individuals who are distributed in the lands between them. This simple model can be understood in a variety of more complex ways—as a combination of costly competitive coercion and administration rather than literal tax competition, as competition over people rather than territory, and as competition between regional and local rulers rather than between rulers and citizens.

The desire to seize this surplus from taxation and governance is what motivates the rulers to collude, dividing territory among themselves to be able reap more of the benefits of governing. Borders can be set anywhere, but to be stable they must be self-enforcing. Collusive behavior can be made self-enforcing by setting the expectation that violations of a border lead to destructive future competition, which deters opportunistic behavior.

We now end the chapter by noting a subtle distinction between two claims. The first is the claim that the territorial state system emerged because rulers sought to establish a cartel in the governance market. The second is the claim that, regardless of its origins, and despite the fact that there are a myriad of different ways to understand it, it is conceptually useful to think of the state system as representing a cartel. These are two distinct claims, with the first claim requiring historical evidence to support it and the second one requiring a demonstration that cartel theory sheds light on many distinct and important features of the system as it took shape.

For the most part, we focused this chapter on the explaining and justifying the second claim.* In Chapters 5, 6, and 7, we offer further demonstration of how the cartel model generates a new and useful understanding of the workings of the state system by examining different aspects of it that the model was not specifically designed to address. These chapters do not rest on the assumption that the system that is in place today *originated* as a cartel, and they can be read independently of the next two chapters, in which we do pursue the first claim that cartel theory explains how the state system emerged in early modern Europe and then spread to the rest of the world with European influence.

---

* We did, however, critique some of the other prominent theories of the state system on both their ability to explain important features of the state system as it exists, and to explain important historical facts.

3

The Cartel Emerges

Where did the cartel system come from? In this chapter, we argue that the origins of the system lie in the political transformations that took place in early modern Europe. We describe these transformations, document their occurrence in some notable cases, and apply the model that we developed in the previous chapter to shed light on these changes. Our theory emphasizes two primary factors—economic growth and improvements in military technology and administrative capacity.

Europe before the Cartel

The emerging states of pre-modern Europe were limited not just in the extent to which they provided governance but also in their ability to project power across distant territories. This meant that powerful actors in the remote regions of a state enjoyed considerable autonomy from their rulers. In the 12th-century, the counts of Holland and dukes of Brittany, for example, conducted themselves as independent princes, paying little attention to the Holy Roman emperor or the French king.[1] Similarly, the dukes of Savoy played the kings of France against the emperor, strategically changing or reinterpreting their feudal allegiance in the process.[2] In even more remote areas, such as Frisia and Switzerland, feudalism had little purchase, and local towns and rural communities governed themselves.[3] Most spectacularly, the Valois dukes of Burgundy used astute diplomacy to build up a large political unit in the 15th century in the borderlands between France and the empire, in spite (or perhaps because) of their status as vassals of both rulers.[4]

The limited reach of rulers meant that the practical consequences of whatever competing influence they had over distant territories with other rulers that rivaled them in power were also limited. It is not surprising that in this situation ruler rhetoric became grandiose to the point of delusion, often claiming dominion over territories that they hardly governed. Such claims

The Cartel System of States: An Economic Theory of International Politics. Avidit Acharya and Alexander Lee, Oxford University Press. © Oxford University Press 2023. DOI:10.1093/oso/9780197632277.003.0003

had ancient roots, going back to the Roman Empire.* The most extravagant of these claims were made by the papacy and the Holy Roman Empire, each of which saw itself as Rome's political heir.**

While the larger polities claimed universal rule, the smaller ones nestled between them claimed a subordinate one. In the feudal arrangements of the Middle Ages, neither the lord nor the vassal possessed full sovereignty in the modern sense of the term. The lord, while asserting preeminence, did not actually control the territories he or his ancestors had granted to the vassals. The vassal, while often enjoying de facto independence, had obligations to the lord and always had to provide for the possibility that the ruler could remove him. The princes and cities of the Holy Roman Empire, for instance, had considerable political authority of their own right, but still acknowledged (and on occasion were forced to confront) the supreme political authority of the empire. In 1792, the empire comprised 80 princes, 120 ecclesiastical princes and prelates, 66 imperial cities, and some 2,000 imperial knights, each claiming some degree of political independence.[5]

In these circumstances, what we would call international relations were hierarchical and mixed up with internal politics. The relations between large powerful polities showcase the confused politics of the era. Both the emperor and the French monarch, for example, considered the duke of Burgundy to be their vassal.[6] Similarly, the war in Normandy between Phillip II of France and John of England (1202–1204) was justified by the French not as a war against a threatening neighbor of equal status but as a conflict with a disloyal vassal to enforce a court judgment, since John's French territories were held "of" Phillip.[7]

The structure of political control that characterized the pre-modern system was often contractual, with promises of protection routinely exchanged for promises of revenue.[8] These arrangements were negotiable and variable. The charters of medieval and early cities, for instance, set out, often in exhaustive detail, the privileges (commercial or fiscal) enjoyed by burghers

---

* Although the Romans did recognize the limits of their influence (they didn't try to conquer areas they felt would be unprofitable) and even withdrew from those like Dacia and Lowland Scotland that were difficult or expensive to administer, they did not, at least explicitly, recognize foreign rulers outside their control as peers.

** Pope Gregory, in the *Dictates Papae* (1075), made an impressive set of universal claims that gave the popes preeminence over all Christian rulers. The Holy Roman Empire made similarly extravagant claims to dominion. Even as late as the 14th century (by which time the administrative machinery of empire was already decrepit) the Latin motto of *Austriae est imperare orbi universo* ("all the world is subject to Austria") continued to feature prominently in the seals and iconography of the Hapsburg dynasty.

and the military, and the tax obligations to which they agreed. Towns, bishops, and secular lords with a strong bargaining position were able to strike unique and advantageous bargains. The Cinque Ports of southern England, for example, were able to win for themselves complete judicial autonomy and freedom from taxation in return for providing the king with a fleet for fifteen days a year.

At the same time, low taxation meant limited services. The agrarian subsistence economies of medieval Europe produced a limited surplus, much of which was absorbed by the local elites that extracted it from the peasantry. Even where they were most powerful, medieval states provided few public goods, focusing on defense and dispute resolution.[9] In areas where local privileges were extensive, even these services were provided by local elites, and the power of the central government (where such a thing existed) was limited. For instance, the bishop of Durham appointed the judges, raised the taxes, and minted his own money.[10]

The Transformation

Economic and Technological Development

The stability of the fractured and overlapping state system of medieval Europe, described above, was upended by the tremendous economic growth that started to take place with the rise of commerce and concomitant improvements in military technology and organization.

Even before the onset of industrialization, several major economic and structural changes had started taking place in Europe as early as the 15th century. Some economic historians have described these changes as the "Commercial Revolution," pointing to the marked improvements in business and finance through the formalization of modern accounting, insurance, and banking.[11] These developments had a major impact on the European economy. Commenting on the structural transformations that took place during this period, Walt Rostow (1959, 4), for instance, wrote that:

> the widening of the market—both within Europe and overseas—brought not only trade, but increased specialization of production, increased inter-regional and international dependence, enlarged institutions of finance, and increased market incentives to create new production functions.

Estimates by Angus Maddison (2007) and others confirm the importance of this period after the 15th century. In Maddison's data, GDP per capita in Western Europe grew by 182% in the period 1820–2000, and by 55% in the period 1500–1820, in comparison to the overall growth of only 38% from 1–1500.[12]

This pattern of growth is also apparent when we focus on the peripheries of specific polities, the areas where a medieval ruler's control was weakest. The urban population in the peripheral areas of France (those that bordered other areas in the Middle Ages but would be eventually incorporated into the French state) was booming throughout the 1400–1800 period, keeping pace with central France despite higher levels of military conflict. This trend is shown in Fig. 3 which plots the total population in French cities with a population over 10,000 in various years for core and peripheral provinces.

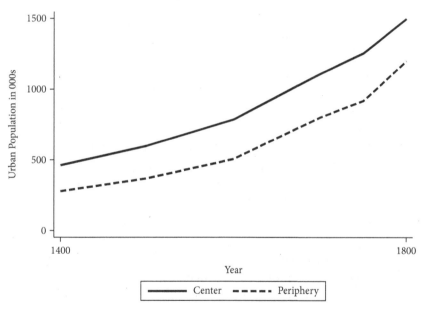

Fig. 3 Total population in French cities with a population over 10,000 in various years, taken from Bairoch (1988). Peripheral provinces are provinces that either bordered a non-French territory in 1477 or are part of today's France, but had not been incorporated in 1477. They include: Flanders, Artois, Hainaut, Cambraisis, Champagne, Burgundy, Lorraine, Alsace, Franche-Comte, Avignon, Metz, Dauphine, Savoy, Provence, Corsica, Roussillon, Languedoc, and Guyenne. Core provinces are the remaining provinces of modern France that were part of the French polity in 1477.

These economic developments brought new challenges and opportunities to European rulers. In the Middle Ages, few governments provided any public services besides defense, dispute resolution, and a basic currency. Over time, however, demand grew for government policies and services to support the new market economy—service such as roads and rural police forces. Moreover, with the growth of commercial activity, even the traditional government service of protection from expropriation became ever more valuable. By the time of the Industrial Revolution, new demands for a wide variety of additional services emerged, including public education, transport, and infrastructure. In England—the first country to industrialize—government sponsored the development of public sewage systems and water lines following the Great Stink of 1858, and established universal primary public education with the Forster Act of 1870. It also enacted new policies regulating labor-management relations, such as the Factory Acts passed after 1802, which protected the interests of labor, as well as the Frame Breaking Act of 1812 and the Malicious Damage Act of 1861, which protected capital owners from violent labor uprisings such as those of the Luddites.

As growth took place, European states also saw an opportunity to increase the revenues they collected from their citizens, in part to finance more and more services. In the period 1600–1780, real French and English state revenues increased by factors of 10.5 and 46.3 and in the period 1833–1990 real French and English state revenues increased by factors of 40 and 16, respectively, while per capita GDP rose by factors of 13.8 and 9.2.[13]

At the same time, the early modern and modern periods in Europe were periods of change in the cost and sophistication of military technology and organization (a development which some historians contentiously call the "Military Revolution") and the development of bureaucratic capacity to support these organizations.[14] The development of artillery and artillery-proof fortifications contributed to enhancing the economies of scale in coercion. Louis IX of France, who was fortunate to retain the services of the Bureau brothers as artillerists, was able to conquer 60 Norman castles in two years, reducing in months a province that had taken the English thirty-four years to conquer using traditional methods.[15]

Even more striking than the improved capabilities of armies was their improved ability to project force over distance. Part of this reflected changes in the means of recruiting and controlling troops. The English, for example, were unable to conquer northern Wales until they stopped using feudal armies (whose service obligation was only 40 days a year) and began to employ mercenaries who could be kept in the principality year round.[16] Similarly, the development of standardized and disciplined forms of military organization such as the Spanish *tercios* and the French *compagnies d'ordonnance* allowed control of remote forces superior to what was possible with feudal armies. Early modern bureaucracies were increasingly capable of paying and feeding such armies outside their home territories. The result was that armies ranged much farther than their medieval predecessors had. The Spain of Phillip II, for example, was able to support armies as far apart as Italy, Belgium, Catalonia, and North Africa, all despite numerous bankruptcies and several mutinies.[17]

How did these economic and technological developments affect the politics of interstate relations? Referring to the model that we developed in the previous chapter, the main implication of economic growth was that it increased the value of governance, and the main impact of improvements in military technology was to lower the costs of governing, especially in distant areas. These changes provided the impetus for border demarcation and the development of a sovereignty norm, as we explain next.

A Model of the Transformation

A simple extension of our model sheds light on the transformation in interstate politics that took place in Europe starting in the early modern period. We explain the transformation by depicting two simple "before" and "after" situations in Figs. 4 and 5, respectively.

The situation before the transformation is characterized by a low value of governance v and costs of governing, c_A and c_B, that are steeply increasing away from the core points of the state, marked A and B in Fig. 4. Here, ruler A's state is the segment from A to Z while B's state is the segment from X to B. This is because it is unprofitable for A to govern beyond Z. To the west of Z, his cost of governing c_A exceeds the value v which is the maximum he could derive from governing in this region. The same is true for ruler B to the west of X, where his cost of governing c_B is too high for it to be profitable to administer this territory. In the Roman Empire, for example, X would be the frontier, and the territory to the west of X would be areas not worth conquering and left to the "barbarians."

In Figure 4, actual states are limited in size and there is a large space between Z and X that is not governed by them, and where powerful local

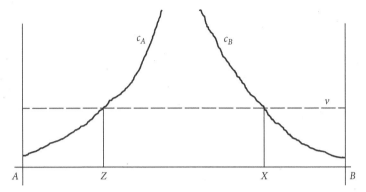

Fig. 4 When the value of governance v is low and the costs of governing c_A and c_B are high and steeply increasing there is a zone between Z and X where neither state A nor state B can profitably govern. The states do not compete to govern in any region of the governance market. A is the monopoly provider west of Z and B is the monopoly provider east of X.

elites who have not quite risen to the status of rulers may have emerged to establish de facto local authority, or even seek to establish themselves as new rulers–a point that we return to in a different context in Chapter 5.*
With such a buffer region between the practical reach of rulers A and B, the rulers will not be competitive providers of governance anywhere. They may draw an arbitrary border at some point between Z and X such that ruler A demands allegiance from vassals that he cannot control to the east of Z, while B demands allegiance from vassals to the west of X.

Or, if the border is hazy, both rulers could demand allegiance from an overlapping set of vassals operating in this region. In fact, it would also not be surprising for either or both of them to claim authority over the entire region Z to X, even though neither has any practical authority over any part of it. Because of the high costs to both rulers of actually governing this region, such claims would be non-threatening because they would have no material consequences: the rulers would find it too costly to exercise control over

---

* Efforts to elevate one's status to formal rulership would fail, however, if there are many of these local elites and the region that each can control is small. That said, our model has no need to draw a distinction between a ruler and such small elites, even though these distinctions were historically customary. A ruler in our model is simply an elite that governs a substantially large region which will eventually grow into a state, as the ruler is able to project greater power over distant areas, squashing other elites who fail to do so.

the residents of this zone, and thus they would leave the space ungoverned. Consequently, each ruler could disregard the competing claims made by the other. In fact, claims by either ruler over the *whole* region A to B could be disregarded by the other for the same reason. The key point is that in a situation where universal claims to authority have no practical consequence, rulers have no disincentive to make them.

The low value of governance v that is depicted in Fig. 4 results from the fact that prior to the economic growth of the post-medieval period, there simply was not very much for rulers to collect in large parts of the world. Likewise, the steeply increasing costs of governing c_A and c_B arise from the fact that primitive military technologies and weak bureaucratic organization make it difficult for states to project their power in distant territories and control these regions.

The economic and military developments that we have discussed above led to important changes from the situation depicted in Fig. 4. With the rise of commerce and industrial production, the value of governance v also rose, and with improvements in military technology and state administration the costs of governing c_A and c_B become less steep. Eventually, the situation started to resemble the one depicted in Fig. 5, which is essentially the same state of affairs as Fig. 1 of the previous chapter. Here, in comparison to Fig. 4, the point Z has shifted far to the east while X has shifted far to the west. Far from there being a buffer of ungoverned space between the rulers, now both rulers can profitably govern in the large area from X to Z and thus they have real potential to compete for authority. If they do compete, they suffer the losses from competition L_A and L_B for reasons explained in the previous chapter.

What does suffering these losses look like in practice? Historically, it meant that lords operating in the regions between X and Z were able to play one ruler off the other and win greater autonomy and control over local resources, thereby depressing the revenue that the rulers could collect from these regions. This would be especially true in the border regions close to Y on either side, where the extent of revenue losses suffered by both rulers is greatest, as Fig. 5 shows. Overall, since the value of governing v is high and the costs of governing c_A and c_B are now much lower, these losses from competition are potentially quite large. In fact, the higher v rises and the less steep c_A and c_B become, the larger the losses are from not cooperating, and it

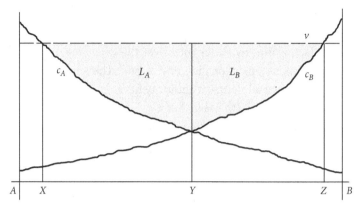

Fig. 5 After the value of governance rises and the costs of governing decline, states X and Y become potential competitors in the large zone between X and Z. The large losses that they incur from competition, labeled L_A and L_B, provide the impetus for a cartel agreement between them, under which A promises not to compete with B in providing governance east of Y and B promises not to compete with A west of this point. A then becomes the monopoly provider west of Y and B the monopoly provider to the east.

is in this situation that the rulers have strong incentives to agree on a border if it helps them recover these large shortfalls.

Since cooperating on a border means recognizing the authority of other rulers outside of one's own territory, rulers now have to be more careful about making claims to lands that are outside of their assigned borders. Other rulers may interpret such a claim as a signal that the ruler is abandoning the cooperation necessary to recover the losses from competition, or they may see it as the ruler trying to shift the border—a possibility that we explore in Chapter 5. Given this, it is not surprising that over the course of history, universal claims to authority would disappear.

Not only that, to cooperate effectively it may not be enough to simply draw the border Y on a map and administer one's region without making periodic cooperative contact with the other ruler. For example, if unruly subjects in the border regions around Y smuggle resources across the border against the wishes of one ruler or both, then the rulers would need to agree on how to deal with this. They may want to prevent citizens who break the law in one state from seeking shelter in the other. They may want to set tariffs on trade, and periodically update these tax rates and methods of enforcement. The rulers would thus want to maintain sustained contact with one other, perhaps through the exchange of permanent ambassadors.

Political Consequences

The economic and technological developments that took place in modern Europe were accompanied by important change in political structure. We discuss three of the main changes as follows—the decline of claims to universal authority, the rise of interstate borders, and the rise of diplomacy.

The Decline of Universal Claims. As overlapping spheres of influence became more common, European rulers took steps to avoid political conflict, increasingly claiming absolute practical control over a finite area rather than theoretical control over an infinite one. This process took off most notably within the Holy Roman Empire, though it had started with the papacy—the two European polities that had made the most extravagant of universal claims.

In the empire, the universalistic rhetoric of the emperor had come into tension with the local authority and particularistic rhetoric of the princes and imperial cities as early as the Middle Ages. During the instability of the 12th and 13th centuries, emperors had granted a wide variety of privileges to the princes and cities of Germany and Italy, which were confirmed in the Golden Bull of 1356. These privileges were extended to the choice of their subjects' religion by the Peace of Augsburg (1555). And, although the autonomous status of the princes was challenged during the early stages of the Thirty Years War (when the emperor used his prerogative to place some Protestant territory under imperial administration), the Peace of Westphalia, which ended the war, put to rest any residual imperial threats to local autonomy.

The papacy's claims to universal secular authority also started to diminish in the Middle Ages. By the end of this period, secular rulers were able to gain authority over the operation of churches in their territories and restrict the claims of the pope to exercise that authority. In northern Europe, the Reformation allowed many rulers to completely disclaim papal supremacy and make themselves the heads of the church in their territories, while other rulers negotiated similar concessions from the Holy See through agreements like the French Pragmatic Sanction of Bourges and the Spanish Patronato Real. In 1683, under the prompting of Louis XIV, the French clergy declared that "kings and princes are not by the law of God subject to any ecclesiastical power, nor to the keys of the Church, with respect to their temporal government."[18]

The Rise of Borders. To solidify their power, the rulers of the new sovereign states of Europe needed a means of demarcating their respective areas of control. Fixed territorial boundaries became the method of choice, allowing much more precise knowledge about jurisdictional responsibilities and violations.

How were these borders drawn? Several examples show that their delimitation and demarcation frequently involved the physical marking of space. We look below at how this occurred on the Anglo-Scottish border in the 16th century, with the creation of the Scot's Dyke, a long earthen mound with a ditch on both sides. Other countries placed boundary markers during the early modern period as well. The Treaty of the Pyrenees (1659) is sometimes cited as the first major treaty to list detailed "metes and bounds," though this dating is almost certainly too late.[19] The 1779 border treaty between France and the Austrian Netherlands was the first in a long series of treaties redefining this particular border to mention topographical boundaries— its predecessor of 1769 had mentioned no unit below the parish, whose boundaries were not defined, and earlier treaties had been based on even larger units, such as the *bailliage*.[20] By contrast, the 1779 treaty was quite specific, mentioning a ditch that separated two villages on either side. This treaty also saw the end of most of the enclaves that had persisted through the Middle Ages, following a process of mutual exchange. In the 19th century, the practice became much more common. The Franco-Spanish border was finally formally marked in the 1860s, while the US-Canadian border was demarcated in Vermont and Quebec in 1818 and in the western part of the border by the Northwest Boundary Survey (1857–61).

Quantitatively measuring the rise of the salience of borders in international relations is a difficult challenge. Fig. 6 depicts perhaps the simplest possible measure of the concept: whether borders were considered worth discussing in international treaties. It shows a running average of the number of treaties mentioning borders (or any of a variety of French or Latin synonyms) per year. While territory frequently changed hands in the Middle Ages, these treaties tended to mention the land of a particular count or abbey rather than a line on a map. But from the figure, we see that mentions of actual borders rose noisily between the 14th and 17th centuries.

Paralleling the rise in the importance of borders was also an increase in the precision with which they were drawn. Unlike medieval boundaries, these new boundaries were more clearly defined and stable, allowing much more certain knowledge about their locations and affording rulers with

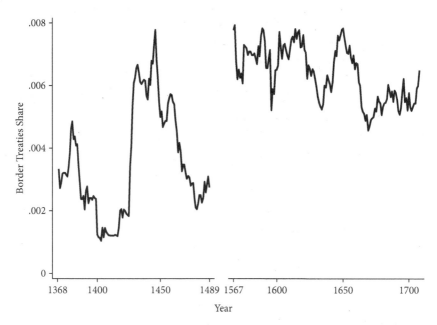

Fig. 6 Mentions of borders in international treaties, 1368–1709. The data are a five-year running average of the share of treaties each year mentioning at least one boundary, calculated from Dumont, de Carlscroon, and Picart (1726), who comprehensively provide the full text of European treaties. Data from 1490 to 1556 are missing.

greater ability to monitor their violations. The process of border demarcation employed modern cartographical techniques.[21] The very process of demarcating linear, consistent boundaries required new inventions like the Theodolite (named in 1571, perfected in 1787), the plane table (1551), and Gunter's chain (1620). Similarly, the drawing of maps aid coordination, allowing negotiators to know exactly where their own control would end and their neighbor's begin, without any local knowledge or expertise and with only limited possibilities for ambiguity.[22]

The Rise of Diplomacy. The emergence of bounded territorial states created a new set of problems. How should polities relate to each other and address issues between them under the new set of norms? Modern states moved to develop institutions for the exchange of information and dispute resolution. Perhaps the most important step in this process was the development of permanent embassies, where the ambassador was not a visitor but a resident.[23]

The development of diplomacy was slow and gradual, and some older hierarchical notions persisted until somewhat recently. At the start of this process, diplomats were ranked relative to each other with empires at the top and republics at the bottom. Britain's representative in Washington, remarkably, was not retitled as an ambassador until 1893. The United States retitled its last legations as embassies as late as 1966. In 21st-century practice, however, nearly all ambassadors are formally equal in status—a reflection of the formal equality of states in the contemporary world.

The gradual but steady trend toward formal diplomatic equality is supported by data from Resat Bayer (2006), which show that the proportion of dyads of European countries in which the two countries had some form of diplomatic relations with each other rose from 57% in 1820 to 78% in 1909, and the proportion of dyads among those with diplomatic relations where each country's representatives were of equal diplomatic rank also grew from 61% to 88% during this period.*

The new diplomacy of the modern era also meant that foreign and domestic affairs became separate spheres of activity in a way they had not previously. In France, the separation of foreign from domestic affairs within the royal secretariat occurred in 1626, but even then the foreign secretary was responsible for the navy and commerce (until 1669), and the internal affairs of several peripheral provinces (until the mid-18th century).[24] In England, the two royal secretaries were split into the northern department (covering northern England and relations with Protestant states) and the southern department (covering southern England and relations with Catholic and Muslim states), and by 1782 the northern and southern departments were reorganized into the Home and Foreign offices.**

Not only did the new diplomatic relations help polities work together, but its development helped clarify the distinction between sovereign and non-sovereign political entities—between cartel members and non-members. The ability to conduct foreign relations was now defined as a function separate from other types of political interaction, and one possible only for sovereign states. In 1461, Louis XI declared that only he could send

---

* Interestingly, some polities that clung to their universal pretensions remained aloof from the practice of posting ambassadors. The Holy Roman Empire never sent ambassadors (though the emperors themselves did as dukes of Austria) and the Ottoman Empire, another polity that claimed universal rule on the basis of religion, did not post an ambassador until as late as 1798.
** See Nelson (1969).

and receive ambassadors, a declaration enforced through threats of exile, establishing for good the idea that "only the king should have a foreign policy."[25]

The Anglo-Scottish Border

Tilly (1985, 174) gives Tudor England as his first example of early modern state-building:

> The Tudor demilitarization of the great lords entailed ... taming their habitual resort to violence for the settlement of disputes. ... In the Marches of England and Scotland, the task was more delicate, for the Percys and Dacres who kept armies and castles along the border threatened the crown, but also provided a buffer against Scottish invaders. But they, too, eventually fell into line.

Tilly was certainly right that the under-governed status of the Anglo-Scottish border was increasingly anomalous in the mid-16th century. However, the borders did not simply "fall into line" automatically, or in response to the use of force. The success of the Tudor and Stuart state-building campaigns in this region required the cooperation of men on the other side and the development of new, mutually agreed upon ways of understanding political authority and territoriality. In order to assimilate the border regions, the two sides had agreed to put limits on their own authority, to act together, and end the ability of the border lords to play one side against the other.

The success of this effort required the development of a new approach to interstate relations. In the 17th century, the norms of the newly emerging state system were still fuzzy and far from universally accepted, and the administrative integration of border regions was the result of long periods in which the relationship between neighboring states gradually became more cooperative. This required acknowledging separate, territorially defined independent states, coming to an agreement on the exact course of the territorial division, and developing the institutions necessary to adjudicate disputes and frustrate the ability of local lords to evade governance. We provide an overview of this process for the British case next.

The Border in the Era of Competition

Administratively, the border region was a weak area for both the English and Scottish states into the 17th century, with powerful local families (the Percys, Dacres, and Nevilles on the English side, the Douglases and Homes on the Scottish) building up fiefs that enjoyed considerably more independence from royal interference than vassals elsewhere.[26] These families also tended to monopolize royal offices in the region and treated these offices as hereditary.[27]

On the English side, this autonomy was sometimes formalized by the granting of "liberties," by which certain areas were exempted from ordinary royal jurisdiction, with courts being answerable to the local lord and doing justice in his name, rather than that of the king. While these liberties were in principle subject to royal taxation, these taxes were often difficult to enforce. For example, in 1336, royal tax collectors told Westminster that they had been unable to enter Hexhamshire to collect, since "the King's writ does not run there."[28]

Other border families, or "surnames," pressed their advantages even further. The Armstrongs, the most powerful family in the Debatable Lands, maintained an armed force of 3,000 men in 1528, and used them to raid on both sides of the border, with the looted cattle being sold on the opposite side with the connivance of royal officials and money being extorted for freedom from raiding.[29]

The surnames eagerly played rulers off each other. Both the English and the Scots governments readily took advantage of civil instability and foreign conflict, sponsoring ambitious rebels. The Black branch of the Douglas family, for example, spent much of the 15th century as English clients, concluding private treaties with the English and receiving military support from them.[30]

Perhaps the most remarkable of the privileges that the borderers enjoyed was almost complete freedom from taxation. In theory, this was a reward for their military service on the borders, but the borderers appear to have much preferred the service—which did not occur in peacetime, did not last all year, and involved profitable opportunities for looting—to paying taxes. In England, the northern counties enjoyed complete freedom from central taxation, and the same was generally true on the Scottish side as well.[31]

Border reivers raided cattle in the Anglo-Scottish border region and sold the raided cattle on the other side of the border. They were thorns in the sides of both the Stuart kings of Scotland and the Tudor kings of England. The governments of Scotland and England eventually agreed that a mutually recognized border (the Scot's Dyke) would help them coordinate in suppressing the reivers. The Scottish and English negotiators, who had more in common with each other than the unruly subjects who inhabited the border region, celebrated their agreement in a series of highly alcoholic banquets. The cost of the banquets became the subject of a minor dispute between the two governments.

Evidence for Cooperation

The administrative integration of the border region was the result of a centuries long effort in which the relationship between England and Scotland gradually became more cooperative. This cooperation involved three steps: (i) an agreement in principal to the existence of separate, territorially defined states, (ii) an agreement on the exact course of territorial division, and (iii) the development of joint institutions to adjudicate disputes and frustrate the ability of local lords to play one side off against the other. We provide a brief account of these three steps.

Mutual Recognition. The confusion over the status of the two polities was eventually resolved by a series of cooperative treaties. The Treaty of Edinburgh-Northampton (1328), for example, elevated the status of the Scottish prince, Robert Bruce, to that of sovereign ruler of Scotland, a land "separate in all things from the Kingdom of England, whole, free and undisturbed in perpetuity, without any kind of subjection, service claim or demand." This recognition forced lords to choose masters, leading to a precipitous decline in cross-border landholding.[32] Despite this, the next century saw continued English efforts to annex Scotland (whole or in part) with the help of disaffected Scottish lords. Eventually, the Treaty of Perpetual Peace (1502), would put relations on a more normal footing, and conclude a marriage agreement between the two royal families.[33]

No subsequent English ruler would question Scotland's status as an independent state, though they would periodically occupy portions of it or attempt to gain control of it through strategic marriages. In fact, even when they occupied southern Scotland, the English never tried to annex it, and the areas they controlled "remained entirely separate from England, both legally and politically."[34] Remarkably, the two kingdoms remained legally separate for a century even after a single monarch (James VI of Scotland, and I of England) took power in both in 1603.

Cooperative Demarcation. Even after the Scots won full recognition of their independence, the boundary was not precisely demarcated and, instead, the Treaty of Edinburgh-Northhampton enigmatically defined Scotland's boundaries as "its own proper marches as they were held and maintained in the time of King Alexander."[35] As an internal English privy council memo noted, "the just bowndes towards Scotland is in debate in diverse places where the two realmes towche, and hath beine cawse of great controversie betwene the nacions."[36]

Changes in population and production made the disputed areas more important over time. The Debatable Lands had, until the early 16th century, been uninhabited, and used only for pasturage.[37] However, sometime around 1516, members of the Armstrongs and the Graham surnames began settling permanently in the region. The English, under Warden William Dacre, provided financial support to the Armstrongs and tacit support for their presence in the Debatable Lands, who they saw as giving them influence on the Scottish side of the border. Once the surnames were established, however, they proved impossible to remove by unilateral action, given their skill in playing the two powers off against each other. For instance, in 1518 the Scottish privy council was informed that while members of the other surnames had given pledges of loyalty, the Armstrongs "ar in the Debatable landis, and agreit [in agreement] with Ingland."[38]

The lawlessness of this region prompted one of Europe's first formal processes of border demarcation. In 1552, the two states appointed a five-man commission to draw a border, with each party appointing two members and the French ambassador serving as a neutral arbiter. A mutually agreeable line was surveyed through the area, giving the Scots more territory but the English control of the main road. The line was drawn on a set of mutually agreed maps and marked with a cross "to mark this line distinctly from the others in the chart."[39] On the ground, the new border was marked by the Scot's Dyke, an earthen mound with a ditch on either side, and terminal stones at each end.[40]

One of the main goals of the division was to end not just the ambiguity over who controlled what territory, but also the possibility that people from one side would be able to play the two countries off against each other. The instructions to the English commissioners are especially interesting in their obvious desire to monopolize all international contact to state officials—banning Englishmen from meeting Scots, marrying them, or holding land in Scotland.[41]

Cooperative Enforcement. Even in places where the borders were clear, their proximity created opportunities for astute locals to rob and murder on one side, returning to sell their loot on the other. To control such raids, the two kingdoms developed a remarkable system of international law enforcement, the March Law, which attained full institutional development in the 1340s, though its roots were older.[42] The law was administered by royal officials, the Wardens of the Marches, who worked closely with their opposite numbers on the other side of the border.[43]

March Law was both customary and defined in "law books of the border," which were periodically compared to each other to ensure conformity.[44] A variety of crimes were covered, including murder, theft, kidnapping, seizure of castles, and illegal cattle grazing. While victims were allowed the (carefully defined) right of hot pursuit, reprisals were strictly forbidden.[45] Instead, disputes were judged on specific "March Days" presided over by the two wardens, with juries made up of equal numbers of Scottish and English jurors. Wardens were responsible for enforcing judgments against criminals on their side of the border, and might pay out of pocket if they were unable to raise the fine from the criminal through their own court system.

During the course of the 16th century, the English and Scottish monarchies began to cooperate more actively to assert their authority in the border region. By the middle decades of the century, relations were downright collegial. In 1567, the earl of Moray, regent of Scotland, wrote to Queen Elizabeth promising to pacify the borders and followed up by suddenly marching upon the borders, where he arrested 34 local men, of whom at least 20 were executed by hanging or drowning.[46] Moray's campaigns against the borderers in 1569 was even more dependent on English support. Douglas Tough and Leonard Walton (1928, 206–7) give a summary that shows how tiresome and violent this type of state building could be:

> Having received a loan [from the English] of £5000 and two hundred Berwick troops he came to Kelso with four thousand men, and having met [English Warden of the Middle March Sir John] Forster, went on and burnt Liddesdale until not a house was left standing in it.... In the middle of September he came again to Kelso for five or six weeks to suppress the outlaws and settle the borders. He made delivery to England for bills [compensation for cross border raids] valued at £1,200.... Then, after taking sureties from many borderers, and, assured of English concurrence against 'recet,' [granting of refuge] he set out for Dumfries, burning on the way....

Interstate legal cooperation extended much further once the two kingdoms came under the rule of King James in 1603, though the proposals for such cooperation predate his accession. A joint border commission was established, even more independent of local elites than the warden's courts had been, but still representing both countries equally. The commission was responsible for the final pacification of the borders, disarming the surnames and executing hundreds of bandits.[47]

Motivations for Cooperation

Why did the English and Scottish, bitter enemies in many other contexts, cooperate in their border policy? The surviving documents emphasize the desire to assert control over their territories by eliminating the border elites. In fact, it is difficult to review the documents without being struck by the dislike, distrust, and contempt of both central governments for the borderers. The wardens, as the local officials on the spot, were well aware that the borderers were using the possibility of adhering to the other side (and by implication, of raiding their current friends) to get what they wanted, but were powerless to act.[48] The men of the borders were "addicted of self-willynes to wrong treade owte the boundes either to their own advauntage" and the "dificultye" they caused was out of all proportion to the value of the lands they controlled.[49]

This point was raised in the Scottish privy council meeting of 1551 which agreed to the partition of the Debatable Lands with England. Instead of discussing the international situation and the gains to relations with England, the Council focused its attention on their exasperation with the area's residents, and the *internal* gains of partition. John Burton (1877, 118–19) quotes the minutes of this meeting, which reflect exactly this frustration:

> Having had consideration of the great and heavy crimes committed upon our sovereign lady's poor lieges by thieves and other malefactors, broken men, and the diverse murders and slaughters committed in the past, and especially by the inhabitants of the debatable land, who by night and day continually ride and make daily plunder and oppressions upon the poor . . . and no victim can get remedied, nor any criminal can be put to due punishment. . . .

The correspondences of the English diplomats also reveals the underlying intentions, demonstrating the fact that both governments were well aware that demarcation was in their interest and not that of border elites. In particular, Dan O'Sullivan (2016) notes that the English diplomats were aware that many of the powerful locals would not look kindly on any such division. Indeed, in a secret correspondence with the Scots, one English diplomat wrote: "indeed the less privy the Borderers be made to the division hereof, the more likely it is that the thing will take place."[50]

Such documents, not intended for publication, provide the best available window into the motivations of early modern policymakers. As the above passage shows, the diplomats involved perceived themselves, in many respects, as having more in common with their fellow bureaucrats on the other side—"men which should have indifferent respect to the quiet and concord of both the realms," than with the border elites.[51] They suggest that underneath the often tempestuous relationship between England and Scotland, ran an important thread of common interest—the desire to control (and tax) their turbulent border subjects.

Besides the increase in law and order, England and Scotland gained financially from the pacification of the borders, though the major gains only occurred after the union of crowns. As George MacDonald Fraser (2008, 362) remarked "it had not escaped the gentry employed in restoring order to the Marches that there was considerable profit to be gained from the operation." He continues to explain how the land of some of the border clans could be expropriated and turned to more intensive agriculture, and how Lord Cumberland was eventually granted the Graham lands, fulfilling his "ambitions to remove the Grahams and replace them with dependable farmers."[52]

In fact, everyone was aware that the pacification meant that the revenue that had previously been retained by the border surnames could be transferred to the crown and its servants. R. T. Spence (1977, 104) describes how Cumberland gained one manor for a rent of £100 per annum, the sum which the commissioners estimated it could be worth if freed "from the malicious bondage of the Grames and their wicked coherents."

The ordinary fiscal structure of the two kingdoms was extended to the border regions, though fierce local resistance made the process gradual. In England, the longstanding exemption of the northern counties from parliamentary taxation was ended quickly after the union of crowns.[53] The courts declared that the customary land tenures of the border should be interpreted using the principles of the "various accepted forms of customary tenure elsewhere in England," with fewer rights for tenants.[54]

Other Cases

We saw in the case of Britain how two neighboring states, England and Scotland, were able to diminish the privileges of border residents and enhance their own authority in the borderlands by formally agreeing on a fixed border between them. We now provide additional evidence of this main implication of our theory—that political consolidation takes place in the peripheral regions of a state as rulers begin to cooperate with their neighbors.

We look, more briefly, at three additional cases: Sweden, Spain, and France. In all three cases, the close temporal association between border agreement and state consolidation is notable. As states cooperate with their neighbors, the privileges won by powerful border elites disappear. There is then a convergence in the autonomy of border zones and core areas, and the states increase the share of revenue they collect from their border regions.

Sweden

In 1660, the Swedish monarch ruled a large empire that included modern Finland and Estonia and large portions of modern Latvia and Germany.[55] As in many other such assemblages, the nobility of the peripheral regions of this empire enjoyed a set of privileges of which the most important were the right to exploit the peasantry. In Livland (modern northern Latvia and southern Estonia), successive Swedish and Polish kings had granted 84% of the land to the nobility as gifts, while retaining only 1.25% for themselves. By contrast, in Uppland (part of Sweden proper), at most 59% of the land had been donated to the nobility and the crown retained 10% of the land. The crown's greater generosity in Livland reflected the desire to retain the loyalty of the nobility in a region subject to constant border disputes with Russia and Poland. Between 1620 and 1660, both Sweden and Poland formally claimed Livland, and fought two major wars over its possession.

Then, in 1660 the Treaty of Oliva finally ceded Livland to Sweden permanently, while Russia guaranteed its border with Sweden at Cardis (1661). After Charles XI of Sweden came of age in 1672, he set out, through his "uniformity policy," to eliminate all political peculiarities among regions under the slogan of "one king, one law, one people." The most important policy consequence for Livland was the *reduktion*, in which the king confiscated all noble property that had previously been given by the crown. Despite protests from the local nobility who referenced earlier royal guarantees made at the time of annexation, the process was successfully completed by the 1690s. The *reduktion* was a financial windfall for the crown, recovering revenues of 5.5 million silver dalers, making the province (previously a financial drain) self-sustaining and forcing it to pay a tax worth 10% of the central budget. By contrast, in Pomerania, the king recovered only a paltry 66,500 silver dalers from the *reduktion*.

These figures support the main prediction of our model—that the profitability of governing border areas should rise precipitously after the border regions gets incorporated through interstate agreements.

Spain

In Spain, the fiscal pressure on peripheral regions was also much lower than in the core prior to state consolidation. In the 17th century, Spain was a composite state including both Castile and the peripheral provinces of Aragon, Valencia, and Catalonia (the "crown of Aragon").[56] These provinces were not subject to Castilian taxation, and enjoyed a set of *fueros* (privileges) that allowed the local nobility to control most posts within the kingdoms and the right to consent to taxation. Though the lack of a developed central accounting system makes quantification difficult, contemporaries and modern historians are in agreement that Catalonia and Aragon had much lower levels of taxation than Castile in the 17th century.[57] As Perry Anderson (1979, 71) notes "nothing is more striking in this respect than the utter lack of any proportionate contribution to the Spanish war effort in Europe during the later 16th and 17th centuries from Aragon."

Particularly in the case of Catalonia, the richest of Spain's peripheral provinces, the reluctance to pressure the local elite came from a fear that they would use their location on the border to call in French troops as allies against Castile. In fact, between 1640 and 1652 the Catalan parliament, the General Estates, had done precisely this after revolting against a royal attempt to create a "Union of Arms" that would have equalized military contributions. Louis XIII of France was declared Protector of the Catalan Republic and Count of Barcelona, while a Franco-Catalan army fought the Castilians. According to Christopher Storrs (2006, 195), throughout the later 17th century, the royal bureaucracy were cautious in their negotiations with the Catalan elite over taxation because they "were constantly aware—and fearful—of the danger of a repeat of the events of 1640–52." This fear was only partly assuaged by the Spanish-French border treaty of 1659, because the administrative weakness and policy drift of the late 17th-century Spanish state made the ministers around the developmentally disabled Charles II ("the bewitched") both suspicious of French intentions and unwilling to undertake major policy initiatives that disturbed centuries-old institutional arrangements.[58]

However, French friendship was ultimately the key factor in the end of the *fueros*. During the War of the Spanish Succession (1701–15), the Catalans sided with the losing (Austrian) candidate against the winning (French) candidate to the Spanish throne. They were defeated, with French military help proving more reliable than Austro-British maritime aid. Now that Catalonia and Aragon were situated between two friendly states with an agreed-upon border, the victors were not inclined to be as generous as they had been in 1652. The Spanish *Nueva Planta* decrees of 1707 (only implemented after the end of the war) abolished the *fueros* of the crown of Aragon, and the administration was reformed to conform to the centralized Castilian model.[59] One of the first acts of the reformers was to establish new taxes designed to equalize the fiscal burden between Castile and the Aragonese kingdoms, with the Valencian version being explicitly called the *equivalente*.

France

Perhaps the most well-known story of state centralization is that of the French state under Richelieu, Mazarin, and Louis XIV.[60] Faced with a powerful nobility, these rulers worked to undermine feudal privileges and traditional institutions while concentrating authority in centrally appointed *intendents*.[61] These efforts occurred in all parts of France, but their effects were especially pronounced in border areas where previous rulers had been generous to the nobility to compel or entice them to accept French rule. Burgundy and French Flanders, for example, had formerly been part of the Burgundian state, and were claimed by the Hapsburgs into the early 16th century. Many of these areas retained representative institutions abolished in interior France, the autonomy of which was an early target of the *intendents*.

The consolidation of the French state, mainly in the 17th century, led to large financial gains for its rulers. Quantitative evidence on the fiscal consequences of the incorporation of border regions in Europe is generally difficult to come by, but 17th-century France is an exception. The data depicted in Fig. 7 show how French state revenues increased over time for three types of French provinces: those that did not border another kingdom during the 17th century, those that did, and those that did border another kingdom in 1600 but not in 1695, due to Louis XIV's annexations. Due to the lack of annual measures of provincial population or economic activity, it is

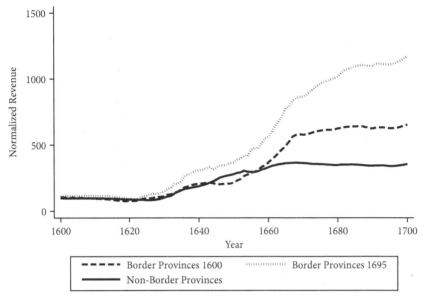

Fig. 7 Trends in French state revenues over the 17th century for three types of French provinces: those that did not border another kingdom during the 17th century (solid), those that did (dotted), and those that did border another kingdom in 1600, but not in 1695, due to Louis XIV's annexations (dashed). The data were collected by Mallet (1789) and digitized and made available by Bonney (1999). All plots are ten-year running averages. For each category of provinces, revenue in 1600 is normalized to 100 to focus the comparison on differential growth rates.

impossible to compute measures of the absolute tax burden. Nevertheless, from these data, we calculate that between 1600 and 1695, nominal state revenue increased by a factor of only 3.81 in non-border provinces, a factor of 6.20 in regions that were border provinces in 1600 but not in 1695, and a factor of 12.05 in border areas, with the fastest rises coming in the middle of the century.[62]

We note that the trends depicted in Fig. 7 do not reflect institutional differences that might have led to *lower* taxation in border provinces, since in the *Ancien Régime*, the peripheral provinces were generally ruled as *pays d'états*, which meant that they could not be taxed without their own consent, while the core provinces were typically ruled as *pays d'election*, which allowed the king to raise taxes at will.* While Louis XIV was quite successful in eroding

---

* A few provinces annexed in the 17th century were annexed as *pays d'imposition*, which gave them an intermediate level of fiscal autonomy.

the autonomy of the *pays d'état* provinces, the institutional difference largely remained intact until the French Revolution.

In addition, it is also worth noting that the larger growth in revenue from the border areas does not necessarily mean that these areas were more heavily taxed than the center. In fact, the qualitative evidence suggests that the opposite was true, and that "prior to the seventeenth century the *pays d'états* generally had more autonomy from the crown . . . which usually allowed them to minimize their tax burden relative to the more centrally controlled *pays d'election*."[63]

Why did this increase in taxation occur when it did? The 17th century—and especially the middle decades—was a period of rapid development in norms of territoriality between France and its neighbors, which in effect gave greater power to the central French state in exercising control over its border regions. Notably, the Treaty of the Pyrenees (1659) ended 24 years of war between Spain and France, and ended Spanish claims to French-occupied territory on both the southwestern and northeastern borders. The southwestern border along the Pyrenees has remained stable since treaty went into effect. On the eastern border, the Peace of Westphalia not only granted new territory to France, but made explicit that several French territories annexed in the previous century, such as the Three Bishoprics of Metz, Verdun, and Toul, were not part of the Holy Roman Empire, giving the "chief Dominion, Right of Sovereignty, and all other Rights" to the French king.[64]

From Bilateral Cooperation to a State System

The examples that we have discussed above are cases in which cooperation between states took place mainly in bilateral fashion. These examples alone do not provide any direct evidence that a sovereignty norm emerged that would define the territorial state system. If such a norm did emerge organically out of the many examples of two neighboring states striking agreements to respect each other's right to rule across a mutually agreed border, it would be very difficult to provide any direct evidence of this. The norm would be something that took shape as states came to a consensus on a common ideology behind these isolated instances of bilateral cooperation. It is even possible that the norm may have emerged unintentionally. We simply do not know.

What we do know is that European rulers did eventually arrive at a common understanding of international order. In fact, the many meetings that they and their representatives attended (such as the Congresses of Westphalia and Vienna) to periodically reorganize the governance market provides us with some evidence that this common understanding was one that the rulers arrived at relatively early in the development of the system.*

Political historians have argued that a main goal of the Congress of Vienna was to suppress democratic movements in the chaos following Napoleon's defeat.[65] It is also clear that the main tool that the negotiators used to try to achieve this collusion was the extensive map-drawing and redrawing that collusively divided the governance market even in places that were distant from many of the states that were represented at the meeting.

Consider the crisis at Vienna over Poland and Saxony. Russia wanted a monopoly on governance in Poland, as Prussia did in Saxony. The other cartel members, however, agreed that Russia would not be entitled to control the entire Polish governance market, and that Prussia would be entitled to just over half of the Saxon governance market, but not all of it. The remainder of Saxony would return to the control of King Frederick Augustus I.[66]

But this is not the only example. The Viennese map drawing exercise extended to essentially all regions in Europe and some outside of Europe as well. It included the transfer of Swedish Pomerania from Danish control to Prussian control, and the transfer of Guadeloupe from Sweden to France, which was asked to compensate Sweden in yearly installments for control over this market—quite like a rental agreement. The Congress also reinstated the Bourbon kings of Spain, entitling them to a share of the governance market in the Iberian Peninsula, and enacted changes in the internal governance markets of Switzerland and the German principalities. Britain was recognized as having a monopoly on governance in southern Africa and South Asia, including the island of Ceylon. Relatives of the Austrian emperor were awarded the rights to govern specific areas such as Duke Francis IV in Modena, and his cousin Marie Louise in Parma. These decisions were made by the rulers of states or their representatives rather than their subjects, many of whom would learn only after the fact that a new monopolist was in charge of governing them. If this is not evidence of open collusion in the governance market, then what is?

---

* Our discussion of interdependent cooperation in the three-state model of the previous chapter provides some foundations for such a process.

In the next chapter, we will look specifically at how governance markets in Africa, Asia, and the New World were divided among European powers. The division of territory in these regions of the world (at meetings such as the Congress of Berlin) provide an even clearer picture of collusion in the governance market, and how collusion became the norm that defines the territorial state system that now encompasses the entire globe.

4

The Cartel Takes Over

At the beginning of the 19th century, the cartel system was in effect mainly in Europe. By the end of the century it had extended over virtually the entire world. This was primarily a function of colonialism, since for many people assimilation to the new world of hard borders occurred when they were conquered. A few East Asian countries maintained their independence but were forced to conform to the expectations of the cartel as it suited European powers. While the cartel system was initially alien to local practice in most of these places, local elites quickly made full membership a policy goal. The cartel system thus remains one of the most enduring legacies of the period of European expansion and growth, though its operation in many parts of the developing world today remains imperfect.

Africa and Asia before the West

While Europe was moving towards a territorial state system in the early modern period, the world outside of Europe was not. In the 18th century, most of Africa and Asia bore a superficial resemblance to Europe in the early Middle Ages. A few large polities claimed very broad or universal dominion, and many smaller ones claimed subordinate status. Moreover, in the many areas inhabited by nomadic, hunter-gatherer, or swidden agriculturalist peoples, there was only limited political organization beyond the village, clan, or band.

Imperial China was the paradigmatic case of the universalizing empire outside of Europe. The emperors saw China as the cultural center of the world and the non-Chinese as inferior "barbarians."[1] As such, they could not accept any outsiders—no matter how powerful they were—as political equals. In fact, they conducted very little exchange with the outside world, including with nearby polities of considerable cultural sophistication such as Korea and Vietnam. To the extent that they did conduct political relations with outsiders, the Ming and Qing structured it through a system of tributary

The Cartel System of States: An Economic Theory of International Politics. Avidit Acharya and Alexander Lee, Oxford University Press. © Oxford University Press 2023. DOI:10.1093/oso/9780197632277.003.0004

exchange. Representatives from other states journeyed to Beijing, bearing gifts for the emperor. While in the emperor's presence, they performed the kowtow—a series of prostrations that signified their inferior status. In the famous Macartney mission to China, the imperial court demanded that the head of the mission, George Macartney, emissary of King George III, kowtow before the emperor, which he refused. In response, the Qianlong emperor's main message back to the British sovereign was to "tremblingly obey and show no negligence."[2] Until the 19th century the Qing never conceded their claims of superiority.*

Other non-European polities made similar claims to universal power, if not always with the éclat of the Qing. The Tokugawa shoguns of Japan proudly refused to follow the other Asian powers in recognizing Chinese predominance, meaning that the two countries had no formal relations.[3] Japanese relations with the Dutch, the only foreign power allowed to trade in Japan after 1636, were humiliatingly hierarchical, with the merchants confined to a small island except during their annual trip to Tokyo, where they were expected to dance and sing for the amusement of the shogun's officials.[4]

Claims to universal authority were also made outside of Northeast Asia. A variety of Muslim rulers claimed to be caliphs—rulers of the entire Islamic world as successors to the prophet. In the early 19th century, the Ottoman Empire, the sultans of Bornu and Sokoto in northern Nigeria, and the Sultan of Yogyakarta in Java all claimed such authority. In the Indian subcontinent, the dominant Mughal Empire also made such claims. As Jos Gommans (2002, 19–20) puts it:

> The frontiers of the Mughal Empire were never lines but always zones... The official Mughal ideology, as expressed in imperial panegyrics and various court-sponsored miniatures, was one of an empire without limits, but with lines fanning out from the imperial centre in all directions towards an endless horizon. In this respect, the names and titles of the

---

* Unsurprisingly, none of these polities willingly recognized territorial limits to their authority. In general, they expanded the limits of their actual administration as far as they could. And, when they could not, they demanded symbolic tribute and fealty from as many polities as they could in the zone beyond that. While the Great Wall of China appears to be the ultimate example of a fixed border, not only did the Qing emperors periodically redefine the administrative frontier unilaterally, but they demanded that the Mongol tribes beyond it pay them tribute (Waldron 1990).

George Macartney, emissary of King George III, genuflects before the Qianlong emperor, as he presents a message from his sovereign requesting the establishment of a permanent embassy in Peking and open trade. Macartney was told by the emperor that his "Celestial Empire possesses all things in prolific abundance and lacks no product," and the mission ended in failure following Macartney's refusal to engage in traditional Chinese diplomatic rituals, which were predicated on the superiority of the emperor to all other sovereigns. Note the diplomats kowtowing on the right.

> Mughal emperors may be illustrative enough: Jahangir, Shah Jahan, or Shah Alam, the first meaning the world-conqueror, the latter two, the king of the world. (pp. 15–20).

In Africa, where population was sparse, the ambiguous nature of frontiers was even more marked. Herbst (2014, 38), for example, has pointed out that "there were few areas where territorial competition was the central political issue because land was plentiful." African states radiated from each ruler's political core into outer zones where the state tended to peter out rather than end; indeed, according to Herbst (2014, 53):

Frontiers tended to be thought of as border regions or zones where more than one polity could actively exercise authority and where the contours of power were confused rather than corresponding to the rigid demarcations of the modern world.

Thus, the reason that many of these empires could claim universal authority without facing any negative political consequences is the same as it was in the European case—that they only governed territory up to a point where no other ruler that rivaled them in power could also govern.

European Influence

Colonial Conquest

It is of course possible that given time and a sufficiently high level of economic growth and military and bureaucratic reform, the rulers of Africa, Asia, and even the Americas might have developed something like the state system that emerged in early modern Europe. But the experiment was never made. Most of the global South entered the cartel system by being conquered by European countries that were already cartel members.

The story of these conquests is well known. Spain, Portugal, England, and France acquired sizable chunks of the Americas in the 16th and 17th centuries, and they and their successor states spent the subsequent centuries expanding into the remaining territories. Britain acquired India in the century after 1757, and combined with the remaining European powers to annex nearly all of Africa and Southeast Asia in a mad rush in the last years of the 19th century—the so-called Second Colonialism.*

Territorial boundaries were a central part of colonial conquest. In many colonial states, they were created long before any effective administrative machinery was established within them. During key moments in the con-

* We focus on the Second Colonialism here. The first (Iberian) colonialism of the Americas mixed features of the medieval and modern state systems. On the one hand, Spain and Portugal were willing to divide the entire world between them along an agreed line under papal mediation (e.g., the Treaty of Tordesillas, 1494). On the other hand, the Iberian powers did not consult the other interested European powers, relied heavily on religious justifications for their claims, and held that their claims trumped those of any other power even when they did not exercise real control.

quest of Africa (most famously at the Berlin Conference of 1884–85) European diplomats sat down and partitioned the continent amongst themselves on a territorial basis. The boundaries they drew were often simply straight lines, reflecting their limited awareness of local geographical and political realities.[5] Despite this, violations of these borders or even of more informal spheres of influence were taken very seriously. The Fashoda Crisis of 1898 almost brought Britain and France to the point of war, until the French withdrew and a new territorial division was agreed on. The First Moroccan crisis of 1905 was similarly prompted by a German state visit to an area the French saw as within their sphere of influence.

For the most part, however, the division of the colonial empires was effected amicably using the diplomatic procedures and norms that Europe had developed over the past two centuries to deal with territorial division within the continent.[6] By this time, the key norms of the cartel system in Europe had set in and each colonial power acknowledged the rule of the others and recognized their own limitations. As Mark Lindley (1926, 210–11) writes:

> In 1885, for instance, Great Britain engaged . . . not to make acquisitions of territory, accept Protectorates, or interfere with the extension of German influence in that part of the coast of the Gulf of Guinea, or in the interior districts to the coast of a defined line [while] Germany entered into a similar engagement in regard to the districts to the west of the line.

The obvious casualties of this process were indigenous rulers, who had no opportunities to play Europeans off each other. The Anglo-German Treaty, for example, declared that "no Companies nor individuals subject to one Power can exercise sovereign rights in a sphere assigned to the other, except with the assent of the latter."[7] Thus, absent powerful allies and military parity, local elites had little alternative but to come to some arrangement with the European power that had claimed them. European governments in Africa and elsewhere responded by providing as little governance as possible while extracting as much as possible.[8] They provided a limited or nonexistent package of government services, little or no infrastructure outside of the export sector, little law enforcement outside of the towns, and the outsourcing of most health and education provision to missionaries.[9]

Cartoon depicting Otto von Bismarck at the 1885 Berlin Conference, cutting the cake of Africa into pieces for European powers to share. Note the sharp divisions between the pieces of cake, and the lack of differences between them.

Involuntary Openings

In early 19th-century East Asia, Europeans faced powers that could not be annexed because they were inconveniently large, too remote to conquer and administer, or because the Europeans could not reach a consensus on who should do so. These Asian powers behaved in ways that did not conform to the cartel model, and European powers had to find other ways to incorporate them into the system. Patronizing rituals might be overlooked, but Chinese claims in Southeast and Northeast Asia, for example, had real implications in light of European ambitions in these regions. To address these issues, the Europeans used the threat of force. They coerced China, Japan, and Korea into becoming members of the cartel that followed the norms of the system.* Putting aside their territorial and economic rivalries, the Europeans were united in their project of forcing the East Asian nations into the state system on unfavorable terms, and cooperated militarily to do so.

---

* China entered the cartel on terms set in the Treaty of Nanking (Britain-China, 1842) and the Convention of Peking (Britain/France/Russia-China, 1860), Japan on terms set in the Treaty of Kanagawa (USA-Japan, 1853), and Korea on terms set in the Treaty of Kanghwa (Japan-Korea, 1876).

For example, after their victory in the first phase of the Second Opium War, the allies—Britain, France, and the United States—were able to dictate terms to the defeated Chinese. These terms included reparations, territorial cessions, and favorable trading conditions, which were standard in such treaties; but some special terms were designed to assimilate Chinese diplomacy to European practice. The fifth article of the Treaty of Tientsin (1858), for example, required the Chinese emperor to nominate a "High Officer with whom the Ambassador, Minister, or other Diplomatic Agent of Her Majesty the Queen shall transact business, either personally or in writing, on a footing of perfect equality."[10] And, with the issue of the kowtow during the Macartney Mission being a particularly sore point, the third article of the treaty aimed to end once and for all Chinese claims to symbolic primacy:

> [The British ambassador] shall not be called upon to perform any ceremony derogatory to him as representing the Sovereign of an independent nation, on a footing of equality with that of China. On the other hand, he shall use the same forms of ceremony and respect to His Majesty the Emperor as are employed by the Ambassadors, Ministers, or Diplomatic Agents of Her Majesty towards the Sovereigns of independent and equal European nations....[11]

In the Japanese case, the opening to the West eventually brought entry into the cartel on terms of full equality, with the final extraterritorial legal privileges for foreign citizens being removed in 1899.[12] Japanese diplomats were received around the world, Japanese political independence fully respected, and Japan was even able to participate in the territorial partition of Northeast Asia as a great power. Similarly, Thailand was able to adopt itself successfully into the cartel and in fact used western territorial norms to justify annexing previously autonomous neighboring areas of Southeast Asia (sometimes with the help of colonial powers) before being colonized itself.[13]

Asian powers were not wholly unfamiliar with the model of territorially bounded sovereignty, and had shown that they could be surprisingly adaptable when they encountered a state of roughly equal or greater power. In the Treaty of Nerchinsk (1689), for example, Qing China agreed to a demarcated territorial border with Russia, and free trade across the border. The language of the treaty avoided the hierarchical language of other Chinese treaties, and the meetings at which the treaty was negotiated were concluded with only minor disputes over protocol.[14] Similarly, Mughal relations with Persia were conducted on the basis of practical equality between the two polities, quite different from Mughal relations with smaller Indian and Central Asian rulers.[15]

In sum, the process by which Europeans arrived at colonial borders and some of their governance practices in the colonies differed from what our model suggests. Rather than emerging endogenously from changes in economic productivity and administrative capacity, territorial division was coercively imposed by external actors. Many of the key aspects of the system reflected contemporary practices in Europe rather than local realities, and thus the cartel system was exported—albeit imperfectly—by Europe to the rest of the world during the colonial period. In the next section, we discuss some of these imperfections.

Imperfect Hegemony

While the expansion of the cartel to the world outside of Europe was impressive, it was imperfect. In fact, there are some parts of the world where the system struggles to assert itself even today. In these parts, governments attempt to exercise some sort of political power outside the boundaries assigned to them on world maps. Many borders are highly contested, and a border is sometimes less a line than a broad zone of disputed and ambiguous political authority. We now examine some cases of the cartel's imperfect hegemony over the world, focusing on two issues: the nonacceptance of the cartel system in one case, and the acceptance of the system where it does not function entirely as it was designed in another.

The Durand Line

Like the 15th-century Anglo-Scottish borderlands, the frontier region between Afghanistan and Pakistan today is a broad belt of territory populated by autonomous, undergoverned elites given to causing trouble in other parts of the region and the world. Despite technical capabilities far beyond what was available to medieval European monarchs, neither the Afghan nor Pakistani states have built up strong state institutions in the border regions. In fact, they have not tried particularly hard to do so.[16]

In many ways, this border that cuts through one of the least-developed parts of the world represents one of the very few exceptions proving the rule that the cartel model has really spread across the globe. The case is especially interesting, not just because the regimes in power have avoided abiding by the rules of the modern cartel but also because it demonstrates how much a thorn in the side of the cartel a remote region of the world can be when it refuses to conform to the standards for cartel membership.

As on the medieval Scottish border, the behavior of these two neighboring states is competitive rather than coooperative. While the two sides have a linear, demarcated border, neither side has been respectful of it. The Afghan state has historically claimed a large part of Pakistan on grounds of shared ethnicity, while the rulers of Pakistan (and, before that, those of British India) have considered eastern Afghanistan to be part of their sphere of influence. Consequently, both states have been forced to give concessions to elites in the regions claimed by the other side.

Causes of Contention. The areas that today make up northwest and eastern Afghanistan are primarily inhabited by members of the Pashtun ethnic group. British colonial policy in the region, like that of their Mughal and Sikh predecessors, fluctuated over time depending on the relative power of London policymakers and local bureaucrats. During some periods, the British actively occupied large areas of eastern Afghanistan, and claimed the right to control Afghanistans's foreign policy. At other times, the colonial government resolutely refused to take responsibility for the Pashtun tribes of the frontier region, preferring instead to attempt to limit their raiding. As C. Collin Davies (1932, 24–36) writes, "a general uncertainty prevailed as to the limits of the two governments, and the tribesmen constantly took advantage of this uncertainty, playing off the one against the other."

In 1893, Sir Mortimer Durand, a British diplomat, visited Kabul and signed a treaty that placed in British territory many Pashtun tribes whom the British had previously not administered.[17] This gave rise to the so-called Durand line, which to this day separates the two countries in the Pashtun ares. In the text of the treaty, the two sides agreed not to govern tribes on the other side of the line:

> the Indian Government will never interfere at any time in the countries lying on that side of the line in the direction of Afghanistan, and that his Highness also will cause no interference at any time in the countries that may be lying outside the boundary line.[18]

Yet the conditions under which the treaty was signed foreshadowed many of the problems that were to follow. On the British side, the government continued to claim the right to control Afghan foreign policy. On the Afghan side, the issues were more severe, stemming from a fundamental objection to territorial division. To make things worse, the areas that the Durand line allotted to Britain were culturally similar to those of eastern Afghanistan, and had been ruled by previous Afghan states. The Kabul government believed that they could administer the region more easily than the British could. Afghan King Abdur Rahman Khan pleadingly wrote to the viceroy: "if they [the frontier tribes] were included in my dominions . . . I will gradually make them peaceful subjects. . . . But if you should cut them out of my dominions they will neither be of any use to you nor to me."[19]

In fact, the surviving evidence suggests that Abdur Rahman Khan only signed the treaty under duress—indeed, the British had already occupied several of the disputed territories before the treaty was signed.[20] The amir may also have felt that demarcation represented a definition of short-term spheres of influence, rather than permanent full control.[21] By 1896, the Afghans were dragging their feet on the demarcation and fomenting revolt on the British side of the frontier. In 1919 Afghanistan unsuccessfully invaded the region, and subsequently in the 1930s supported a movement calling for an independent Pashtunistan.[22]

The independence of Pakistan from Britain strengthened opposition to the Durand line in Afghanistan even further. In 1949, King Zahir Shah formally cancelled all treaties between Afghanistan and colonial India. To make real their claims, throughout the middle decades of the 20th century the Kabul government actively intervened in matters of governance among the tribes on the Pakistani side of the Durand line. As Elisabeth Leake (2016, 150) notes, "Pakistani and Afghan agents struggled to gain an upper hand in the tribal zone, as each plied Pashtun tribes with promises of economic and political aid in return for their opposition to or support for, respectively, Pashtunistan."

Immediately after independence, the Afghans supported the establishment of Pashtunistan regional governments in the tribal areas that clashed with the Pakistani military. However, the process degenerated into a bidding war, in which in the words of Leake (2016, 192), "the Afghan government could not afford to offer the same material incentives as the Pakistani government."

Since 1979 the civil war in Afghanistan tended to both distract the Afghan government from irredentism and weaken the attraction of Afghan rule for residents of the border region. However, the Afghan government's official position remains that same in the 21st century as it was in 1949: the Durand line is invalid and the Pashtun-speaking frontier areas are not part of Pakistan. For its part, the Pakistani government has also been a less than ideal upholder of the norms of state sovereignty. The Pakistani army violated the Durand line to attack unfriendly tribes at various points during the 20th century, almost precipitating war on several occasions, and it is an open secret that it continues to provide support to insurgent groups in Afghanistan to the present day.

Consequences of Contention. Like the medieval English and Scottish states, both the Afghan and Pakistani states compete for the allegiance of the Pashtun tribes outside their territorial borders. This competition has had consequences for the levels of governance provided in the frontier zone. The Pakistani state, the winner of this bidding war, taxes very little in the region, while spending vasts amounts of money in the region. The result has been beneficial for the elites of the region, who enjoy a level of autonomy and freedom from fiscal burdens that are much higher than they are for local elites in other parts of South Asia.

The Durand line placed on the British side both the Pashtun-speaking plains districts (known as the Khyber Pakhtunkhwa Province or the North-West Frontier Province, NWPF) and the Pashtun-speaking foothills (the "Tribal Agencies" or Federally Administered Tribal Areas).* Not only was the NWFP a subject of special administrative attention, it was also in a relatively privileged financial position, receiving net subsidies throughout the colonial period.[23] In 1932 provincial expenditure stood at 36 million rupees, while revenue stood at only 8 million.[24] The Central Provinces (far from any border) had seven times the population but cost only three times as much to administer.

The tribal areas were governed even less. The residents of these areas paid no taxes, though there were some attempts to collect salt taxes on the region's border.[25] Despite this, residents of the tribal region could travel freely in British India and join the colonial army, and the colonial state

---

* For the sake of consistency, we use the terms NWFP and FATA throughout. In 2018, the Pakistani government announced plans to administratively merge the two areas.

A *jirga* on the Pakistan-Afghanistan border is an assembly of local tribal leaders that settles disputes and legislates in the region relatively independently of the Afghan and Pakistani governments. Such regions demonstrate that not all border regions of the world (especially the developing world) have been fully incorporated into the cartel system of states. The process of incorporation continues.

paid pensions to local leaders in the tribal regions in return for keeping the peace, carefully adjusted to reflect their relative influence.[26] Criminal law in the tribal regions was governed by the Frontier Crimes Regulation, rather than the ordinary courts. Crimes were tried by tribal *jirga* (councils that run independently of the state) under traditional customary law, under which defendants possessed no rights to appeal, present evidence, or retain counsel.[27] Since there was no police force, punishment was collective, with the army and militia arresting the relatives of perpetrators, or blockading whole communities.[28] While it is doubtful if ordinary people benefited from this system, it clearly benefited local leaders (the *maliks*) who were best positioned both to manipulate the *jirga* in their own favor and to profit from mediating the confrontations with the colonial state.[29]

This system continued almost unchanged after independence. Remarkably, until 1996, residents of FATA did not enjoy the right to vote, which was restricted only to the maliks, and the Frontier Crimes Regulation was still in force until 2018 despite complaints that it made FATA residents into second-class citizens.

In consequence, the tribal areas are the center of a wide range of economic and political activities that would be illegal anywhere else in Pakistan. The frontier is a center for kidnapping and auto theft, where people and assets seized in other parts of Pakistan are held in the tribal districts and ransomed, out of the reach of the police. Opium cultivation and processing are common in the province, as is the transit of opium grown in neighboring areas of Afghanistan.[30] FATA is also the center of a flourishing trade of illegal arms particularly of AK-47s and Lee-Enfield rifles. In 2017, there were 600 arms factories in the region.[31]

The fiscal position of FATA is, in theory, enviable. Residents of FATA continue to pay no taxes, and in fact the 2018 constitutional amendment that abolished the separate status of FATA kept these tax exemptions intact.[32] Electricity, when available, is free, "an expense that represents thirty-percent of the average household costs in the rest of Pakistan."[33] The Pakistani state also continues the colonial policy of subsidizing maliks financially in return for keeping peace. The government of Zia ul Haq controversially began subsidizing local religious figures as well, which has been suggested as a major factor in the rise of the the political salience of religion in the province.[34]

Perhaps the best-known consequence of the state's withdrawal from the tribal regions is the presence of militant organizations such as Al-Qaeda and the Taliban.[35] For our purposes, two points are worth noting about these organizations. First, their presence in the region is a product of voluntary state weakness rather than a lack of coercive capacity. These organizations have at one time or another benefited from the tacit acceptance or active financial support of the Pakistani state, and in fact Pakistani softness on these organizations has been condemned internationally.[36] Second, the presence of these organizations is closely linked to the ineffective international border. Al-Qaeda has used FATA as a refuge after being chased out of Afghanistan. The Afghan Taliban in particular were viewed by some elements of Pakistani intelligence as allies who are capable of maintaining Pakistani influence on the other side of the border, or at least of weakening the Afghan state to the point where it is incapable of raising the Pashtunistan issue.[37]

The Weak States of Africa

According to our theory, there are two types of zones where states provide relatively low levels of governance: (i) areas where the potential governance markets of states do not overlap, making them materially indifferent to what occurs there, and (ii) areas where the potential governance markets of states overlap and where they are unable or unwilling to cooperate, leading to competition. The first situation corresponds to Fig. 4 of Chapter 3 and the second to Fig. 5. The border between Afghanistan and Pakistan discussed above is an example of the second type of situation. It is an area where the authority of both states is relatively weak in part because of competition—the two neighboring states cannot agree on who should govern. Many border zones of Africa are examples of the first situation, where neither state can provide a high level of governance profitably.

Previous work in African politics has demonstrated that African states often do not collect significant quantities of direct taxes from their citizens, do not possess a monopoly of coercive force, and provide poor or nonexistent governance.[38] Authority is delegated, formally or informally, to local elites, who exercise it on a small scale subject to very weak accountability.[39] This pattern has persisted throughout African history and was even more extreme in the colonial period. It is also widespread spatially, being not just confined to border areas but prevalent in most parts of Africa outside the immediate neighborhood of the capital and areas of natural resource production. For example, outside of a small radius of Mogadishu, the Somali state does not provide much, if any, governance, while South Sudan is divided among a kaleidoscope of weak armed factions.

Another extreme example comes from the northeastern region of Central African Republic (CAR) which has never been governed by a central authority.[40] Today, state authority in this region continues to be weak and, for most of the past two decades, the country has suffered from civil war with the northeast being controlled by groups that do not recognize the central state in Bangui. There are no paved roads and few schools and the state is generally absent from this region, as "the president and ministers in the capital do not see it as their job to govern or regulate the hinterland."[41] In consequence, the residents of the northeast have no relationship with the CAR government. As Louisa Lombard (2020, 24) writes:

Most of the people in the area lack a national identity card. Many have no birth certificate either. Some make the trek to the capital to procure one, but travel to Bangui is arduous, expensive, and time-consuming, with no guarantee that one can navigate the bureaucracy on arrival. People in the capital assume that people from the northeast are foreigners (and dangerous to boot), so they might summarily reject an application from someone from there.

For our purposes, such cases of state weakness in Africa are especially interesting because of the peculiar apparent stability of the state system in the continent—and in particular, the persistence of the artificial borders that colonial powers drew. Unlike in Europe, African borders have not adjusted to changes in political reality. New states have not emerged to govern in undergoverned areas. Even if border regions in Africa on the ground may bear a passing resemblance to the borderlands of medieval Europe, on maps drawn since the 1960s, African borders have looked as stable as those of contemporary Europe.

This stability of African borders is a product of the fact that they run through under-governed areas. States do not contest them because they are not particularly consequential, and because the winner of such a contest would gain only some poor, sparsely populated land that produces little revenue. In the case of the CAR's northeast region mentioned above, for instance, population density has historically been very low—only about 1 person per square kilometer—and natural resources are scattered and modest. For this reason, even the French colonial regime was uninterested in governing it.[42] The same is true for the present CAR government and the neighboring states (Chad, Sudan, and South Sudan) just across the international border. These states have shown no desire to incorporate the region.

The situation in such regions corresponds to Fig. 5 of the previous chapter, where the value of governance is low relative to the costs of governing and a nominal border with little practical significance is drawn arbitrarily anywhere between the points Z and X. Even the very arbitrary borders that the continent inherited from the colonial period do not prompt interstate conflict because they divide space that state governments cannot profitably govern and thus care little about. According to the logic of our model, for the same reasons that universal claims had no bite in pre-modern Europe (and therefore rulers had no reason to contest them) many African borders have been stable precisely *because* they have little practical significance.[43]

The Cartel Outside of Europe

The spread of the cartel system to the rest of the world outside of Europe was the result of colonial conquest and neo-colonial coercion. But the cartel's operation today outside of Europe and European offshoots in North and South America and Oceania remains a mixed bag.

Many of the polities of East Asia embraced the cartel system and (for the most part) it works there today mostly as it was intended.[44]

Many of the weak states of Africa have accepted the system as well, but its operation there does not entirely follow the logic of the cartel model that we have developed. African borders have been exemplary in their levels of stability and mutual recognition, but the process of limiting the power of local elites has been slow, as the low economic productivity of these areas has not provided sufficient impetus to expand governance. As a result, these lightly governed areas are often the bases for rebellions against states or secessionist efforts to create new states that might govern more effectively— an issue that we examine in the next chapter.

And then there are parts of the post-colonial developing world today where the cartel system was never accepted, even by the rulers. The example of the Afghan-Pakistan border, for example, shows that when mutual recognition cannot be imposed by force, interstate relations and borderland politics can devolve into the competitive anarchy that our model predicts when states fail to collude. Some of the most vexing problems in world governance today, such as the rise of global terrorism and the emergence of the Islamic State, are closely associated with the nonacceptance of the cartel model around the world. We discuss this again in the final chapter.

5

Challenges to the Cartel

Cartels are inherently unstable—plagued by the temptation of their members to cheat and the inability or unwillingness of the other members to detect and punish the cheating. They also face the challenge of deterring entry to their industry by new competitors. (OPEC, for instance, has had great difficulty in maintaining high oil prices in the face of unregulated production by both its members and new producers.) And yet the territorial state system has so far proven to be remarkably stable. While states occasionally seize territory from each other, and new states do emerge, such events are increasingly rare and have not undermined the overall stability of the system. How do we reconcile this stability with our argument that the territorial state system represents a cartel?

In this chapter we examine some of the threats to the stability of the state system and describe some of the ways in which states have responded to these threats. We focus on three questions.

First, why is it that centuries of conflict and territorial redistributions have not undermined the state system? Since the early modern period, the map of the world has changed regularly, sometimes quite dramatically. States have conquered other states and transferred territory amongst themselves both violently and peacefully. Yet, even after the bloodiest conflicts such as World War II, the fundamental norms of the system have prevailed. Why haven't such conflicts destabilized the state system so much as to obliterate it completely?

Second, as all cartels deal with the threat of entry, so too does the state system. Populations living in a region of a state that differ in language, culture, and political loyalty from the populations of the state belonging to the dominant culture are relatively easier for regional elites to govern than for national elites. Why haven't the world's secession movements led to opportunistic entry into the state system through the creation and rapid multiplication of new states in places like Somaliland, Catalonia, Quebec, and Scotland? And why hasn't the persistent threat of such entry undermined the state system? Existing states seem to have successfully countered

The Cartel System of States: An Economic Theory of International Politics. Avidit Acharya and Alexander Lee, Oxford University Press. © Oxford University Press 2023. DOI:10.1093/oso/9780197632277.003.0005

many of these threats, deterring entry into the governance market from a multitude of the cartel's competitors.

Third, the state system, like other cartels, operates at the expense of its customers (or at least many of its customers). By design, it has enabled those who control states to better exploit its citizens. But with the advent of democracy in the 19th century, political power shifted in many countries from the previous ruling classes to the broader citizenry. Why haven't these citizens demanded an unraveling of the state system and opened up the governance market to competition from a greater number of providers? That a system which apparently exploits so many of its citizens could survive despite democracy presents a peculiar puzzle.

We investigate these questions in this chapter. We first provide some theoretical background to these three threats to cartel stability: conflict, opportunistic entry, and the potential demand for competition in the market for governance that comes with an empowered citizenry. We argue that the incentives to collude are so strong that the cartel has been able to survive periodic border revisions. They have also been strong enough to incentivize unilateral or bilateral military action to crush new entrants. Furthermore, since the cartel benefits some even as it exploits others, pivotal citizens in a democratic state that redistributes tax revenue back to them may have incentives to preserve the cartel just as strong as those of authoritarian rulers.

Territorial Disputes

Our model of the state system is built upon a theory of cooperation among states rather than the conflict between them that is at the center of most theories of interstate relations. But history is full of instances of border disputes and wars that have resulted in redistributions of territory. At least 67 wars from 1651 to 1950 resulted in redistributions of territory, and territorial disputes have been the key predictors of international conflict.[1] In addition, while many territorial redistributions have taken place following violent conflicts, there are also several instances of negotiated peaceful transfers under the threat of force. In 1940, for example, the Soviet Union was militarily stronger than it had been during the early 1920s and pressured Romania into ceding Bessarabia (modern Moldova). During the First World War, Austria-Hungary, distracted on other fronts and with its institutions weakened, offered Italy sizable territorial concessions in return for peace—offers that were eventually rejected as insufficient. A rearmed Nazi Germany successfully extorted sizable amounts of territory from Austria, Czechoslovakia, and Lithuania in the late 1930s.[2]

These disputes were not the result of ambiguous border agreements but rather a desire to revise clear existing borders. The Nazi annexation of the Sudetenland from Czechoslovakia in 1938, for instance, was not based on confusion about where the border was or whether Germany had agreed to it, but rather the insistence that the area belonged to Germany on linguistic grounds, and the confidence that Germany's renewed military power was sufficient to disregard an agreement made in a period of weakness after World War I. Similarly, the various redistributions of colonies that occurred following European conflicts in the 1714–1914 period had little if any justification besides the economic and military strength of the victorious powers. It should be no surprise, therefore, that strategic or economically valuable territories tend to be fought over more than other territories.[3]

Territorial disputes and war present a challenge to the cartel system. If states have the power to revise borders in their favor through war or the threat of it, a militarily powerful state might constantly seek to encroach on its neighbors, or even conquer them entirely. This could undermine the cooperation that exists among states. The question that we are concerned with then is how our model handles the fact that territorial disputes, including violent ones, are an unmistakable part of life in the world. How does the cartel theory of cooperation fit with the fact that territorial conflict takes place?

A Model of Territorial Shifts

We present a simple extension of our model that addresses the issue of territorial disputes. Recall that in the model the border between adjacent states occurs at the point at which their costs of governing intersect. But what happens if costs change? Advances in military and administrative technology have continued to lower the costs of governing, especially farther away from the core areas of a state. We can understand this as states developing ways of exerting military power more effectively, or developing better state institutions that enable them to govern at lower costs. This fact alone, however, would not necessarily change the rationality of forming a cooperative agreement with one's neighbors. In fact, it may make cooperation even more

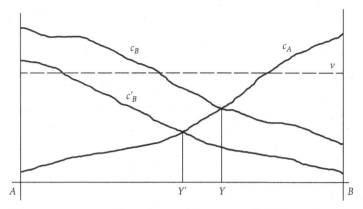

Fig. 8 *B*'s governance costs have dropped from c_B to c'_B, shifting the joint profit-maximizing boundary from *Y* to *Y'*. Will original boundary *Y* stay in place, or will *B* initiate a conflict to move the boundary to *Y'*?

profitable, since states could leave the tax rate the same and internalize the savings from the reduction in governance costs.

But the capacity to govern has not developed evenly across states. The more economically and politically advanced states have been the developers and early adopters of new governance technologies while other states lag behind. Their costs have declined more substantially than those of their competitors. As costs shift, the joint profit-maximizing boundary, which we conjectured is focal, may also shift. Put another way, changes in the relative power or administrative efficiency of states lead to shifts in the position of the efficient boundary.

We depict in Fig. 8 an example of this situation where state *B*'s cost of governance has declined from c_B to c'_B while *A*'s cost has remained the same at c_A. Consequently, the joint profit-maximizing boundary has shifted west from *Y* to *Y'*. The question then is whether the historical boundary *Y* remains in place or whether the states somehow shift the boundary to the new joint profit-maximizing one, *Y'*, by redistributing some of *A*'s territory to *B*— specifically, the region between *Y'* and *Y*. Is the historical boundary focal, or is the new joint profit-maximizing boundary focal?

If the two states considered the new joint profit-maximizing boundary to be focal, they would have to institute a mechanism to coordinate a switch to it. The mechanism would have to work in the presence of uncertainty and asymmetric information as well. In particular, suppose any changes in the states' costs of providing governance are private information. For example, in the case of the figure, only B knows that its bureaucracy has become more efficient, or that its army had become more powerful. B would have to persuade A that indeed its costs have dropped, which could be difficult. The capacity of government is typically hard to measure.[4] B would have to communicate not just its efficiency in ruling the territory it has, but in ruling territory that it does not currently administer, and which might differ from its core territories in a variety of ways. Moreover, B would have an incentive to persuade A that its costs have dropped even if they have not, making any attempt at communication non-credible. A state, for instance, might parade its military power in the hopes that its neighbor will grant it territory, but the neighbor has no way of knowing whether this is just a bluff. In fact, since they must make calculations of relative rather than absolute power, A might also suspect that B is inaccurate in its appreciation of A's own military and administrative capabilities.

What is missing for B is a mechanism by which it reveals that its governance costs have indeed dropped only when they really have. War may serve such a purpose. In the case where B's costs have dropped, the value of the territory in dispute is high—at least higher than if B's costs had not dropped. The territory that B would like to gain is the interval between Y' and Y. Let us call the net value of the territory to B in the case where costs have not dropped to be V, and the net value in the case where its costs have dropped to be V'. What we are saying is that $V' > V$. If the cost to B of fighting a war to shift the boundary west is W, where $V' > W > V$, then B would be willing to fight the war *only* in the case where its cost of governing has dropped, and not in the case where it has not. War may then serve as a revelation mechanism that allows B to credibly reveal that its costs have dropped. The crucial point is that B is willing to suffer the costs of war over a piece of territory only when its costs of governing it have declined, and will usually be successful in the resulting war when this is the case.[5]

After the war is over, we should expect the cartel to quickly reestablish itself. The profits from cooperation are simply too large to give up for vague regrets. Indeed, there are many examples of losing nations accepting the results of violent and traumatic conflicts. Denmark no longer claims the provinces around Malmo in southern Sweden. Spain no longer claims Portugal. Mexico no longer claims Texas and California. Turkey no longer claims Syria and Iraq. And Germany no longer claims the Sudetenland; or, for that matter, East Prussia and Silesia. Where disputes do persist, it tends to be because of claims pertaining to ethnicity and national identity, a factor we will explore in greater detail in the next chapter.[6] Similarly, winning powers, once they have seized all they can administer, become champions of the state system.* Thus, even when states in our model contest and go to war over territory, this occurs within an equilibrium of long-term cooperation.

An Illustration: The Atacama Desert

To see the logic of our argument at work more closely, consider the case of the boundaries between Chile, Bolivia, and Peru in the Atacama Desert.[7] Upon independence from Spain in the 1820s, all three nations claimed the desert as theirs. This did not become a major source of conflict for the next 40 years, because the desert—one of the driest parts of the entire world— was almost completely uninhabited. In the framework of our theory, it was a space where the economy was too weak to support governance provision and where conflicting and overlapping claims could therefore coexist.

Recall that conflict occurs in our model when changes in the relative efficiency of the states combine with changes in the value of the territory— that is, if V' defined above is lower than the cost of war W but grows to be higher. In the 1860s, the rise of nitrate (saltpeter) mining made the desert one of the most valuable regions in the entire world and a key source of revenue for all three countries. Bolivia and Chile attempted to settle their disputes with an innovative attempt at non-territorial jurisdiction, agreeing that between the 23rd and 25th parallels (the "zone of mutual benefits") they would jointly collect taxes and spilt them (1866). However, the agreement quickly broke down over Bolivian efforts to raise taxes unilaterally, and a new treaty (1874) divided the territory but agreed that Chilean mining companies in the area would pay low taxes. It was Bolivia's violation of this provision (the "ten cent tax") that provoked Chile to begin the War of the Pacific or Saltpeter War (1879–82).[8] Chile would have been highly unlikely to go to war over the region if the desert had remained worthless.[9]

Whatever the legal claims, it was the superior efficiency of the Chilean army and navy that eventually enabled Chile to conquer the region. Bolivia

---

* This is the basis of the classic distinction in international relations between a status quo power and a revisionist power (e.g., Carr 1946). It is also related to the kind of organized hypocrisy that Krasner (1999) uses to describe the concept of modern territorial sovereignty. While everyone tacitly acknowledges the underlying principles of the state system, they also frequently violate them, and yet somehow these frequent violations have not undermined the espousing of these principles.

had a small army that played only a minor part in the war, while Peru's large army was poorly equipped with only a third the number of conscripts as the smaller Chilean one.[10] Bolivia had no navy, and the Peruvian navy was eliminated after dogged resistance, allowing the Chileans to defeat the Peruvian army and occupy most of Peru. Peru agreed to cede its portion of the Atacama to Chile in 1884, though a provision that some parts of the ceded region could choose their government through a plebiscite would cause controversy until the disputed area was split in 1929 with the help of American mediation. Bolivia refused to sign a treaty until 1903, when it formally ceded the region in return for some limited coastal access.

While there remains considerable popular resentment against Chile in both Bolivia and Peru, the Chilean seizure of the Atacama has become a stable, generally recognized feature of the international system.* Without war, it would have been impossible for Chile to convince the Peruvian and Bolivian elite that it was more capable of exerting political and military power in the region than they were—indeed, this is why prewar efforts to divide or share the area had always foundered.

Opportunistic Entry

An important threat that any organized cartel must grapple with is that of opportunistic entry. If the cartel succeeds in profiting from exploiting its customers, then there is room for others to enter its market and steal some of these profits. The state system is not any different.

In this section, we explore the challenges that existing states face in suppressing entry in the governance market from opportunistic challengers—lords seeking to become rulers, regional leaders seeking to secede from the nation, and petty rulers seeking to acquire recognition from their peers as equal states in the modern system. While not all such attempts have failed, they have faced sustained and effective resistance, both military and diplomatic, from existing states.

In many cases, entry deterrence means simply that governments suppress rebel groups within their own territory. The United States opposed the

---

* Bolivian attempts to renegotiate the treaties, for instance, were unanimously dismissed by the International Court of Justice in 2018.

secession of the Confederacy; the Nigerian government opposed the session of Biafra; and even the feeble Congolese government opposed the secession of Katanga. However, even states that are not involved in these affairs have been reluctant to embrace putative new states. While in all of these cases the secessionist state sought international recognition, in none of them was it able to gain the formal diplomatic recognition of the great powers despite some of these powers expressing sympathy for the secessionist cause. While Biafra was recognized by five small states, its failure to secure recognition from any of the major world powers has effectively squashed its hopes for independence.[11] The Confederacy's failure to gain international recognition is also considered to be a major cause of its military defeat.[12]

In some cases, the suppression of secessionist independence movements has extended even further. Secessionist groups like the Liberation Tigers of Tamil Eelam in Sri Lanka, the Kurdistan Workers Party in Turkey, and Chechen rebels in Russia have been labeled as terrorist organizations by many Western countries, severely restricting their ability to operate and raise money abroad. In some cases, hostility to secessionism has led non-involved powers to give military aid to states to suppress them or even commit their own military forces. The recent international military effort against the Islamic State and the UN-led intervention that ended the Katangese secession are examples, as is the massive aid provided by the United States to the Philippines to fight Muslim rebels.

Even when states have direct material interests in the success of a secessionist movement, the precedent that secession sets is very often too disquieting for states to embrace openly, since they know that they themselves might subsequently face such claims. For instance, it is more than remotely possible that the Catalan independence movement figured into Spain's reluctance to entertain the wishes of some prominent Scottish leaders to find a way for Scotland to remain a part of the EU following Brexit.[13] Even in the 1860s, imperial Russia was concerned enough about the Confederacy setting a precedent for Polish secession that it sent a fleet to protect Union ports during the civil war, despite the vast ideological and geographical differences between the two countries.

Nevertheless, in some instances secession does succeed—the dismemberment of the Soviet Union and decolonization movements in Africa and Asia provide some prominent examples of secession waves.[14] Other notable examples include the independence of Bangladesh, South Sudan, Eritrea, and East Timor. It is our job to understand the unique features of these exceptions to the general rule that successful secessions are rare.

A Model of Entry Deterrence

Consider a variant of our baseline model in which a potential state located at C between states A and B finds the opportunity to enter the state system by creating a new state between A and B. We depict this in Fig. 9. C's costs of providing governance are given by the two dashed lines that meet at the point C. Since C is a potential new state, it does not have access to the same level of military and bureaucratic technology that makes it cheap to govern distant places, but between X and Z it would govern more profitably than both A and B—the increase in joint profit is given by the shaded area. If C were allowed to enter the state system, it might establish its own state between X and Z. A would rule to the west of X, B to the east of Z, and C would rule in between. However, allowing C to enter the system reduces A's and B's profits. If there is a way for A and B to deter entry from C cheaply, then they would want to do so.

Suppose that A and B must each decide how much to contribute to deter entry from C. We can think of this as funding the military force necessary to coerce C out of the governance market. Let us assume that to successfully

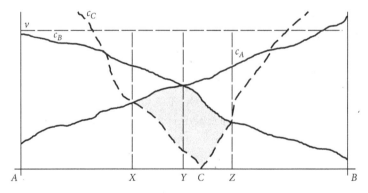

Fig. 9 C is an aspiring ruler seeking to establish a new state between A and B. C's cost of governing is labeled c_C and depicted by dashed lines emanating out of the point C. X and Y mark the boundaries of a potential state C that would increase overall joint profit maximally. This resulting increase in joint profit is the size of the shaded area.

deter C, a total contribution of d is needed. If d is met then C is deterred; otherwise, C enters and sets up a new state. Suppose that if C enters and A and B lose territory as a result, their profits drop by the amounts K_A and K_B respectively. If $d > K_A + K_B$ then the total contribution needed to deter entry is so high that A and B will not stop C from entering: they are unwilling to contribute the amount needed to prevent entry. If $d < K_A$ then A is willing to contribute the full amount d to deter entry if it expects B to not contribute. Similarly, B is willing to contribute the full amount to deter entry if $d < K_B$ and it expects A to not contribute. In these cases, the prediction is that C will not enter, since one of the two states can deter entry on its own.[15] Intuitively, when the tax revenue from a marginal area is high, states are willing to individually fund the cost suppressing secession movements.

On the other hand, if d is larger than both K_A and K_B but smaller than the sum $(d < K_A + K_B)$, then A and B can prevent entry from C if they both contribute enough to meet the d threshold, and neither is willing to do it alone. In this case, there are equilibria in which C is deterred, and ones in which C is not. If each of A and B expect the other to contribute the agreed share, then C will be deterred. But if they both expect the other to not contribute, then neither will contribute, leading C to successfully enter.

This extension shows that in some circumstances, entry cannot be deterred because the costs of suppressing the entrant are high in comparison to the losses that existing states can recover from maintaining their exclusive control of the governance market. In other circumstances, states can deter entry without working together because the cost of suppressing the potential entrant is low while the value of doing so is high. And in a third set of cases, the existing members of the cartel need to work together to deter entry. In this instance, the states face a coordination problem: if they each expect the other to do their share in suppressing entry then they will succeed, but if they do not trust each other to do their part then they will fail in suppressing entry into the system.

Since the coordination problem can be resolved in either of two ways, there is reason for states to create institutions that facilitate coordination in the interest of the members of the existing cartel. In the subsequent chapter, we argue that international institutions like the United Nations and the Organization of African Unity serve this purpose, among others. However, before that we discuss a few examples of entry deterrence—of polities that attained all the institutional attributes of states but failed to secure admission into the cartel, as well as one that succeeded despite the attempts by its competitors to block entry.

Examples of Successful and Failed Deterrence

We start by giving two examples of successful deterrence in Africa: the case of the Rif state in Morocco in the early 20th century, and the deterrence of Somaliland from attaining statehood today. We then discuss how European powers allowed Belgium to join the state system.

The Rif State. Many attempts to deter entry into the state system require the participation of only one state. When the state whose territory the new state would come from is able to defeat the secessionists militarily, there is no need to call upon the entry-deterring features of the international system. However, inevitably, some states will be so poorly run, and some secessionist movements so well managed, that only the cooperation of the target state and its neighbors can stop them. Morocco in the 1920s provides a striking case of the necessity for such coordination in deterrence.[16]

Morocco had been partitioned between Spain and France in 1912, with the Spanish taking the north of the country. Based on the relative military and administrative power of the two states, the arrangement was generous to the Spanish, a product of the fact that the other great powers (in particular Britain) wanted a buffer between French territory and the strategically important strait of Gibraltar.

Spanish rule was, however, unpopular and weak outside a few coastal towns. This contributed to the success of Abd el-Krim (1882–1963), a charismatic former Spanish official, in raising a revolt in 1919 in the under-administered interior; and in 1921 he inflicted a devastating military defeat on the Spanish at Annual, killing 13,000 Spaniards and confining the survivors to a few coastal cities. The Spanish were subsequently able to retake some of the coastal plain and constructed fortifications to secure it, but showed no capacity (or desire) to retake the Rif mountains.

In his new territory, Abd el-Krim established the Republic of the Rif, with himself as prime minister. The Republic was anxious to assume the trappings of modern statehood, issuing paper money, organizing a regular army with uniforms and monthly pay, establishing a centralized bureaucracy, constructing roads, and creating the beginnings of a state-run educational system. Citing his administrative successes and military achievements, Abd el-Krim unsuccessfully sought diplomatic recognition from the other European states, particularly Britain. The influence of international norms, though, would be striking. The Rif Republic was widely acknowledged to be able to provide governance more efficiently than the Spanish had, but no other state was willing to recognize it as a peer.

While the other powers were passively hostile, the French, who shared a border with the Republic, were actively hostile. The French were conscious of the threat that a popular and stable Berber state posed to their own control of border areas. This led the French government to join with the Spanish in a joint military effort to defeat the Rif Republic, conducted primarily in Spanish territory by primarily French troops, employing a quarter million men and poison gas. Abd el-Krim was exiled to Reunion, and Spanish rule was reestablished in northern Morocco.

The Rif state's experience is notable for two reasons. First, while many potential entrants to the state system spend their whole existence as guerrilla movements without lasting institutions (or deterred entirely from establishing the incumbent state), the Rif state was well developed and certainly more capable of mobilizing the resources of the Berber tribes than its Spanish colonial rival. Second, the French were willing to pay an enormous cost (almost a billion francs and over 8,000 dead) to maintain Spanish power in Morocco. Rather than recognize the Republic, seize the Spanish zone for itself, or simply push the Berber forces across the border, it chose to reestablish the status quo ante bellum, contenting itself with defeating the Moroccan attempt to establish a new state.

Somaliland. The Rif's experience may (at least in some part) have been a product of the attitudes of European powers during the colonial period. But there is a contemporary state that is an even better example of our entry deterrence logic: the Republic of Somaliland, which has all of the institutional attributes of statehood but none of the international ones. For while the Rif Republic spent its whole existence at war with a fairly well-institutionalized internationally recognized claimant, the government of Somalia that is recognized by the international community as being in control of Somaliland has actually been incapable of administering it and has for nearly three decades left Somaliland to its own devices.[17]

Somalia is a fusion of two colonial units, British Somaliland, which mostly coincides with today's Somaliland and Italian Somaliland (ruled by the

All cartels deter entry from market competitors. The cartel of states is no exception. Somaliland has been denied entry into the cartel even though it effectively functions as an autonomous and independent state with democratic elections. Above is a picture of a Somaliland woman casting a vote in 2012.

British after 1941), which consists of the rest of present-day Somalia. The British zone, while smaller and poorer, was more homogenous in clan demographics, and the British policy of benign neglect had tended to preserve traditional clan institutions.[18]

After independence, the two regions were ruled by a unified government until 1989 when Siad Barre, the dictator of the Somali Republic, was overthrown and the Somali state rapidly collapsed. In the south, this led to anarchy and contention between a changing set of clans, militias, and warlords which has never been fully resolved. Somaliland, by contrast, created its own government after a consensus-based process in which clan leaders played an important role. They gradually established secure control within their territory, which they have defended against incursions from neighboring separatist quasi-states. At the same time, they have not attempted to claim any area of former Italian Somaliland.

The Somaliland government is well institutionalized by African standards. There is a regular army, a currency, and state-run school system. Taxes are regularly collected. The economy, based on livestock and remittances, is relatively prosperous, and piracy is not common. Perhaps most remarkably, Somaliland regularly holds free and fair elections.[19]

How has such a poor and unrecognized polity been able to run its territory with such success? A key reason is that it has a high level of information about and consent within the society it is governing—what one observer called "an unprecedented degree of interconnectedness between the state and society."[20] This is based on a system of consultation with clan assemblies, the *beel* system, which resolves many local disputes.[21] Even the tax system is based on less coercion and more persuasion than those of comparable African states.

On the other hand, the main thing that is lacking in Somaliland is international recognition: in the eyes of the international system, Somaliland is just a breakaway region that ought to be under the control of the government of Somalia, a government that controls no territory in Somaliland, has not been democratically elected, and whose direct practical authority is confined to a small area around the capital.

In fact, many in the international community regard the independence of Somaliland as a bad precedent.[22] Given the artificiality of most of the colonial boundaries in Africa that post-colonial states have inherited, the number of potential claimants to statehood on ethnic or historical grounds is large, and many states fear creating undesirable expectations for their own minorities—a view that has become the official view of most international institutions.[23] While some governments are willing to give aid to Somaliland's government or establish an informal diplomatic presence, no state has extended full diplomatic recognition to it.

Belgium. The creation of modern Belgium shows the intimate involvement of the international community in the creation of new states and its occasional willingness to bend the no-secession-without-consent norm if it suits the interests of the most powerful cartel leaders.[24] In the 16th century, the modern Netherlands and Belgium were ruled by a single ruler, the Hapsburg king of Spain. A revolt against the Spanish led to a protracted war (1568–1648) which in turn led to the partition of the Low Countries between the areas the Spanish were able to retain (roughly modern Belgium) and the area in which the rebels were successful (roughly the modern Netherlands). The fact that Belgium became overwhelmingly Catholic under Spanish pressure while the Netherlands became primarily Protestant entrenched the division.

For the next two centuries Belgium became a territorial bargaining chip, acquired by Austria (1714) and France (1795). At the Congress of Vienna (1814–15) the great powers of the period (Britain, Austria, Prussia, Russia) decided to place Belgium under the control of the Netherlands. The primary calculations were international in nature, and focused on the powers' desire to punish France, which had been recently defeated in the Napoleonic wars, and build up the Netherlands as a counterweight to it.

The anti-Catholic and centralizing policies of King William I alienated most Belgians, and in 1830 a popular revolution (touched off by a rowdy demonstration after an opera performance) overthrew the Dutch government and occupied most of the major cities. Since the Dutch controlled a large regular army and the Belgians only a poorly organized militia, most observers and King William himself assumed that they would be able to reoccupy the country eventually. After a period of military buildup and attempted conciliation (in the Ten Days Campaign of August 1831) the Dutch army defeated the rebels, and appeared poised to overrun the whole country. The Dutch, however, were not allowed to complete their victory. A French army invaded Belgium, and the Dutch, unable to defeat a great power without allies, agreed to a British-mediated ceasefire. The French would return again in 1832 to remove the last major Dutch garrison, in the citadel of Antwerp.

The Dutch and French interventions occurred in the context of fevered international diplomacy. Representatives of the four Vienna powers and France had met in London immediately after the Belgian revolt, and would continue meeting on and off for the next two years. Their interests diverged. Prussia, Austria, and Russia, to different degrees, supported the restoration of Dutch rule, fearing that a successful secession would create an undesirable precedent in other parts of Europe, particularly Poland.[25] France, politically and militarily resurgent since Vienna, saw the Belgian Revolution as an opportunity to either annex large portions of the country or, failing that, to create a politically weak Belgium over which it could exercise influence.[26] Britain saw a French-controlled or influenced Belgium as a major political and military threat, but believed that the revolution itself demonstrated that a united Netherlands was not capable of excluding French influence. As the London conference protocol stated:

> The events of the last four months have unhappily demonstrated that . . . the union of Belgium with Holland is destroyed; and that it now becomes

indispensable to have recourse to other arrangements to accomplish the intentions which the union in question was designed to carry into execution.[27]

The compromise that resulted, the Treaty of XVIII Articles, reflected British preferences. Belgium was declared to be perpetually neutral and all the powers guaranteed to respect its neutrality. As events would prove, this was not an empty guarantee. British intervention in World War I was primarily justified as an attempt to honor Britain's obligation to defend Belgium against foreign invasion. After some controversy, the Belgians elected a king acceptable to the powers—a minor German prince who only a few months before had refused their offer of the throne of Greece.[28] The powers also set the frontiers of the new state without consulting either the Belgians (who lost some territory they had occupied during the revolution) or the Dutch (who were deprived of half their territory without the opportunity to fight). However, the Ten Days Campaign made both sides realize they could not challenge the powers' will, with Holland eventually accepting a slightly revised treaty in 1839.[29] While the Belgians had been successful in gaining their own country, they had succeeded only because the most powerful members of the international system saw a Belgium created on terms that they chose as more conducive to their interests than partition or Dutch repression.

The Democratic Political Economy of the Cartel System

So far, our model has referred to rulers and citizens separately. Rulers are the providers of governance, and citizens are the consumers. But one may wonder whether this metaphor should apply only to a time when this distinction is clear. In today's world, there are numerous democracies. The Economist Intelligence Unit (EIU), for example, classifies 75 states as full or flawed democracies. The proliferation of democracy, which started in the late 18th century, presents some potential challenges for cartel theory.

The main issue is whether the spread of democracy would lead to an unraveling of the cartel system, as citizens, now in power, demand more competition in the governance market. Democracy, it has been argued, is accompanied by greater demand for policies that favor citizens who were historically exploited by the state.[30] But it is curious that even with the advent of democracy very few citizens are interested in changing the overall system by which governance is provided.

Is our model—which makes a sharp distinction between those who govern and those who are governed—still an accurate representation of how things work today, particularly in the democratic world? Alternatively, if our model is a reasonable approximation for the period prior to the 19th century, but has become less accurate with time, then what are the implications of this for the cartel system?

A Simple Model

We now add a simple political economy of democracy to our baseline model. We do so in a rudimentary way that does not capture all considerations; nevertheless, the extension allows us to get at some of the key ambiguities concerning the effects of democracy on the governance market.

Consider the baseline model of Chapter 2 partially redepicted in Fig. 10. Recall that under the cartel agreement ruler A governs to the west of Y and earns a profit equal to the sum of the two shaded areas; let us call this profit Π_A. Under the cartel agreement, each citizen receives a payoff of 0, paying

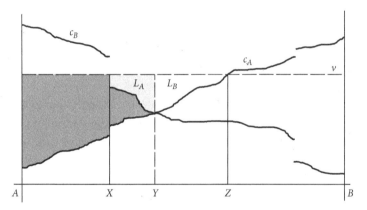

Fig. 10 If state A is a democracy that redistributes its net taxes back to the populace, then its citizens will divide the sum of the two shaded areas in this figure among themselves. Opening up competition in the governance market will benefit citizens living to the east of X since they will pay less in taxes (by a total amount equal to the light shaded area marked L_A) but will harm those to the west of X since their net transfers will be lower.

exactly the same amount for governance as the value that is derived from it—the monopoly price of v.

Suppose then that the ruler of A is overthrown and democracy is instated. There are now at least three ways in which the state may act as the agent of the people. We describe these in turn.

The first way is that the cartel agreement between the two states, A and B, is maintained. Those that come to power in state A (such as a democratically elected president, a prime minister, the legislature, etc.) continue to set prices in the governance market and engage with state B exactly as the previous autocratic ruler of state A did. However, since state A is now a democracy, it is unreasonable to assume that these democratic leaders keep the profits that the state earns from taxing their citizens; after all, this would make these politicians very poor agents of the people. Per the standard models of the political economy of public finance, let us assume that the net taxes collected are redistributed evenly to the citizens in the form of lump-sum transfers.[31] Let the mass of individuals from A to Y be $\mathcal{Y}$. Then each citizen of A claims, and receives, $\Pi_A/\mathcal{Y}$ amount of the dividend. We call this the *redistributive policy*.

The second possibility is that the state acts as the agent of the people by earning no profit, and therefore not redistributing. In this situation, the citizens earn different payoffs: each citizen at each location earns the value of governance minus the cost of supplying governance to that location. Each location receives back from the government exactly the amount of governance that it paid for in taxes. If the citizens are uniformly distributed and since the cost of governance c_A is increasing, the median citizen is the one located at the midpoint of A and Y, which we denote m_A. The citizen located at m_A earns $v - c_A(m_A)$.* Under this policy the cartel agreement between the two states remains in place in the sense that B is not an active seller in A's governance market, and vice versa, but public finance in state A is different than it would be under an autocrat. We refer to this as the *non-redistributive policy*. Note that this policy will be much less advantageous to border residents than the redistributive policy, since the cost of governance is highest in their region.

A third possibility is that the citizens of A support a policy of opening up competition in their governance market and allowing ruler B to be a

---

* If the agents are not uniformly distributed, then the median will not occur at the midpoint, but this will not affect the main conclusions that we draw.

competitive seller of governance in their state. In this case, the politicians in state A would manage the public finance of the state by providing governance competitively and redistributing the profits back to the citizens as in the redistributive policy described above. But in this case, their profit will be only $\Pi_A - L_A$. The primary beneficiaries of such a policy will be the citizens who live to the east of X, who instead of paying v for governance will only pay c_B.* We call this the *competitive policy*.

Our baseline model remains a reasonable description for democratic states if the redistributive or non-redistributive policies are chosen, because those are cases in which the cartel agreement between states to not provide governance in each other's markets is maintained. If the citizens of state A choose the competitive policy, however, then there is a tension between democracy and our model: the devolution of power to the citizenry that comes with democratization leads to an opening up of the governance market in some areas, especially those near the border.

So what can we say about the conditions under which the competitive policy will be chosen? Let us refer to the region west of X as the core area of state A and the region between X and Y as its periphery. If the median-income citizen belongs to the core area, then his payoff under the competitive policy always falls short of what he gets under the redistributive policy: the core citizen will prefer his government to provide governance as a cartel member and redistribute the profit, rather than open up the governance market to competition from foreign providers.** Opening up competition does not help citizens in the core area since it does not affect how much they pay for governance, but it does lower the amount that the state can collect from the periphery and redistribute towards them. While authoritarian rulers may use the increased taxation in peripheral areas that the cartel makes possible for their own consumption, in a democracy this money can be used to benefit the core.

The literal interpretation of our public finance accounting is that democratic governments exploit the citizens of the periphery by denying them the benefits of competition. However, a less literal interpretation would be more insightful. As we discussed in previous chapters, in practice the benefits

---

* Recall that under competition we said that the lower-cost seller serves the market by selling at a price equal to that of the higher-cost seller.

** Note that if the agent with the median income is located at m_A, his income is only the tax dividend $(\Pi_A - L_A)/\mathcal{Y}$ if he is in the core area (i.e., if m_A is to the west of X) and it is the surplus from economic activity plus the tax dividend $v - c_B(m_A) + (\Pi_A - L_A)/\mathcal{Y}$ if he belongs to the periphery (i.e., if m_A is to the east of X).

of competition tended to flow to regional elites (such as the surnames of the Anglo-Scottish border or the maliks of the Afghanistan-Pakistan border) much more than to ordinary individuals in these regions. These elites, unconstrained by any form of democratic accountability, often pose a burden on their neighbors. The ordinary people of such a region might prefer citizenship in a democratic state to competition, since in a democracy they would gain from redistribution some of what they pay in taxes (or even more than what they pay). It is notable, for instance, that ordinary people in the frontier regions of Afghanistan were generally in favor of the 2018 repeal of the Frontier Crimes Regulation, which had given maliks powers of jurisdiction and prevented the application of ordinary Pakistani law.[32]

What we have said so far assumes that the government is controlled by the core. If, instead, the pivotal citizen belongs to the periphery, then her payoff under the competitive policy could be greater than the payoff from both the redistributive or non-redistributive policies. The idea is that under the competitive policy, the peripheral citizens get to enjoy the benefit of competition in the governance market *and* the benefit of redistribution from the core area to the periphery. The state is not able to collect much from citizens in the periphery, due to competition with the other state; on the other hand, it collects substantially from its core area.

However, the scenario in which the median voter is located in the periphery was probably uncommon, at least in the early days of democracy.* Moreover, in cartel theory, the center, or central zone, of a state is not necessarily the geographical center, but rather the place where it can tax most efficiently relative to its competitors.[33] These areas also tend to be the political centers of the state and home to the citizens who exert the most influence on government policy (which, in a flawed democracy, may not be the median voter).

In sum, the distinction that our baseline model makes between those that govern and those that are governed may not be relevant in today's world of many democracies. The outcome of our baseline model in which citizens are exploited by their rulers and receive a low level of welfare also loses its relevance under democracy. But as our extension shows, it does not follow from these facts that the cartel system—by which we mean the efforts of those

---

* In addition, peripheral regions rarely if ever join a center and pay a monopoly tax rate voluntarily—they are forced to do so. For the peripheral median voter condition to apply, at some point the periphery must have been conquered by a center that was inferior to it in population and has been repressed by that center since that time. While this may be possible, it is more likely that if this occurred, the boundaries of states would be reconfigured to turn these peripheral areas into the core areas of new states. The larger peripheral unit would eventually win independence from the smaller core unit and establish a new state with the old periphery as a new core.

who wield power in states (be they autocratic rulers or pivotal voters) to reduce competition in the governance market—would necessarily unravel.

That said, it is interesting to note that in the last few decades most Western democracies and many other polities around the world have decided to open up their borders to greater competition in the governance market—through globalization policies such as free trade and the easing of restrictions on labor and capital mobility. Whether they have done so because these are the policies that a majority of their voters prefer is an interesting question.[34] Regardless, we conclude with a much more limited claim that suffices for now: while democracy, under some conditions, may generate political pressures against the cartel system, democracy alone is not a sufficient condition for the system to unravel.

Democratic Repression in Practice

Consider the example of the participation of Catalonia in a unified Spain. In Chapter 3, we discussed how in the 17th century the Catalans had been able to use their peripheral position in Spain, and the possibility of alliance with the French, to secure concessions in taxation and autonomy from the Hapsburg regime in Madrid. In the 18th century, the Bourbon rulers, secure in their alliance with France, reduced Catalonia's privileges and created a harder border between Spain and France. This policy of centralization was pursued by various Spanish regimes during the 19th century and energetically by the Franco regime in the mid-20th century, which tried not just to ensure that the Spanish government's policy was the same in Catalonia as in other regions, but also to inculcate a Spanish national identity that would make secession less likely.[35]

While the reasons for this consistent policy of the Spanish government may in part have been ideological, there is a strong material logic as well. Catalonia has always been more economically prosperous than the rest of Spain and has since 1714 always paid a disproportionate share of Spanish taxation. In 1890, Catalonia made up 10% of the Spanish population, but contributed 27% of total taxes.[36] In 2014, it made up 16% of Spain's population, contributed 20% of its taxes, and received 14% of public expenditures.[37] The tax payments of Catalonia mean that the Spanish state is able to spend more on whatever its leaders wish, be it palaces, wars, or hospitals, than would be possible based on the taxes of the rest of Spain alone.

The restoration of Spanish democracy in the 1970s led to a renewed demand for a separate Catalan state. However, while authorities in Madrid have been willing to grant Catalonia a much higher level of autonomy than under Franco, they have been strongly resistant to granting independence or even full fiscal autonomy. An attempt to extend Catalonia's autonomy was limited by the Spanish Supreme Court in 2006, and an attempt to declare independence in 2017 was repressed by the police, with the leadership of the regional government being arrested and the powers of the regional government being suspended.

Spain is hardly the only example of a democratic nation willing to use force or the threat of force to maintain control over a region where a large section of the population does not wish to remain part of it. The United States fought a long and bloody war to retain control of the South, confounding observers who expected them to let the secessionists depart in peace. India has fought a whole series of secessionist and irredentist conflicts throughout its history, including in Kashmir, the Punjab, and Nagaland.[38] While democracies may be less likely than dictatorships to violate the human rights of those who advocate for secession, it seems they are no more likely to agree to a diminution of their territory.

In fact, there are some reasons to think that democracies are *more* likely to resist new entrants to the governance market or territorial revision among the existing states. First, democracies are more successful in war, making secession or attacks and land grabs by neighboring dictatorships less likely to succeed.[39] Second, democracies are also less likely to go to war with each other than other pairs of states, making territorial revision among democracies less likely. And, finally, democratic leaders may also be more accountable, creating higher domestic costs for territorial concessions.[40]

Democracy and Competition

Democracy does not autonomically lead to changes in the governance market that increase competition while retaining existing territorial boundaries. In particular, democracies often restrict immigration to their countries—competition in the governance market that takes place through the movement of people. The mechanism is straightforward. If democracies redistribute the taxes they collect, then existing members of the population have an incentive to restrict the entry of people who will take a share without making a commensurate contribution in taxes, or are expected, rightly or wrongly, to do so.* In American immigration policy, this opposition is encoded as the public charge rule, and investor and skill-based visas. In Canada, it is encoded as a point system that favors immigration by wealthy and productive individuals over others.

On the other hand, globalization in governance is in some ways a response to the development of democracy or the threat of democracy. While the cartel may have originally developed to transfer resources to the elites of large states, under democracy the borders of the state system can become a prison, trapping these elites in tax and governance regimes set by voters who are disproportionately poorer than they are. Competition enables the elites, even those located far from a border, to escape the system that their predecessors created and reap the benefits of competition in the governance market. As long as the rich have disproportionate political power, this dynamic is likely to continue, undermining the fiscal basis of states.

At the same time, many subgroups of voters in advanced industrial democracies like the US and those of Western Europe perceive themselves as gaining comparatively little from free trade policies and globalization, and possibly coming out on the losing end. Donald Trump and UKIP leaders tapped into this perception. As we explained above, voters in a democracy may support or oppose greater competition in the governance market depending on how the benefits of this competition are distributed in the population. We referred to core and periphery voters as the key groups. But when competition in the governance market takes place in the more abstract space of policies that regulate the world economy, the distinct groups of winners and losers from specific policies cannot so easily be identified and may not correspond so cleanly to geographic regions. We explore this further in Chapter 7.

The Secession of Poor Regions

Given our model, it would not be surprising if democracies were more willing than non-democracies to allow a region to secede when the region trying to do so is poorer than the center. While a dictator will have incentives

---

* On the flip side, democracies may have a corresponding motive to admit high-skilled immigrants who bring in more in taxes than they will receive in benefits. This cost-benefit analysis has been an important part of the debate around high-skilled immigration in many Western societies. We discuss this more in Chapter 7.

to rule an area from which he can extract a tax surplus, even if it is very small, the citizens of the rich regions of a democracy that suffer a high tax burden may wish to limit the number of net recipients of the state's finances. By allowing a poor peripheral region to secede or be annexed, they reduce the political pressures to subsidize these poor regions.

For this reason, it is notable that the major 20th-century examples of peaceful territorial loss by democracies—the split of Czechoslovakia, the split of Serbia and Montenegro, etc.—all involved territories that were either similar to or poorer than the core region, in terms of GDP per capita.

This dynamic also helps explain the two large-scale episodes of new state creation during the 20th century: the independence of most of the West's colonies and the independence of the republics of the former Soviet Union. Unlike most episodes of new state creation, these episodes (with a few crucial exceptions) were peaceful and involved the consent of the larger power. As the extractive policies of the high colonial period became increasingly unacceptable in the years following World War II, colonial powers found it impossible to maintain their democratic values and levels of redistribution while ruling large, poor overseas empires. Western democracies faced the prospect of having to assimilate the colonies into their own polities, which would have involved enormous costs in transfers, either spent in the colonies or on citizens of the colonies who chose to move to the metropole. In fact, these empires were so large that any policy giving colonial citizens full political rights would have given them political control of the empire.

Charles de Gaulle's acid dismissal of the possibility of keeping Algeria French sums up the problem as contemporaries saw it:

> Do you think the French body politic can absorb ten million Muslims, who tomorrow will be twenty million, after tomorrow forty? If we integrated, if all the Arabs and Berbers of Algeria were considered French, would you prevent them to settle in France, where the standard of living is so much higher?[41]

Non-democracies did not face this consideration as strongly. It is notable that the major authoritarian colonial power, Portugal, resisted decolonization by force until the frustrations of conflict led to its overthrow.* Similarly, in the Soviet Union the authoritarian regime was willing to rule the periph-

---

* In fact, there is only one historical case of unilateral decolonization by a fully undemocratic regime: Spain's 1968 withdrawal from Equatorial Guinea.

eral republics by force, while the democratic regime allowed these nations to secede peacefully.*

Thus, our hypothesis is that democracy was an important factor in one of the most striking developments of the state system of the last century: the vast expansion of the number of states. If entry deterrence is successful, the number of states should change little over time, as no new states are created and old states are preserved by the norms of the system. There have been long periods when this prediction held true, notably the late 19th century. However, since 1914 the number of states has nearly tripled in three major episodes—a modest rise in the period immediately after World War I, an enormous one in the period of decolonization after World War II, and a small rise associated with the fall of the Soviet Union. The trend is depicted in Fig. 11.

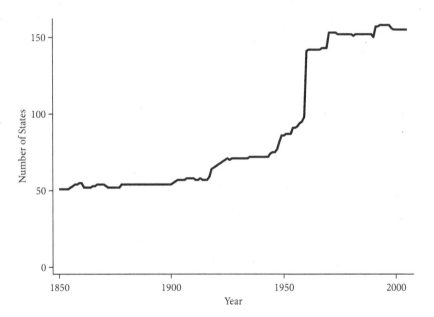

Fig. 11 The number of states over time since 1850, taken from the Polity IV dataset (Marshall, Jaggers, and Gurr 2002). Only states with a population over 500,000 are included.

---

* That said, we should note that while the vast majority of the Soviet republics were poorer than the core republic, Russia, or had very similar incomes, the three small Baltic republics were in fact richer.

Outstanding Questions and Potential Limitations

We have proposed three reasons why a governance cartel should collapse in short order. We have argued that one of these, democracy, may not really be an obstacle to the functioning of a cartel. The other two, opportunistic entry and border disputes, can also be managed—the first by informal norms and unilateral enforcement by the other powers, and the second by the swift reestablishment of territorial norms after conflict.

On the issue of border changes, however, some important questions remain. In particular, our model explains how a joint profit-maximizing boundary might be implemented as a focal solution to dividing borderlands between two cartel members. But in the case where governance costs change, it does not resolve the question of whether the historical boundary is focal or the new joint profit-maximizing boundary is focal. It is common for historical boundaries to persist, since parties might find them easier to coordinate on than the changing joint profit-maximizing boundaries, which are debatable and change frequently.[42] If this is the case, then it could be that many of today's boundaries were once joint profit-maximizing but are no longer joint profit-maximizing today.*

Given the costs of shifting borders, especially when war is necessary to do so, states may prefer a "good enough" boundary hallowed by time, even when it means that the more efficient state is receiving less in taxes than it otherwise would. In particular, the argument that changes in relative costs should easily translate into shifts in borders may seem to overstate the fluidity of the system, since there are many cases where states with very different levels of institutional efficiency border each other without territorial change—the Mexican border since 1848 is a good example. In the next chapter, we will discuss two additional reasons for the persistence of historical borders: nationalism and international institutions.

Another limitation is that border disputes do not always indicate a failure of the broader coordination mechanisms of the territorial state system; they often are a consequence of disagreement about which division was coordinated on in a previous period. This may be why border conflicts are often called disputes. Frequently, such disputes stem from technical problems

---

* Relatedly, the artificial borders that European powers used to divide territory in the colonies are perhaps not joint profit maximizing today, and perhaps never were from the perspective of self-governance. But they may be focal, as discussed in Chapter 4.

such as unwritten agreements, poorly written agreements, or boundaries not being demarcated on the ground. In such cases, the parties to the dispute agree to the underlying rules of the cartel. They simply disagree on how these rules apply in their particular case. Alternatively, a border may be so new that the parties are uncertain whether the other state is a reliable partner or whether an old border or a new one is being negotiated. Or, they may disagree about the legitimacy or existence of the agreement.[43]

For disputes of this nature, it is not clear that strengthening the norms of the cartel would help resolve them. On the other hand, border disputes such as these are unlikely to be the source of the cartel's unraveling. Instead, as we will argue in the final chapter, the present and future challenges to the cartel lie elsewhere—not in conflicts over physical territory.

6

Resilience of the Cartel

The late 19th century and early 20th century could have been an extremely unstable period for the cartel. Rapid changes in relative wealth and military power created incentives for powerful nations to try to increase their share of the governance market through conflict and coercion. Meanwhile, numerous rebel groups and non-state actors attempted to join or subvert the state system by taking over a portion of the governance market, and the rise of democracy threw into doubt the assumptions of a system based on the cooperation of rulers against their people.

But, if anything, the cartel remained remarkably resilient in this period. Territorial wars are now rare, and while the entry of new states occurred at many critical moments in the 20th century, it happened almost always with the cooperation of the other states involved. Most violent conflict now occurs within states rather than between them. Between 1945 and 1999, there were five times as many intrastate conflicts as interstate ones.[1] Even in Africa, a continent of weak states, state creation occurred with the consent of the international community. State revenues, rather than slipping due to competition, are at all-time highs, particularly in the democratic states.[2]

In this chapter we discuss two developments that help explain this stability. First, despite the rapid changes that took place in the technologies of governance, there are good reasons why boundaries now shift rarely. With the rise of global trade and the shift from land and natural resources as the main source of income to more mobile forms of capital (such as financial and human capital), the relevance of geographic borders has declined enough that competition in the new governance market has started to take place more at international trade talks than on the battlefield. To the extent that a state's share of the governance market shifts, it now shifts in a more abstract space of policies that govern the location of economic activity, migration, trade barriers and restrictions, and tax regimes.

At the same time, contributing to the stabilization of the cartel starting in an earlier period was the fact that states invested heavily in the creation of national identities and attachments, which have had a direct effect on the

The Cartel System of States: An Economic Theory of International Politics. Avidit Acharya and Alexander Lee, Oxford University Press. © Oxford University Press 2023. DOI:10.1093/oso/9780197632277.003.0006

costs of governance. Whether they made these investments to stabilize their borders or this stabilization was an unintended byproduct is immaterial. Ultimately, a major effect of these investments has been to lower the cost for each state of governing its own citizens while simultaneously increasing the cost for other states to govern these same citizens.[3]

The other key development which contributed significantly to stabilizing and institutionalizing the cartel system in the face of challenges was the rise of international institutions. The norms of the state system discussed in the previous chapters were often ambiguous. States must be recognized, but what is a state? Unilateral land grabbing must be avoided, but how can self-defense be separated from aggression? Even if norm violations are clear, multilateral enforcement can be difficult to coordinate.

International institutions provide a partial solution to this coordination problem. Institutions such as the United Nations, European Union, and Organization for African Unity serve as arbiters of membership in the state system, and help define both the norms of the system and particular relationships between clusters of states in far greater detail than ever before. Occasionally they have even helped coordinate multilateral responses to state failure and violations of the cartel's norms.

Nationalism

One of the key factors that made the *realpolitik* of the 18th century possible was that populations could easily be transferred from one ruler to another. In today's world, these transfers have become much rarer due in some part to the fact that most (though certainly not all) populations have been inculcated with strong national attachments. In fact, one of the most salient effects of nationalism has been to create a steep jump in each ruler's governance costs that occurs right at the boundary of the nation-state. This jump has contributed to the stabilization of borders and in turn the strengthening of the cartel.

The creation of national identities presents a unique feature of the state system as a cartel. While some firms do attempt to create brand loyalty in a bid to extract more of the consumer surplus (and simultaneously raise the cost for potential competitors to attract their customers), nothing they do compares in scale or effectiveness to the loyalty that states and their rulers have managed to create by investing in efforts to nationalize their populations. This critical feature sets apart the state system as a cartel from other economic cartels. De Beers may have successfully persuaded many consumers that "a diamond is forever" and even that the diamonds produced by it or other cartel members are of relatively high quality; but very few consumers are willing to die for the right to buy diamonds let alone the right to buy them from De Beers specifically. By contrast, many citizens are willing to die rather than be ruled by alternative states.

At least in Europe, nationalism and national identities coevolved with the state system. As rulers had an interest in dividing the governance market by drawing borders, they also invested in the creation of national identities to reinforce these borders, which in turn has contributed to the stability of the original borders over time. To develop these national attachments, rulers promoted a national language that is distinct from the language used by their neighbors.[4] They also invested in national school systems that teach children to identify with their state and not other states.[5] And they placed symbols of the nation—flags, statues of fallen heroes, etc.—in public places and demanded that they be venerated.[6]

Eugene Weber's (1976) description of this transition in rural France remains classic. As late as the mid-19th century, peasants, particularly in the south, did not have any special affective link to the Paris-based state, identifying instead with their village or province. Weber writes that in 1856 a historian from Marseille "still spoke of 'the Frenchman' and 'the French' as if they were a race apart (and not a very nice one)."[7] However, things changed rapidly during the late 19th century under the impact of universal primary education, universal conscription, and the broader literacy and awareness that accompanied these changes. Peasants began to identify with the French state and, as World War I would show, to sacrifice their lives for it. Moreover, they began to speak French in preference to patois, and to follow fashions from Paris rather than local customs. All of these changes reflected the deliberate policy of the school system, which constantly urged teachers to emphasize "the teaching of national history and ... the way it has been used to develop patriotic feelings."[8]

Even without deliberate policy, the creation of hard borders and institutionally unitary states tended to encourage a psychological identification with these institutions. As Benedict Anderson (2006, 57–58) remarks, the government official's:

colleagues, [are] from places and families he has scarcely heard of and surely hopes never to have to see. But in experiencing them as traveling companions, a consciousness of connectedness ("Why are we ... here ... together?") emerges.

Some readers may wonder whether we are reversing cause and effect, and may ask whether nations create territorial states rather than the other way around. But, as we argued in Chapter 3 the state system is typically thought of as originating in the early modern period (if not before) while the classic accounts of nationalism, from those of Weber (1976) to Ernest Gellner (1983) and others, describe the rise of the nation-state as taking place largely in the 19th century with the growth of conscription and primary schooling. Because of this, territorial divisions are likely to have reified national identities rather than the reverse. We do not deny that the original costs of governing individuals could incorporate governing costs that vary with ethnic, linguistic, and religious attachments. But to say that these attachments mattered at the onset of state building is different from saying that the creation of national identities, more specifically, was an initial driver in the development of the state system.

In what follows we use our model to depict how the creation of national attachments stabilizes borders. It is worth emphasizing that we are not making the claim that rulers invested in nationalism for the purpose of stabilizing borders or strengthening the cartel. Our claim is much weaker: for whatever reason they invested in the creation of national identities and whether or not they were even aware of all of the consequences of their investments, their efforts have contributed to the stabilization of borders and indirectly to the strengthening of the cartel.

A Model of the Effects of Nationalism

The creation of strong national attachments makes it easier for rulers to govern their citizens and harder for other rulers to govern the same population. In the context of our model, this amounts to decreasing the cost of governing one's own population and increasing the cost for other rulers of governing the same population. The overall effect of this is to make borders resilient to small short-term changes in costs of governing that would lead rulers to want to revise the boundaries between their states.

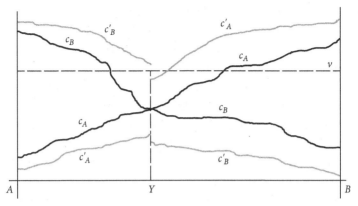

Fig. 12 The effect of nationalism on governance costs is to lower the cost of governing one's own population and increase the cost of governing the citizens of other states. Thus c_B drops to c'_B east of Y and c_A drops to c'_A west of this point, while c_B rises to c'_B west of Y and c_A rises to c'_A east of this point. The effect is to create a discontinuity in costs exactly at the boundary Y, which makes the boundary resilient to further small changes in cost caused by incremental improvements in governance technology.

Figure 12 depicts the logic. In the figure, as in the baseline model of Chapter 2, the boundary between the two states A and B is set between the rulers at Y, the point where their costs of governing c_A and c_B intersect. Over time, however, rulers invest in the creation of national attachments. They promote a national language that is distinct from the languages used by disparate ethnic groups. They invest in standardizing national schooling, in national monuments and symbols of pride, and in writing and disseminating stories of a shared history. These investments reduce their costs of governing their subjects. Within their territories, the costs of governing shift down from c_A to c'_A in ruler A's state west of the point Y and from c_B to c'_B in ruler B's state to the east of Y.

At the same time, the same investments make it costly for rulers to govern the subjects of other rulers. c_A rises to c'_A to the east of Y, and c_B rises to c'_B to the west of Y. The effect of this, depicted in the figure, is to create a sharp discontinuity in the new costs of governance. This discontinuity occurs exactly at the border Y, even though no such discontinuity existed there before under the old costs. Unlike the discontinuities arising from rivers, mountains, and other such geographic breaks, this continuity is man-made. It represents the idea of North Dakotans feeling that they are American and desiring to be part of the United States, and Manitobans feeling that they are Canadians and desiring to be part of Canada.[9]

Thus, instead of interpreting the governance costs in our model as purely exogenous, we can understand them to also reflect actions by citizens who may revolt against or shirk their obligations toward a state that they do not identify with. The most important gain to the state in governing a population that strongly identifies with it is in its superior ability to maintain a monopoly of violence and suppress conflict. Peripheral areas populated by minority ethnic groups are more subject to civil wars than other areas.[10] Areas inhabited by populations where even a minority identify with the nationality of a neighboring state are prone to irredentist conflicts. Examples include interwar Yugoslavia's problems in Macedonia and the United Kingdom's problems in Northern Ireland.

For our purposes, the important consequence of the discontinuities in governance costs created by national attachments is that the joint profit-maximizing boundary of the state becomes insensitive to small changes in the cost of governing. For example, ruler B's cost of governing c'_B may shift down somewhat due to improvements in administrative technology or state capacity, but so long as the shift is relatively small, the joint profit-maximizing boundary will remain at Y. When citizens are strongly attached to a particular state, they are unlikely to prefer to be governed by a foreign state, even one that is more administratively efficient.

This logic would continue to hold even if national attachments did not create discontinuities in the costs of governing but rather steep continuous changes. In this case, the joint profit-maximizing boundary would move with incremental improvements in governing technology. But the movements would be small enough that with any fixed costs (such as the cost of war) in attempting to move the boundary, the gain from doing so would not be worth it.

One final aspect of the creation of national identities that is worth mentioning is that it has the potential to eliminate what we referred to in the previous chapter as the periphery region—the region in which competition between rulers works in lowering the revenues that can be extracted from citizens. With investments in national identity creation, all regions, even previously peripheral ones, become part of the core, as is the case for state A in Fig. 12. In the figure, once B's cost rises from c_B to c'_B to the west of Y, no amount of competition between the rulers benefits any of the citizens belonging to A.

Why is this observation important? Recall that one of the important necessary conditions for the citizens of A to demand competition in the governance market under democratic institutions was that the median voter of A belonged to the periphery. Without a periphery, this condition cannot be met. Thus, one effect of the creation of national identities can be the removal, or lowering, of democracy's threat to the cartel system. Again, we do not argue that this was an intentional goal of rulers when making their decisions to invest in the creation of national attachments, but it may certainly be a consequence of it.[11]

An Illustration: Nepal and Sikkim

Between 1947 and 1975, there were three independent states in the foothills of the central Himalayas: Nepal, Bhutan, and Sikkim. All three countries were independent monarchies, with Bhutan's and Sikkim's dynasties dating to the 17th century and Nepal's to the 18th. Relative to their neighbor, newly independent India, the military power of all three nations was derisory. India had a population 40 times Nepal's and 2,600 times Sikkim's. It also had a relatively modern bureaucracy and army, inherited from British rule, while all three Himalayan kingdoms were inefficient states hobbled by the remains of patrimonial state building.[12] Moreover, given the inaccessibility of their borders with China, almost all foreign trade for all three kingdoms had to flow through India, making them acutely vulnerable to Indian pressure. In the context of cartel theory, all three states existed in the zone in which an efficient neighboring power might have been able to govern them cheaply.

Sikkim eventually succumbed to this pressure. It had existed as an independent protectorate under British suzerainty during the period of colonial rule. This policy was continued by the Indian government following the 1950 India-Sikkim Peace Treaty which explicitly ceded control over the kingdom's diplomacy and national defense to India. Sikkim's domestic affairs were governed by the monarch (the Chogyal) with the aid of an unelected state council established in 1953. In 1968, an anti-India protest broke out in Gangtok, Sikkim's capital, in the wake of events following border clashes between Indian and Chinese troops at the Sikkim-Tibet border in the previous year. Indian troops were sent to suppress the protest and periodically returned to Sikkim for the next five years. Finally, in 1975 they surrounded the royal palace, disarmed the guards, and arrested the Chogyal. The state council then announced that the king had been deposed and declared the result of a referendum in which 99.55% of voters allegedly voted for Sikkim to be incorporated as a state of India. Within a few weeks the Indian parliament passed an act finalizing Sikkim's admission as an Indian state.

The same path might have been followed in Nepal. Anti-India protests like the 1968 protests in Gangtok have periodically taken place in Kathmandu and other Nepali towns. After 1975, the term *sikkimikaran* in Nepali, or Sikkimization in English, became common in Nepali newspapers and for-eign policy circles as a reference to Indian expansionism in the Himalayas. The Indian foreign policy establishment has similarly asserted that a precept of India's foreign policy, especially under the "Indira doctrine" set by Prime Minister Indira Gandhi, is that all Himalayan states are squarely within the Indian sphere of influence. Yet, India has never tried to incorporate Nepal, or Bhutan for that matter, as it did Sikkim.

What explains the difference? The key fact is that a sense of national identity had already been inculcated in the Nepali population even prior to Indian independence while no sense of Sikkimese national identity existed.

Nepali rulers started to invest in promoting a sense of Nepali identity in the late 18th and early 19th centuries when they commissioned local poets and writers to write panegyrics to Nepali Gurkha soldiers. The Nepali government established the first national newspaper in Nepali, the *Gorkha-patra*, in 1901. In 1913, it established the *Nepali bhasha prakashini samiti* (Publication Board of the Nepali Language) to publish books in Nepali for schools and colleges. Radio Nepal was established in 1951, giving the Nepali government a voice even in the most remote areas. A national curriculum for primary education was standardized in the 1950s, which included the policy of making Nepali the medium of instruction even though a number of local vernaculars were (and still are) spoken across the country. Nepali speakers in India established the *Nepali sahitya sammelan* (Nepali Literature Conference) in 1923 and published books such as *Nepali bir haru* (Heroes and Builders of Nepal), glorifying Nepal's history of independence. Unlike Sikkim, Nepal in 1975 already had a political establishment, opposition, and civil society. Nepal established diplomatic ties with the United States in 1947, became a member of the United Nations in 1955, and was elected as a non-permanent member of the Security Council from 1969–70. Sikkim, on the other hand, never joined the UN.*

* Bhutan also joined the UN (in 1971) but its foreign policy is largely influenced by India, which is the only country besides Bangladesh to have an embassy in its capital, Thimpu. Moreover, unlike Nepal, Bhutan does not have diplomatic relations with any of the five permanent members of the UN Security Council.

A strong sense of national identity in Nepal means that the costs to India of taking over Nepal and governing it are high. Riots broke out throughout the country in 2000 with protestors burning tires and effigies of Bollywood actor, Hrithik Roshan, after he allegedly made disparaging comments about Nepal. Movie theaters across Nepal temporarily banned Bollywood films. Similar protests had taken place the previous year after another Bollywood actor, Madhuri Dixit, remarked that she thought Nepal was a part of India.

In Sikkim, efforts to promote a Sikkimi identity were not nearly as effective. Sikkim's official government ideology was linked to Buddhism, a religion practiced by only a minority of the population.[13] The Choygal's attempts to promote nationalism were either ethnically divisive or regarded as being appealing only to the small middle class. As a result, many Sikkimis, in particular Nepali speakers, welcomed Indian annexation, which they saw as replacing an old-fashioned and ramshackle government with a more modern one—one that could offer expanded employment opportunities.[14]

Indian policy towards the smaller South Asian nations matured during the tenure of Indira Gandhi in the 1970s and in the 1980s. This was a time of great activity in South Asian regional politics, encompassing the separation of Bangladesh from Pakistan, the Indian takeover of Sikkim, and India's support of Tamil separatists in Sri Lanka.[15] But by this time, Nepali national identity had already developed to a point where the costs to India of governing Nepal were too high for it to be worth it to take over Nepal. In fact, in recent decades Nepali ethnolinguistic nationalism has spread even to *Indian* states, with, for example, many of the residents of Darjeeling seeking to establish their own state of Gorkhaland separate from West Bengal.[16]

International Institutions

The Problem of Coordination

In previous chapters, we have frequently referred to the norms of the international system. These norms—in particular, the sovereignty norm that states should not attempt to govern territory outside their borders—are important because when they are violated, states often resort to competition and war.* In some cases, attachment to the norm is so strong that even non-victims can have an incentive to punish norm-breakers because of their interest in maintaining the stability of the system (recall the interdependent mode of cooperation that we described in Chapter 2).

In practice, however, determining norm violations is difficult. Borders may be poorly demarcated, and what one side interprets as an incursion, the other may view as a policing action to protect its authority within its own territory.[17] Even if parties agree in principle that certain actions violate norms (e.g., OPEC members producing more than their quota), in practice detecting and punishing these violations is difficult and can easily degenerate into retaliatory behavior that undermines the cartel agreement.

In the 19th century, statesmen recognized the possibility that even minor disputes, either in the colonies or in the European periphery, could unravel the state system. German Chancellor Otto Von Bismarck famously predicted that "One day the great European War will come out of some damned foolish thing in the Balkans."[18] The solution adopted by these statesmen was the Concert of Europe, a term used to describe a series of informal arrangements made by the great powers to settle disputes multilaterally and defend the broad contours of the cartel agreement.[19]

This informal system, however, had some important flaws. Ad hoc meetings took quite a bit of effort to arrange. Since there were no formal mediating

---

* Most of the other norms including the inviolabilty of embassies, the laws of neutrality, the laws of the high seas, etc. are extensions of the sovereignty norm.

roles, success was dependent on the presence of a few strong personalities such as Bismarck or Austrian Chancellor Klemens von Metternich. And since the objectivity of these mediators was more than a little questionable, the legitimacy of conference decisions in the eyes of the other participants was also in doubt. In July 1914, with Bismarck dead, the world was treated to a demonstration of the flaws of this informal system, as the Germans dismissively rejected British offers to host and mediate a conference to resolve the dispute between Austria and Serbia.

It was the failure of these informal efforts to prevent World War I that led to the creation of the League of Nations. The innovation emerged from a simple question asked by the leaders of the cartel: what if the cartel organized a central office to reduce transaction costs and solve coordination problems? The League, however, was ineffective at preventing the next major threat to the cartel in the form of World War II. Much of its failure stemmed from the fact that it was charged with coordinating a global consensus that did not exist. The United States, emerging as a dominant world power, never joined the League and the Soviet Union and Germany were not present at its inception. Nevertheless, although we now remember the League as a failure, it is wrong to judge it so harshly. The basic theoretical principles on which it was founded were sound, and they were what laid the foundations for its successor organization, the United Nations.

The United Nations

Very often when an institutional innovation fails, its designers are so quick to abandon it that even its strengths are discarded and forgotten in the frenzy. Not so with the League of Nations. The idea of a central organization dedicated to looking after the interests of the cartel was so remarkably sound that the basic principles behind the institutional innovation of the League managed to rise from the ashes of World War II in the form of the UN.

The UN today is the headquarters of the cartel, not terribly different from the way OPEC is the headquarters of the cartel of oil producers. Membership in the UN is a sufficient, and in most cases also necessary, condition for international recognition. In 2020, among the many states of the world there were only four UN members or observers whose status as states was not recognized by more than one UN member (Israel, Palestine, North Korea, and China) and only three non-members recognized by more than one member (Taiwan, the Western Sahara, and Kosovo).

The UN also helps develop, disseminate, and interpret norms about what constitutes contravention of the cartel. Like its predecessor, the League, it collects and publishes copies of all international treaties as required by its charter. Without any coercive power of its own to enforce these norms, it acts mainly as a body that facilitates coordination among the most powerful cartel members. This can be seen from the design of institutions that govern it. Five of the world's most powerful states have permanent status on the Security Council and exercise veto power. Any resolution that is not in the interest of any one of them is unlikely to pass. On the other hand, when the five are mostly united in their goals, a resolution is unlikely to fail. Compare, for instance, the response to the Iraqi invasion of Kuwait to the otherwise quite similar Russian invasion of Crimea.*

To elaborate on this idea, we look at the role of the UN in coordinating the entry of new states into the cartel during the period of decolonization, which is suggestive of two points. The first is that even in the 20th century, coordination was necessary for the cartel leadership to make important distinctions between those who have the right to enter and those who do not. For example, while it might seem obvious to some that armed groups seeking Corsican or Breton independence from France were rebels (or, worse, terrorists) worthy of international sanctioning while rebels seeking Vietnamese or Algerian independence from France were freedom fighters worthy of international recognition and aid, this was a distinction that required constant articulation and policing, not least to keep France from attacking countries that aided the Vietnamese and Algerians and to keep other nations from aiding the Corsicans and Bretons.[20]

The second point is that even among the most powerful states it is the global superpowers whose interest the UN will coordinate. Although the entry of new states into the cartel during the period of decolonization involved the dissolution of the British and French colonial empires—two

---

* The 1990 Iraqi invasion of Kuwait, for instance, was four days later condemned by the Security Council, which placed economic sanctions on Iraq. Three months later, the Council voted to authorize the use of force to drive Iraq out of Kuwait. This was enforced by an international coalition led by the US and comprising several dozen nations.

The reestablishment of the Kuwaiti government despite their own extreme military and administrative weakness also shows how small and powerless states, which might have been easily gobbled up in the 18th century due to a failure of the great powers to coordinate a response, can safely survive in the modern world because international institutions like the UN lower the odds of such a coordination failure.

The cartel at work: The United Nations Security Council.

powers that had and continue to possess veto power in the Security Council—these old powers were on the decline while two other powers, the Soviet Union and the United States, were ascendant. These emergent superpowers lacked large colonial empires of their own and believed that any attempt to upload colonialism through force would be destabilizing. More importantly, they had good reason to think that they could exert just as much (if not more) influence in the newly independent nations than they could in the colonies of other powers. Both nations thus pressed for the independence of the colonies through actions both open (verbal condemnations) and covert (US denial of Marshall Aid, Soviet aid to guerrilla groups).[21] Through the UN, they coordinated the entry of these new nations into the state system.[22] A similar thing happened when the USSR faded from its role as a global superpower, and its member states obtained cartel membership as independent nations.[23]

These examples are particularly revealing because they represent important exceptions to the entry-deterrence objectives of the cartel. They suggest that the UN really is a body that serves the interest of the most powerful cartel members rather than one that upholds the principles of cartel governance in all instances.

In addition, the fact that powerful states are the key actors shaping both international organizations and the state system as a whole—and will occasionally break the underlying principles of collusion—is not any different from the management of economic cartels by the largest and most powerful producers. In fact, economic cartels also distinguish between players sufficiently powerful to break the cartel unilaterally (dominant firms) and others that are expected to always follow the norms (fringe players).[24] De Beers, for example, was ruthless towards smaller competitors during its period as a global cartel leader in the diamonds market but treated the Soviet Union, which controlled a potentially decisive 17% of the world market, with kid gloves.[25] The dominant role of Saudi Arabia in OPEC is also widely acknowledged and the Saudis are often able to alter OPEC policy in response to their own domestic needs.[26]

Beyond Territorial Governance

In this chapter, we have discussed two aspects of the international state system that have stabilized the cartel's division of the governance market, both of which also distinguish the state system from economic cartels that tend to be more unstable. First is the creation of national identities that have resulted in a strong brand loyalty that citizens have towards their own states and governments, diminishing their desire for more competition in the governance market. Second is the use of international institutions that make cooperation explicit, rather than tacit.

Although we have emphasized mainly the role of international organizations like the UN in coordinating action in the governance market, it is also important to acknowledge that these organizations work in several other areas. We highlight three of these. First, they advance the interests of the cartel leaders on other issues unrelated to territorial governance. The suppression of nuclear proliferation through treaties like the Non-Proliferation Treaty is one example. Second, not only do these organizations serve coordination purposes, they also seek to resolve collective action problems. The organization of periodic meetings (Rio, Kyoto, Paris, Copenhagen, etc.) to address the existential threat of climate change is perhaps the most prominent example of this.

Third, international organizations help coordinate the interests of a broad set of political and economic elites who govern and influence these organizations, not always as perfect representatives of their fellow citizens. The WTO is a good example. In the past few decades, the WTO (and its predecessor, the GATT) has coordinated the lowering of international trade barriers, enabling nations to take advantage of the efficiency gains from trade. As we discuss in the next chapter, this has been mainly an elite-led project with powerful corporations lobbying for favorable terms in these trade agreements while popular opinion is often in opposition. The irony is that, in some cases, nationalist attachments have become so strong that many popular movements now advocate for the closing of borders and for the cartel to operate as it did historically by limiting competition in the governance market rather than opening it up. In the next chapter, we discuss this interesting dynamic within the framework of cartel theory.

7

The Cartel Today

Throughout this book we have argued that cartel theory provides a useful lens to view the relationship between states and between individuals and the states that govern them. In our theory, states provide governance to their citizens as monopolists in geographically segmented markets, and they collude to restrict individuals from receiving governance from more than one provider.

This portrait of the state system as a set of local monopolies of governance continues to be relevant today, but its workings have become more complicated with the major technological and economic changes that we have witnessed in the last century. As we alluded to at the start of the previous chapter, the space in which states compete in the governance market has transformed from the simple and concrete space of physical territory to the increasingly more abstract space of complex policies that regulate today's world economy.

These developments have been driven mainly by the massive declines in communication and transportation costs and advances in finance that took place in the last hundred years. Sea freight costs, for example, are now only 20% of what they were in 1930, facilitating greater trade and distance between the locations of production and consumption. Passenger air transport costs and international calling costs have declined by an even greater amount.[1] People can now travel by air to any country in the world and remain in touch with friends and family at home through video calls and instant messaging.* Improvements in financial technology through the creation of new financial instruments and with the help of digital technology have led to an unprecedented globalization of finance. Banks can now collect and transmit information instantly and safely, enabling them to operate

---

* When one of the author's great-grandfathers came to the United States from Norway in the 1880s, the trip took several weeks and cost half a year's income for an agricultural laborer. When the other author's father first came to the United States from Nepal a century later, the trip took roughly 24 hours and under $2,000—still quite a bit relative to the per capita income of Nepal, but not a large sum relative to US per capita income, which made the trip worthwhile. Not coincidentally, there were three times as many migrants in 2017 as 1962 (OECD migration dataset).

The Cartel System of States: An Economic Theory of International Politics. Avidit Acharya and Alexander Lee, Oxford University Press. © Oxford University Press 2023. DOI:10.1093/oso/9780197632277.003.0007

internationally. Individuals can use their credit cards anywhere in the world and keep track of their expenses. They can learn about investment opportunities and living conditions in other countries through internet research. They can move money across investments in one country to another with the click of a button on a personal computer.

To analyze these developments more systematically, economists point to the rise over time of three important measures of globalization—financial integration, trade openness, and international migration.[2] These measures actually peaked at the start of the 20th century, another period of globalization fueled by technological innovations like the steam engine and political developments like the broad adoption of the gold standard and the creation of large colonial empires.[3] But as the cartel reasserted itself following the end of World War I, they declined during the middle of the century and have risen again steadily over the last several decades.

Even more so than during the first major wave of globalization in the late 19th and early 20th centuries, the persistent removal today of the technological and informational hurdles to crossing an international border (whether physically or digitally) has challenged the historical cartel system in which rulers divided the governance market geographically and restricted their citizens from access to the services provided by other states. It is true that all states continue to suppress movements of labor and capital through citizenship and immigration laws, tax treaties, currency controls, and other regulations; but many have ultimately relented to pressures of technological progress by increasingly opening up their economies. This has led, effectively, to an increase in competition in the governance market. If a state does not provide good governance at a low cost to its citizens, these citizens will want to move themselves or their businesses abroad. Immigrants have left their homes in search of better opportunities and living conditions for themselves and their families. Money, intellectual property, factories, machines, and the inputs and outputs of production are all on the move, as businesses and individuals search for better investment opportunities and regulatory environments across the globe.

In this chapter, we discuss how these developments have led to a more complex governance market and the ways in which the cartel has continued to try to control and segment this new market. We then turn to some of the political challenges that the cartel now faces in this environment. We focus on four key challenges: (i) the issues around international migration, (ii) the issue of failed states that serve as breeding grounds for terrorism and groups such as the Islamic State that have no intention of abiding by the norms of the cartel, (iii) the rise of new powerful actors within the cartel (China) and the tensions between them and existing leaders (the United States), and (iv) transformations in the mode of international conflict, which in an increasingly interconnected world can take the form of economic and cyber-warfare. After discussing these issues, we end with some brief speculative remarks on how the cartel might adapt to address them along with the other major challenges of our time, such as the management of environmental externalities across borders and the existential threat of climate change.

A More Complex Governance Market

In Chapter 2 we hypothesized that one reason why the market for governance was divided geographically was the importance of land and natural resources for production. If the state system were being created for the first time today, with land being relatively less important than other forms of capital, it is not clear that rulers would opt to divide the market solely along geographical boundaries. The governance market has transformed significantly, and is now much more complex. At the turn of the 20th century, just under three-quarters of American GDP derived from agriculture and mining, and much of the rest of the world was even more agrarian. Today, more than three-quarters of the American economy is driven by manufacturing and services. Moreover, as Fig. 13 shows, the share of services has been increasing while even the share of manufacturing has been on the decline. The economies of the vast majority of rich and middle-income countries (save a handful that are based on oil) rely very little on land and natural resources. Value, in these economies, is not as rigidly tied to specific locations as it once was.

As a consequence, states are now dividing up a much more complicated governance market. To say that a country is entitled to a certain share of the governance market today is not just to say that it is entitled to a certain amount of territory in a certain part of the world; it also means that the country is entitled to put in place a certain set of policies that enable it to claim this share, and that the policies of other countries will not interfere with its ability to do so. With certain favorable policies in place, a country can attract businesses to invest in its economy. It can attract workers to relocate there and pay taxes to it rather than to a different state. With the diminished

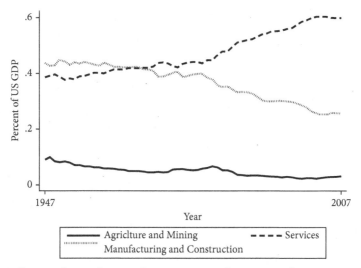

Fig. 13 Shares of agriculture and mining, manufacturing and construction, and services in the US economy from 1947 to 2007. Data are from the Bureau of Economic Analysis.

importance of agriculture and mining, laying claims to a certain territory is less important than laying claims to the right to regulate one's economy in a certain way and participate in international commerce on favorable terms. It is no wonder that interstate wars have declined while the degree of engagement at trade talks has increased.

Dividing the New Market

The fact that such a large share of the world economy is no longer location-specific has presented a new set of issues for the cartel. In today's global economy the efficiency advantages of freer trade and more open borders are substantial, as economists have argued.[4] Cartel leaders have recognized that to actually reap the full-scale benefits of economic and technological development, some degree of openness of borders and integration of the world economy is necessary.[5] To put it simply, if free trade policies are efficiency-enhancing then the cartel is losing money by restricting competition in the governance market. At the same time, however, too much competition could result in a race to the bottom that diminishes the revenues that these cartel elites can appropriate by colluding. The challenge for the cartel is to figure out what kinds of policies are optimal given how this tradeoff between the benefits of economic openness and the costs of race-to-the-bottom competition has changed over time.

The policy that the cartel has settled on to resolve this tradeoff is what Joseph Stiglitz (2002) calls "managed trade." In the second half of the 20th century, the cartel started to dismantle trade barriers, but it did so in a slow and controlled fashion. It operated through international institutions like the GATT/WTO that coordinate trade policies in formal meetings that take place periodically at various cities around the world, as well as more informally through organizations like the World Economic Forum that since 1971 has brought together a wider array of cartel leaders (and the interests they serve) at its yearly meetings in the resort town of Davos in Switzerland. It is at these meetings that the cartel elite mingle, share information, and form the camaraderie that provides the relational basis for collusive behavior.[6] The benefits of this kind of coordination have been spectacular. The cartel has managed to regulate today's complicated governance market in creative new ways that enable it to resolve the efficiency/race to the bottom tradeoff described above. What has resulted is a system of managed trade, rather than a system of genuine free trade. Stiglitz (2002, 20) puts it bluntly:

> If [a free trade agreement] were about free trade, it would be short, a few pages—each country gives up its tariffs, its non-tariff barriers to trade, and its subsidies. The Trans-Pacific Partnership . . . ran upward of 6,000 pages.

Under managed trade, countries make deals that increase competition in some sectors, but not others, and as a result benefit certain sets of consumers and producers, but not others.[7] For example, free trade policies have promoted the shift in manufacturing industries from developed countries like the United States to developing countries like China and Mexico. Corporations and the typical consumer may have benefited by being able to produce and buy the same goods at lower costs, but manufacturing workers in developed countries have lost their jobs while workers in developing countries have gained employment and raised their living standards.[8] At the same time, subsides to farmers in developed countries have persisted despite calls from the developing countries to end these protectionist policies.[9] American farmers have benefited from this protection while Indian farmers still do not have free trade access to the American food market.

Trade, therefore, has the potential to create winners and losers. Under a full-scale free trade agreement like the one Stiglitz posits in the quote above, it may be difficult to predict who these groups of winners and losers will be. Managed trade, by contrast, *picks* the winners and losers.

Cartel theory provides a simple explanation for why trade is managed rather than made genuinely free. Managed trade is the way in which the cartel optimizes the benefits of free trade against the costs of race-to-the-bottom competition in the governance market.

In addition, there are also at least two other reasons why it is important for the cartel to manage trade. One of the most important functions of any cartel is to determine the share of the market accruing to each member. The governance cartel targets each state's share of the world economy. Actual free trade could alter these shares in unpredictable ways. Even if the cartel could predict the shares of the world economy that go to each member state, these shares may be incommensurate with the previous distribution of the market or with each state's economic and political power. The whole point of a cartel is to carefully manage what share of the market (i.e., what share of total potential profit) each member receives. Trade must be managed to target these shares.

Secondly, trade must be managed because each cartel member serves the interest of a select group of domestic constituents, whom we can think of as being the principals for whom politicians act as agents. In a perfectly functioning democracy, this is the electorate.[10] In less than perfectly functioning democracies, this may be wealthy individuals or large corporations that exert their influence on public policy.[11] In autocracies, it is the leaders, land and business owners, and other powerful members of the ruling elite. Trade must be managed not just to calibrate the shares of each state but also the benefits to each of the important players within states. This helps to ensure that trade policy serves the domestic interests that each state's trade negotiators represent at the bargaining table.[12]

What we are saying is that the leaders of states are responsible to certain domestic constituents who exercise political power. These powerful constituents collude, through their political agents, at the expense of other citizens. The term "ruler" that we have used in our model refers precisely to these powerful actors. As we mentioned before when discussing democracy, the absolute rulers of the past have been replaced by democratically elected politicians in many countries, making it difficult to ascertain who is exploiting whom through the collusive cartel arrangement. But one way to identify the sets of individuals that the term "ruler" metaphorically represents is to work back from the sets of individuals that have benefited and suffered from managed trade.

Managing Competition in the New Market

In our model of the state system, the key consequence of competition in the governance market is the reduction in taxes that states are able to extract from those citizens who can potentially take advantage of such competition. With the rise in governance competition fueled by globalization, states today compete vigorously to attract businesses to their countries by offering more favorable tax rates and regulatory environments. This includes laws governing the treatment of workers, such as minimum wage laws, laws guaranteeing humane working conditions, and environmental protections.[13]

The extent to which this increased competition has depressed tax collection is difficult to estimate. But anecdotes reveal the ability of corporations to take advantage of the growth in tax competition in spectacular ways. Many have employed creative accounting techniques to move to low-tax jurisdictions without actually moving any of their physical production. For example, using base erosion and profit shifting (BEPS) tools, a company might declare all its intellectual property to be owned by a subsidiary in a low-tax jurisdiction and pay it royalties, or arrange it so that a subsidiary in the low-tax jurisdiction is owed interest at artificially high rates from other subsidiaries.[14] The Apple corporation, for example, using the "double Irish" and "Green Jersey" BEPS arrangements, was able to move most of its profits to low-tax Ireland from high-tax America. The arrangement became notorious after an internal accounting maneuver (a $300 billion purchase of intellectual property) resulted in Irish GDP increasing by 26.3% in a single quarter.[15] Many countries like Ireland take this deal even when tax competition results in small increases in government revenue because they prefer the small stream of revenue they obtain to having the corporation locate elsewhere and earning no tax revenue from it as a result.[16]

This kind of global competition in the governance market has the potential to harm and benefit citizens differentially. Those that gain from tax competition include the owners of large multinational corporations like Apple, and the 60 profitable Fortune 500 companies that paid no taxes on a total of $79 billion in profits.[17] Those that get the short end of the stick include the overwhelming majority of workers and small businesses who have a harder time moving abroad to shop for more favorable governance policies. If their state lowers taxes to attract business, workers and small businesses may end up either receiving poorer quality services or having to pay more to make up the difference. If their state chooses to let the businesses locate elsewhere, tax revenue will still fall, and workers may lose employment opportunities as well.

Not surprisingly, economic elites—the winners from increased competition in the governance market—tend to be enthusiastic supporters of globalization.[18] They argue that it provides businesses (that they own) an alternative to tax regimes that may be extortionate and governments that may be inefficient. They also argue that such competition in the long run makes governments more efficient, providing better services at lower costs. They point to many examples (most of East Asia since the 1970s, for instance) where the need to attract investment has been a major driving force in institutional reform, bettering the lives of citizens in those countries and bringing them into the world economic system as participants with a shared interest in economic stability and peace.[19] Economic elites argue that it is the anti-globalization populists who are openly scheming to collude against them, restricting their ability to shop for better deals in what ought to be a free and open governance market. According to them, it is they that represent the individuals in our model who are potentially exploited by ability of rulers to restrict competition in the governance market.

On the other hand, many members of the anti-globalization movement who claim to represent the interests of the workers and small businesses in rich countries deplore the race to the bottom in taxation and regulation. They see it as benefiting large multi-national corporations and wealthy individuals at the expense of ordinary people.[20] Politicians like Bernie Sanders (I-VT) and Elizabeth Warren (D-MA) in the United States have called for policies reimposing tariffs, regulating the repatriation of profits, and coordinating efforts to curb tax avoidance across borders through international treaties and organizations.[21] Among the more widely discussed policy recommendations made by Thomas Piketty (2018) in his book *Capital in the Twenty-First Century* was a coordinated global wealth tax that would be designed to give elites nowhere to hide their money.

While some commentators have denounced such proposals as fanciful ideas rooted in the socialist dream of world government, many at least recognize the importance of the problem that has given rise to such demands.

Dani Rodrik (1997, 81 and 73), for example, warned us more than two decades ago that "the ability of firms to play national tax authorities off each other is a source of negative cross-border externality, as it undercuts the revenue sources needed to maintain social and political cohesion" and "the mobility of capital and of employers both aggravate the risks immobile groups face and render it more difficult to generate the public resources needed to finance social insurance schemes." Year after year, the IMF and OECD put out reports on the extent of taxes that are evaded by corporations and individuals exploiting the new growth in competition in the governance market. They propose that governments coordinate to suppress such activity.[22] Just last year, 136 out of 140 members of the OECD/G20 Inclusive Framework on BEPS pledged to introduce a minimum corporate tax rate of 15% starting in 2023. The agreement was specifically designed to discourage tax evasion by individuals and corporations capable of moving their money abroad.[23]

Much of the tension between the viewpoints of the economic elite and anti-globalization populists lies in the fact that while the efficiency gains from competition are long-term and uncertain, the distributional costs are immediate. For example, only those who own mobile capital can benefit from the increasing ease with which these assets can be moved across borders.[24] How governments respond to these countervailing political pressures thus depends on the degree to which the owners of mobile capital are influential in policymaking vis-à-vis labor and other interests. In many democracies, the wealthy have disproportionate influence over the political process through mechanisms such as lobbying and campaign contributions, and are able to prevent the implementation of policies restricting tax evasion.[25] Even dictatorships may also see the benefit of open competition in the governance market insofar as they enable the rulers themselves to move assets away from the risk of expropriation by future rulers.

Whether proposals to coordinate taxation of the wealthy will succeed will depend on how politics unfold, and who comes to power in the future. If left-wing populists that seek to make the corporations "pay their fair share" come to power, then they will be the rulers in our cartel model. If they succeed in coordinating and implementing their anti-globalization policies in sufficiently many powerful countries, then they, as the rulers of the cartel, will have successfully colluded against the corporations. If, on the other hand, individuals who have the resources and will to avoid taxes are in power (or influence public policy through their lobbying efforts and campaign donations) then they will be the rulers. Competition in the governance market will be enjoyed only (or primarily) by the wealthiest individuals and corporations. This will represent a different kind of collusion by the cartel's leaders against the masses. Who exactly is colluding against whom in the cartel model depends on who is in power, and whose interests they serve.

Political Challenges

Immigration

We have discussed the ease with which capital can be moved across borders these days, but it is not just capital that is on the move. More people are moving across international borders today than ever before. High-skilled workers from developing countries have emigrated to places where their productive skills earn the greatest returns (the "brain drain"). Wealthy entrepreneurs and asset holders in rich and poor countries alike have migrated to places that provide greater security, tax relief, and a more welcoming politics. Displaced individuals and those whose personal lives are under threat in their home countries have sought refuge in places that provide better security and human rights protections.

One key motivator for migration is the vast differences in the *quality* of governance across states, not just the differences in how much individuals are asked to pay for this governance. Many states with low fiscal capacity simply do not have the administrative ability to coerce their citizens to pay taxes and therefore cannot provide high-quality governance, including protections from terrorists, warlords, human traffickers, and other criminals. When we look at measures of perceived "quality of governance" and new migration, we see a robust positive correlation between immigration and governance quality: people have chosen to leave countries where governance is poor and enter countries where it is better, and they have done so in large numbers. The correlation is depicted in Fig. 14.[26]

Our model can help make sense of this pattern while also revealing the nuances in understanding the migration decision and how it relates to the workings of the governance market. In our model, we assumed that the value of governance that states can provide is fixed and constant in distance while the cost of providing this level of governance varied. This of course was a simplifying assumption. In reality the value of governance that a

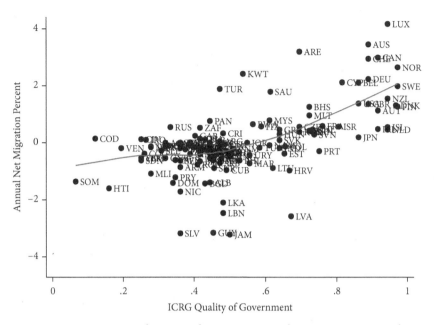

Fig. 14 Net migration and perceived governance quality in 2017. Perceived governance quality is the index reported in the International Country Risk Guide.

state can provide also varies with geography and across states: some states are efficient and capable of providing high-value governance, while others can only provide lower-value governance for the same cost.

Consider now a variant of our baseline model in which there are two versions of state B: one that, like state A, provides governance that has value v to its citizens and another that is a more inefficient state that is only able to provide some value v' that is less than v.[27] Fig. 15 depicts these distinct cases. In the first case, the joint profit-maximizing boundary is Y. Let us assume that this is the original border between the states. In the second case, there is a region between the states, namely the region between Z and X that neither state A nor state B can profitably govern. We use this variant of our model to help make sense of the factors affecting the migration decision and the relationship between governance quality and net out-migration.

If states act as monopolists that do not redistribute what they collect back to the population, then the net value of being governed is zero for individuals in any state. In this case, no citizen has any incentive to migrate. Let us then proceed by starting with the assumption that states A and B in the figure redistribute what they collect back to the population as untargeted lump sum

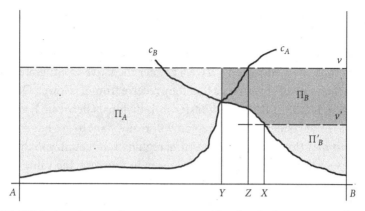

Fig. 15 If B is a weak state that can only provide a level of governance that is valued at $v' < v$ but claims all of the territory east of Y, then it may not provide governance at all to citizens between Y and X. These citizens then may have an interest in migrating.

transfers, as described in Chapter 5. We could also assume that these states do not redistribute all of what they collect, or they redistribute some but not very much of what they collect. This will not matter for clarifying our main ideas. What we need is that not all of the citizens' surplus is extracted by the states, and assuming that all of it is redistributed back keeps the accounting simple.

With this assumption, consider first the case in which state B can provide governance of value v, and recall that the value in transfers (or public services) that are received by each individual governed by state A is the value of the light shaded area, Π_A, divided among the mass of individuals who live to the west of Y. Analogously for state B, let Π_B denote the sum of the two shaded areas east of Y, and Π'_B denote just the lighter shaded area. These are the net revenues collected by the state for the two cases where the values of governance that B provides are v and v' respectively.

If B provides a value of governance equal to v and governs up to the boundary Y then the value to an individual east of Y from being governed by B is Π_B divided among the mass of individuals who live east of Y. If this per capita value is comparable to the per capita value from being governed by A, and migrating from B to A has some fixed cost, then these individuals will not want to leave state B. On the other hand, if the value of being governed by B falls substantially short of the value of being governed by A, then individuals governed by B will want to emigrate to A.

Next, suppose that the value of governance that B provides falls to v' from v. If B continues to provide the transfer to individuals between Y and X then the value of belonging to B's state for any individual east of Y is now much smaller. These individuals now have a greater incentive to emigrate to state A, since the value of governance that they receive from B is lower. Of course, B may simply not provide the transfer to individuals between Y and X, in which case the residents of this region will really want to get out and move either east of X (for instance from a rural region of the country to the capital city) or west of Y to A's state. However, even in this case, the value of being governed by B for individuals east of X may still have dropped, in which case even citizens who live east of X will want to move to state A.*

This accounting suggests a rationale for why we see the correlation between quality of governance and net out-migration. The point is very simple: if the value of being governed by another state is significantly higher than the value of staying at home, then people will bear the costs of migration and leave. In today's world of ever-declining travel costs, even small differences in the value of governance between states can result in significant migration pressures. For larger differences, such as the difference between a country in which citizens are killed by criminal gangs with impunity and those where they face protections from the state and enjoy the rule of law, migrants are prepared to bear extraordinary costs and risks.

Finally, let us return to the point we made above that a similar but more complicated calculation would apply to the emigration decision in cases where full redistribution does not take place, or if transfers are targeted. Autocracies generally redistribute less than democracies, and if state B were an autocracy or a flawed democracy that gave back less to its citizens than the full amount it collects in net tax revenue, then the incentive for these citizens to migrate to A would be even higher. This is one purely economic reason why out-migration pressures may be greater for autocracies than they are for democracies, all else equal. But it also suggests that the possibility of international migration puts pressure on autocrats to give up more to their citizens if they do not want to lose their populations to out-migration—particularly the

---

* Formally, suppose that the citizens are a continuum of unit mass distributed between the locations A and B depicted in the figure. Let $\mathcal{Y}$ denote the mass of individuals east of Y. Supposing there is a mass $\mathcal{X}$ of individuals east of X, each would receive value $\Pi'_B/\mathcal{X}$ from state B after the drop in governance quality from v to v' if this state decided to neglect its citizens who live west of X. If $\mathcal{X}$ and $\mathcal{Y}$ are close relative to the difference between Π_B and Π'_B then $\Pi'_B/\mathcal{X}$ may be much smaller than $\Pi_B/\mathcal{Y}$, in which case even individuals east of X are tempted to leave state B for state A (or other states).

Interstate migration, facilitated by the lowest costs of human travel in history, is affected by the uneven levels of governance that the member states of today's cartel provide. This includes migration of refugees, and low- and high-skilled workers alike, all seeking better governance in the form of greater personal and job security, and higher qualities of life in their new homes.

most talented individuals who have the resources and willingness to leave, and who have skills that other countries would like to take advantage of. If autocratic rulers have to compete in the governance market to keep their citizens from leaving, then they must either provide them with good reasons to stay or expend more resources to coerce them from emigrating.[28]

This argument explains how regime type could influence the emigration decision, but a similar logic also applies to the way regime type affects the immigration decision. If state A is a democracy that provides large welfare benefits to its people, then the temptation for individuals from B to move to A is even greater. If the welfare benefits are large enough, even citizens with low skills might move to take advantage of these benefits. This suggests that there could be a kind of sorting taking place in the migration decision, where the least redistributive states receive only relatively skilled immigrants and the countries that provide the greatest welfare spending end up taking a broader cross-section of migrants.

Our discussion, we should note, simplifies the decision to migrate considerably, boiling it down to a simple cost-benefit calculation. In reality, this decision is not purely economic. Nationalism, for example, is a non-economic force that makes people unwilling to migrate even if the costs of migration are low. Other related factors include the linguistic and cultural barriers that many immigrants face when they move to unfamiliar places. The strength of these barriers varies across countries. The barriers are low in certain countries like the US that are multicultural, relatively welcoming of immigrants, and where English, the world's lingua franca, is the main language. It is no surprise, then, that so many people from around the world (including one of the authors of this book) have chosen to emigrate to America.*

In fact, one of the most important factors (which may not be purely economic) that constrains the level of immigration that a country is willing to accept is its internal politics. As much as unfavorable politics in one's home country can be a push factor in the migration decision, politics in the destination country can be a barrier as well. We mentioned before that in many rich countries, citizens and businesses that benefit from employing immigrants are typically in favor of immigration. But an important interest group that is opposed to immigration is the group of economically vulnerable low-skilled citizens who fear that immigration will reduce their real wages if they have to compete with them for jobs.[29] In most democracies, the views of these citizens are politically significant, and the critique of immigration has become a central talking point for right-wing populists, from Donald Trump to the campaign for Brexit in the UK and the French National Rally.[30] Their anger has become a source of tension in the politics of these countries and has raised the political barriers to immigration even as the economic barriers have fallen. Political pressures like these are what led to the creation of sophisticated bureaucratic regimes to control the movement of people into wealthy democracies in the 20th century. These regimes are exceptional in historical terms. In the years before World War I, no European country other than Russia required a passport for entry.

---

* In addition to all of this, even the purely economic calculation of whether or not migration pays is a much more complicated one than we have discussed, and as an empirical matter, emigration to gain higher-quality governance is difficult to distinguish from emigration to take advantage of economic opportunities. We have not made a conceptual distinction between the two in our model in some part because high-quality governance is an important contributor to the creation of economic opportunities and income (Acemoglu, Johnson, and Robinson 2005; Rodrik, Subramanian, and Trebbi 2004). The United States is both better governed and richer than El Salvador, but it is likely richer than El Salvador *because* it is better governed.

Right-wing populist leaders like Nigel Farage of the United Kingdom Independence Party claim that loose border restrictions, free trade, and international organization membership serve the interest of the cartel elites at the expense of the citizens of democratic nation-states. They draw their support from voters who see themselves as unlikely to be net beneficiaries of global labor market competition and free trade and those strongly committed to traditional ideas of the bounded nation-state.

Failed States

Inequality in state strength has existed throughout history, and in fact even today's weak states are probably stronger than some of the weakest states of prior centuries. However, the problem of weak states today is compounded by the interconnectedness of the world and the ease with which bad actors such as international criminals, terrorists, and drug and human traffickers can move from place to place.[31] Witness, for example, the spread of groups using terrorist tactics across the world, from the Middle East to Southeast Asia and across the globe. The externalities they create can be significant even if these bad actors do not move physically, as is evident from the problem of cyber-attacks. While some of these attacks are state sponsored, many attackers operate from the soil of weak states that do not have the capacity to find and stop them even if some have the willingness to do so. When a state becomes so weak that it cannot govern at all in some regions, it is referred to as a failed state.[32]

There are two ways to think about state failure in our model. One is that the value of governance that a state can provide (in principle) stays the same, but the cost of providing it increases everywhere. Suppose that this happens for the state governed by ruler B in our baseline model of Chapter 2. The cost c_B rises everywhere to a level such that this ruler's cost now intersects v at a point east of Y in Fig. 1. This may then lead to a transition from the situation in which states govern the whole interval between A and B in that figure, to one in which there is a region just east of Y in which ruler B was previously providing governance but now does not consider it profitable to do so. We can think of state failure as taking place in this region if it is left ungoverned.

The second way to think about state failure is that the costs of governing remain the same for both rulers, but the value of governance that ruler B can provide drops from v to v' as we described in the previous section and depict in Fig. 15. Now again there is a region from Y to X in which B does not find it profitable to govern. State A may not provide governance in this region (even though it could profitably govern up to Z) because it continues to respect the interstate boundary Y. And even if it did decide to step in and govern up to Z, the region from Z to X is unprofitable for either state A or B to govern. The result is the same: a region is created that no existing state would like to govern. Such ungoverned regions exist around the world from the peripheral regions of the Democratic Republic of Congo to the borderlands of Myanmar.

When state failure causes such a governance vacuum in an entire region of a country, its consequences can be severe for the neighboring countries and even others not sharing a direct border with the failed state. State failure in Afghanistan and Northwest Pakistan, for example, enabled Al-Qaeda to grow its presence and plan attacks against the United States from its base in that region.[33] State failure in the Niger Delta region resulted in it becoming a base for piracy targeted at the ships of neighboring countries. State failure in parts of Colombia and Venezuela has turned these countries into bases for international drug production and trafficking.[34] State failure in Somalia in the early 1990s led to the costs of governance rising for neighboring Kenya, which had to house and feed substantial flows of refugees and suffer terrorist attacks by Al-Shabaab, a non-state Islamist group based in Somali territory.[35]

Even more distant governments were affected by the weakness of the Somali state, since they had to pay the costs of protecting their Indian Ocean trade from Somali pirates. State failure in Syria overwhelmed the administrative capacity of many countries in Europe and the Middle East to deal efficiently with the swell of refugees at their borders.

There are no easy remedies to state failure. Sanctioning a failed state for the criminal activities that are planned and perpetrated inside its borders can be counter-productive. In many cases, the failed state government may be just as eager as its neighbors and the broader international community to find and root out these criminals. Offering positive incentives to the failed state to extradite or punish the perpetrators will also not work, since the very fact that they are weak means that they may not have the capacity to find and punish them even if they have the willingness to do so.

In many instances, neighboring states and the international community have dealt with state failure by stepping in to provide governance in the ungoverned region. In the model described above, for example, state A could literally take over the ungoverned region from Y to X which would include governing the region between Z and X at a loss—an example of this is the recent Turkish occupation of northern Syria during its civil war. Or it could provide governance in this region through an international intervention, as with the extended NATO interventions in Bosnia, Kosovo, and Afghanistan, the UN intervention in East Timor, and the British intervention in Sierra Leone. However, the reality is that if a new state does not emerge to govern this region, and state B simply cannot govern it at a profit, then such interventions (if they have an end date) will not provide a permanent solution to the problem of state failure.[36]

In some cases, the international community has tried to remedy state failure by making costly investments to strengthen the failed state, seeking to establish institutions that will live beyond its presence.[37] But as the American experience in Afghanistan has proven, this kind of nation building is not easy in unfamiliar environments, in which local institutions are dysfunctional, and where the intervening states face an armed opposition. The Americans spent $2 trillion over a period of 20 years in Afghanistan, and as they were leaving the Taliban returned to power in 11 days.

A final possibility that may work in some cases could be for the cartel to ease its strict policy of deterring entry into the state system, as we discussed in Chapter 5. If a new state emerges in the region between Y and X to govern at least the space between Z and X at a profit, then both state A and state B

should want to recognize it and welcome it into the cartel—and more so if leaving the region ungoverned generates the kinds of negative externalities that we have mentioned above. The problem with this policy, however, is that in many of the most vexing cases of state failure, the cartel has good reason to be suspicious of the motivations of the new entrants. In some cases, the potential entrant clearly signals that it has no intentions of abiding by the norms of the cartel. The Islamic State, which emerged in northern Iraq and Syria, for example, has sought to re-establish an Islamic caliphate covering the entire world, calling for a return to a system of religiously based, universal sovereignty that has had little purchase in international affairs since the 19th century. They are thus not even potentially assimilable to the values of the cartel.

Power Shifts

A third challenge facing the cartel lies in adapting the norms and governance infrastructure of international political economy to the upcoming changes in economic structure taking place across many countries. As lower-income countries gain in economic power, the current high-income leaders of the cartel not only face the pressure to accommodate the interests of these countries to a greater extent; they also face the challenge of setting (or strengthening pre-existing) norms that shield them from opportunistic behavior by the rising powers.

As developing countries like China and India grow, they will claim more of the abstract governance market that has been the focus of this final chapter—not necessarily more territory, but a larger share of the world's resources and production. This means that a country's share of the governance market changes even if borders remain stable. If the cartel seeks to control these changes, then it may be vulnerable to conflict among its members that could threaten its traditional operation.

The most likely such conflict is between the United States, which has led the cartel since World War II, and the fastest-growing rising power, China, which has steadily increased its influence over world affairs in the last few decades. China's Belt and Road Initiative and its effort in creating the Asian Infrastructure Investment Bank, for example, are part of its ambitious plans to grow its influence over the governance market and rewrite the rules of the game that were set mainly by the Americans after World War II. China is already the largest economy in the world in terms of both purchasing power and goods traded, and as it grows it will seek to correct any asymmetries between its economic power and its political influence.[38]

Policymakers and political scientists alike have pointed to the rise of China as being the most important trend in international politics today. Some even highlight the possibility of great danger to the world associated with it. Graham Allison (2017), for example, frighteningly predicts inevitable war between China and the United States.[39] Of course, it is possible that these dangers are overstated, as many of us would like to believe.[40] But even if they are, it will still be important for the cartel members to carefully manage their relations with each other as power shifts continue to take place in world politics.

To illustrate the point, we focus on just one of the complex issues that have arisen in the relationship between the United States and China—the fight over intellectual property, and whether intellectual property rights are rights that the cartel should protect at all.

Technological developments and globalization have led to major sectoral shifts that have taken place in developed and developing countries alike. Many of the world's modern economies shifted their economies first from agriculture to manufacturing and more recently from manufacturing to services. A hundred years ago, 70% of American workers worked in agriculture; today, the American service sector takes roughly 75% of labor employment. Even the once powerful manufacturing sector accounts for less than 10% of labor employment in the United States today.* To a large extent, manufacturing has either become automated or has moved from the developed countries to the developing countries of Asia and Latin America.[41]

Many services will eventually be automated, and it will be cheaper for Americans to buy these services from other parts of the world. Self-driving cars will ultimately eliminate the need for human drivers, while telemedicine and remote-controlled robotic surgery will enable doctors and nurses in places as distant as India to serve patients in the United States without either of the two parties having to leave their countries of residence. Eventually the developed countries will have to make the transition from a service

---

* The share of manufacturing in the United States dropped steadily from 25% of GDP to 12% from the end of World War II to 2010. The share of agriculture dropped in the same period from 8% to 1% while the share of finance industry, on the other hand, rose from 10% to 22% in this period, and professional, business, educational, and health care services rose from 5% to 22%. These figures are from the Bureau of Economic Analysis.

economy to one that is primarily a knowledge economy—a place where ideas are developed and inventions are made at such a rapid pace that the goods and services that these ideas provide will have to be built and provided by machines or workers in developing countries. The growing focus of investors on the many small startups of Silicon Valley already point in this direction. The history of economic progress and periodic sectoral shifts points to such a transition as being inevitable.[42]

As this transition occurs, the importance of intellectual property rights for developed countries like the United States will become paramount. A country whose economy is built primarily on the creation of new ideas has to be able to appropriate the value of these ideas. It is no surprise, then, that the most developed countries have worked hard to define and popularize the relatively abstract concept of intellectual property rights around the world. Today, firms in developing countries already pay large sums in royalties to those in developed countries that hold patents for new drugs, technologies, and methods of production, even when these methods and technologies are already well understood.[43] But, despite this, the concept of intellectual property rights has not achieved the kind of universal acceptance that would be necessary for developed countries to make the transition to becoming predominantly knowledge-based economies. While the concept of physical property rights goes back millennia, the origins of intellectual property rights are at best a few centuries old.[44] Even today, it is not clear that the concept has much purchase in many parts of the world. Consider for a moment whether the villagers of South and Southeast Asia, or the goods traders of Africa, would have as clear a concept of intellectual property as they do physical property.*

As developing countries like China continue to grow in economic and political strength, they may not want to abide by the rules set by the developed countries on issues like intellectual property rights. If they expect their economies to be made up mainly of manufacturing and services (rather than knowledge) for much of the foreseeable future, then they will have little

---

* And yet, not transforming into a knowledge-based economy may not be a realistic option for the developed countries. Krugman (1979) explained the reasoning behind this more than 40 years ago in his North-South model of product cycle trade, writing that "North must continually innovate not only to maintain its relative position but even to maintain its real income in absolute terms." If our predictions about economic structural change hold up, then according to his model, intellectual property will be an important source of real income for North.

interest in accepting the idea that intellectual property rights are real rights that ought to be protected. The challenge for the developed countries is that stealing intellectual property is much easier than stealing physical property: you simply learn how the technology works, put it to use without paying any royalties, and then deny all wrongdoing. There may be no traceable conclusive physical act of theft that can be caught on camera, no place where the stolen goods are physically hidden that could be discovered. American law enforcement has already identified China's theft of American technology as the biggest threat to the United States.[45] If China stops honoring intellectual property and simply denies the accusation of theft, it is not clear that the United States could (or would) do anything other than perhaps try to punish it through sanctions that could lead to a trade war, which we have already seen would be costly for both sides.[46]

The issue of intellectual property rights is just one of many complicated issues that will confront the cartel as the world governance market continues to increase in complexity. It is an interesting issue in its own right, but we have discussed it mainly because it illustrates the kinds of political challenges that the cartel will face as some very important power shifts take place.

New Modes of Conflict

In this chapter, we have recast and reinterpreted the governance market so that the line segment between rulers A and B in our model reflects the more abstract space in which production takes place, with new sources of revenue for states—human capital, intellectual property, and financial assets, besides simply physical territory. What implication does this have for interstate conflict? What could war look like in such an an abstract space?

We approach these questions by thinking of war also in somewhat abstract terms: war is a costly endeavor in which two or more sides vie for control of a source of value. Land is an important source of value, but it is not the only source. As other sources (particularly those that are less tied to physical geography) become more important, it is natural to expect that some wars will be fought not to gain new territory but to gain control of a larger share of world GDP via other means, besides territorial conquest. In particular, economic wars (such as trade wars) are also costly wars, often with the aim of achieving some policy outcome that is in the economic interest of the nations who initiate them (regardless of whether the strategy is effective or sensible).*

Moreover, as the goals of conflict become more abstract, it is also reasonable to expect that the way wars are fought—the weapons used—will also be different. In distant history, wars were fought primarily on land using guns and canons. Then came tanks, battleships, and aircraft. In today's interconnected world, there are yet newer technologies of warfare and destruction that have kept pace with developments in the technologies of production. Today, economic and cyber-warfare can also be enormously destructive, with their ability to destroy many billions of dollars worth of value, and thus take a heavy albeit indirect toll on human lives and livelihoods. As the space of competition in the governance market has grown more abstract, it is natural that the manner of fighting within this space should also become more abstract in the process.

Already, we have seen signs of states starting to appreciate these changes and embrace the new technologies and tools of conflict. Although many observers point to Russia's 2014 takeover of Crimea and its 2022 invasion of Ukraine as surprising evidence that the era of conventional war is not over even in an advanced region of the world like Europe, what is more noteworthy than Vladimir Putin's attempt at a 19th-century-style land grab has been the West's response. NATO countries and their allies—at least up to the time of this writing—did not send troops to fight the Russians on the ground, or even try to dominate the skies by setting up a no-fly zone. Instead of fighting a conventional war, they initiated a devastating economic war. Vladimir Putin himself, appreciating the severity of costs inflicted upon him, his regime, and state, referred to the West's sanctions as "akin to a declaration of war." Of course, it remains to be seen whether this kind of response can be effective as a deterrent.**

But regardless of how the Ukraine war unfolds, it is a false optimism to think that even the most intense economic warfare of the future could only have relatively benign consequences. Highly interconnected economies have

---

* In a recent study, Fajgelbaum et al. (2020) estimate that the tariffs imposed by the Trump administration in 2018 and the retaliatory tariffs imposed on US goods resulted in short-term losses to US consumers and importing firms of 0.27% of GDP. Tariff revenue and gains to domestic producers did not make up for all of these losses, as aggregate real income was still $7.2 billion lower.
** The challenge for sanctions and other such collective security arrangements is the urge to free ride, since states may be unwilling to pay the costs of conflict when their interests are not directly at stake. Not all states have participated fully in the sanctions. For example, many states that rely on Russian oil and gas (or that see opportunities in free riding) have been reluctant to cut their business with Russia.

a lot to potentially lose from conflict. Hard-fought economic wars could send millions of people into poverty, lowering a society's overall health, wellbeing, and even birthrates. Such wars could lead to more rapid out-migration of the most skilled citizens in countries that are expected to lose these wars. These citizens may be a source of tremendous economic value, and the costs of economic warfare could be especially high in countries that rely heavily on global markets to support their economies. The indirect effects of economic warfare may appear less gruesome than those of conventional warfare, but this does not mean that their effects can be ignored.

Put differently, war is about imposing costs and limiting the ability of the adversary to impose costs. In war, sites of economic value (buildings, factories, bridges, and other infrastructure) are destroyed and lives are lost. As globalization continues and the world becomes even more interconnected, the potential for one side to inflict costs upon another without having to engage in conventional war-fighting only grows. In a world without such interdependence, conventional war is the main mode of warfare precisely because there are few other ways to inflict such severe harm. This was the case historically. But it may be a much less accurate description of our current and future world.

The Future of the Cartel

Our central claim in this book has been that the international state system represents a governance cartel—an oligopoly of states colluding to exploit their citizens. From the onset, we have contrasted this system of governance to a hypothetical alternative system of governance provision in which states compete to provide better governance at lower cost to citizens around the world. But we never considered the opposite counter-factual of a global monopoly—the case of a single world government. In these concluding pages, we ponder such a governance structure with the intention of understanding how that system might fare in dealing with the many challenges that the cartel faces today.

Consider the challenges associated with globalization that we have described in this chapter. Globalization is a trend that has moved the existing state system more in the direction of a competitive governance market rather than a single monopoly. Does it then follow from this that the problems associated with globalization would be mitigated if the world were to move more in the direction of a global governance monopoly?

First let us take the issue of tax evasion through the use of offshore accounts in tax havens. It is plausible that under a monopoly world government, the use of tax havens would decline as coordination across regional authorities increases. Piketty's (2018) global wealth tax, for example, would be easier to implement. It is certainly true that in many federal structures, tax competition across domestic jurisdictions exists. Delaware, for example, is considered a domestic tax haven within the United States.[47] But with a powerful enough central government regulating such competition, it is plausible that the extent of internal tax competition would be lower than it would be if no such central authority existed.

Moreover, such a central monopoly may allow greater labor mobility across borders, just as Americans in California who find work opportunities in Texas can take these opportunities without having to acquire new employment authorization. The unequal treatment of labor and capital, pointed out by Margaret Peters (2017), would be mitigated, which in turn could mitigate some of the political tensions caused by globalization. With the ability of people and money to move more freely from place to place, governance quality may also become less uneven across regions. The ratio of GDP per capita between the richest and poorest American states, only 2.25, is dwarfed by the corresponding ratio between the richest and poorest countries, which is over 100.

For similar reasons, policing of international crime (international terrorism, human and drug trafficking, etc.) may also improve as the monopoly government not only provides better coordination across regions, but also creates a central policing authority that has the ability to capture and punish criminals anywhere in the world without having to calculate the risks of violating a nation's sovereignty in pursuit of these bad actors. The American operation that killed Osama bin Laden on Pakistani soil would not have had to be as covert, and his whereabouts might have been discovered sooner. There may also be less fear of conflict breaking out over such acts.

Finally, such a central authority may be well positioned to address the most pressing global problem of our time—the existential threat that we face from climate change. In fact, even the cartel, as a collusive arrangement that requires some level of cooperation across states, should be better suited to addressing this collective action problem than a competitive governance system. Imagine trying to coordinate action to address this challenge in an alternative world where every state is a competitive supplier in the governance market and there is no coordination among these suppliers. A monopoly government may be even better suited than a cartel if it can pass binding international laws on how different regions of the world should share the burden of mitigating the risks of a climate catastrophe.

Let us be clear that we are not advocating for a single world government to solve these problems. After all, the world could probably not handle such a radical institutional innovation given the obvious strength of nationalist attachments. But even if it could, the danger is that a single monopolist could be extremely coercive and exploitative, as individuals would have nowhere to escape persecution or poor governance. Nothing would be worse than a powerful but corrupt and despotic world government with no alternative.

Instead, what we are testing in this thought experiment is the logical coherence of our theory. The question that we are answering is whether the problems associated with increasing governance competition would be mitigated by in fact reducing governance competition, independent of the concern that reducing this competition may result in newer, different problems. Our answer is that, yes, many of the problems associated with increasing competition could in theory be mitigated by reducing competition, even though in practice there are likely to be other costs and risks that clearly outweigh these benefits. This is an important logical check on our theory.

More importantly, this fanciful thought experiment guides us to a more pertinent and broader question: Moving forward, how much competition in the governance market is ideal? On what dimensions should states compete, and on what dimensions should they not compete? How could institutions be designed to strike the right balance?

These are difficult questions with no clear answers. But one institutional innovation that interests us is the European Union. The EU has certainly been under stress lately with the exit of Britain, the economic difficulties faced by many of its southern European members, which have strained relations with their northern partners, as well as other political tensions having to do with the rise in immigration in past years. Today, it looks like the EU might be failing. But even if it does fail, lessons must be learned from the experiment. After all, the League of Nations failed but its basic idea lives on in the form of the UN. The Holy Roman Empire collapsed, but the norms of sovereignty that were practiced under its *landeshoheit* system are an integral part of the cartel's norms today.[48] Are there aspects of the EU project that provide a blueprint to the way not just Europe but the entire future world could be governed?

The most fascinating aspect of the EU is that it performs some of the functions of a state without being fully a state. The EU has significantly eased restrictions on capital and labor flows within its borders and adopted a common policy with respect to trade and competition outside the bloc. It coordinates and funds scientific and technological research (through projects such as the European Research Council, the European Space Agency, CERN, and Airbus) that many of its small member states would not otherwise have undertaken to the same proportionate degree if they had to fund these projects alone. It places regulations on agriculture, safety, the environment, and energy, among many other policy areas. It also manages a common currency and monetary policy within the bloc. It does all of this in a region of the world where nationalist attachments have been strong and two major wars were fought not long ago that ravaged the continent.

The EU experiment gives us a glimpse of what an alternative arrangement to the existing cartel system could look like. But how far can such an integration process go? To what extent can the whole world become as integrated as Europe is today? And how soon could this be possible? Will it ever be possible? If nationalist attachments get even stronger, and skepticism of international institutions grows even more intense, then political opposition to both monopoly and competitive governance provision may strengthen as citizens view both of these ways of organizing the governance market as leading to an unwanted softening of today's borders. Borders may be here to stay, even as we enter a world in which they make little sense.

The Pacific end of the US-Mexico Border Barrier, Tijuana.

Notes

Chapter 1

1. See, e.g., Pierson (2000); Page (2006); North (1990).
2. Fernandez and Rodrik (1991) argue that when this happens a majority of voters may oppose efficient policies.
3. These claims are based on US immigration trend data reported by the Migration Policy Institute and available at https://www.migrationpolicy.org/.
4. This calculation is for the year 2000 and based on the data in Schultz (2015).

Chapter 2

1. See also Olson (1993); Gambetta (1996); Bates (2001); Hobbes (1651); Rousseau (1762).
2. Milgrom, North, and Weingast (1990) and Greif (1993).
3. Federal Trade Commission (1948, 25–26).
4. Jacobs, Friel, and Raddick (2001, 80–95).
5. See Edelstein (2017) for a related discussion of the importance of time horizons in international relations.
6. Herbst (2014, 38) writes that "property rights over people were extraordinarily well developed in Africa compared to other parts of the world."
7. This important question was raised by Ruggie (1993), who asks why spatial delineation emerged as opposed to what he calls other "heteronomous" forms of organization. It is also the subject of some recent works, such as Kadercan (2015).
8. Elliott (2002) and North (1981).
9. We use the term focal in the informal sense of Schelling (1960). A focal border, like a focal point, is the option that the parties will choose from a number of possible self-enforcing alternatives.
10. They use this term from Hobbes (1651) to refer only to dictatorial states.
11. There are, of course, many other theories that we do not discuss including Wallerstein's (1984) world systems theory, Hobson and Sharman's (2005) theory of hierarchical sub-systems, and Deudney and Ikenberry's (1999) theory of interlocking institutions, to name a few. Kang (2010) also offers a theory of the state system based on the East Asian model, but this is discussed as an alternative to the system we have in place today. We have chosen the three sets of theories that we critique because of their sustained prominence in the literature and because they provide the opportunity for a wide range of criticisms, many of which cover these other theories as well.

12. The origins of the Westphalia hypothesis lie in a 1948 article by the jurist Leo Gross (1948) who pointed mainly to three articles in the Treaties of Onasbruk and Muenster that comprise the Peace as laying the foundations for the modern state system. These are Article 64, which states the rights of princes to choose the official religion of their principalities, Article 65, which states that they may conduct their own foreign policy, and Article 67, which states that they can set domestic policy.

13. There is no evidence that any historian, diplomat, emissary, or ruler prior to Leo Gross (the originator of the Westphalia hypothesis; see the previous note) cited the Peace of Westphalia as a source for the norm of territorial sovereignty, rather than a legal precedent affecting particular territories.

14. A closely related argument is that the ideas about territory and technologies for demarcating space changed in the early modern period, making modern territoriality ideologically possible. Political geographers have been especially active in examining the ways in which ideas about territory and territoriality evolved over time (Agnew 2009; Larkins 2009; Elden 2013; Branch 2013). They argue that territorial sovereignty was an idea that had to be constructed. However, relative to Philpott (2001), the geography literature is less explicit in stating that these ideological changes *caused* the state system to develop, instead focusing on describing the ideological changes that occurred. Other authors that emphasize the importance of ideas include Bull (2012) and Phillips (2010).

15. For evidence on this, see Gennaioli and Voth (2015) and the references therein.

16. See Bueno De Mesquita (2013) for a review of these theories.

17. For a relatively recent articulation of these ideas, see Wagner (2010). See also the historical discussion in Rendall (2006).

18. Scheve and Stasavage (2010).

19. In fact, the so-called "gunpowder empires" of the Ottomans, Safavids, Mughals, and Qing used the new technology to repress local rulers and build large polities that explicitly claimed universal dominion (McNeill 1989).

Chapter 3

1. Sumption (2009).
2. Cox (2015).
3. Vries (2015).
4. Vaughan (1965).
5. Lee (2005, 71).
6. Holzgrefe (1989) and Vaughan (1965).
7. Bradbury (2015, 145–55).
8. These obligations were expressed through reciprocal oaths of vassalage, typical of the feudal system (Bloch 1939). An inferior lord (vassal) might make a contract with a superior lord, receiving from him protection for himself and his lands. On the other side of the coin were the obligations that vassals owed to rulers. In the feudal system, these obligations were usually payments in kind, either in agricultural

produce (for payments from peasants) or military service (for payments from less powerful members of the military class). In later years, many of these obligations were commuted to cash payments, but the basic ideal of military protection in return for money and service remained.

9. Strayer (1970).
10. Lapsley (1900).
11. Lopez (1976) and Beniger (2009).
12. While these figures are European averages, growth was also notable in the border zones between the major European polities in the period before the development of states. Especially important was the belt of relatively urbanized territory running between France and the Holy Roman Empire, through modern Italy, western Germany and eastern France, and the Low Countries. This region, Stein Rokkan's "city-studded center," benefited from being on the direct route from the Mediterranean ports to northern Europe, and was the fastest-growing part of Europe during the Middle Ages (Rokkan 1975). Also, Maddison (2007) estimates that per capita GDP in modern Belgium grew by 105% between 1000 and 1500, while in modern Italy it grew by 144%, the highest figures for any countries. Many of the small polities in this territory would be targeted for absorption by the French and Hapsburg monarchies during the early modern period.
13. See Bonney (1999) for these figures.
14. Parker (1996) and Brewer (1990).
15. Oman (1968, II:226).
16. Oman (1968, II:64–67).
17. Parker (2000).
18. Quoted in Jervis (1872, 50).
19. See Reeves (1944, 537) and the sources therein.
20. Hadley (2006, 120).
21. See Branch (2011; 2013) and also Biggs (1999) and Pickles (2004).
22. Branch (2011; 2013) takes the argument even further, arguing that map making *caused* the change in attitudes toward borders; see also Pickles (2004). In our view, as provocative and interesting as this claim is, it is too strong. Many intellectual changes fail to generate political results when there is no incentive for elites to hold to them.
23. Like many aspects of modern diplomacy, this practice was initially developed in 15th-century Italy (Mattingly 1955). Anderson (2014, 6–7) cites Nicodemus of Pontremoli, Ambassador of Milan in Florence for two decades beginning in 1446, as the world's first de facto permanent ambassador, and the duke of Savoy's embassy to Rome in 1460 as the first embassy to be officially described as permanent.
24. See Roosen (1976, 36).
25. Quoted in Anderson (2014, 4–5).
26. Fraser (2008).
27. See Neville (1988); Rae (1966); Tough (1928).
28. Quoted from Holford and Stringer (2010, 177). A more tangible mark of autonomy was the high level of private fortification (both legal and illegal) in the border zone, where "nearly all men of any wealth at all occupied bastle [fortified] houses"

(Dixon 2016, 127). Similarly, a 1461 royal law designed to limit aristocrats granting livery (the main means for the building up of late feudal private armies) specifically exempted the largest border lords, "whose livery, mark, or token may be given, borne, and used from [the river] Trent northward at such time as is necessary to raise people for defence of the Marches" (quoted in King and Etty (2015, 160)).

29. Maxwell (1896, 161).
30. King and Etty (2015, 74–81).
31. See Watts and Watts (1975) for the English case and Goodare (1989) for the Scottish. The larger lords sometimes passed some of these gains on to their tenants, in the form of tenancy arrangements that were much more favorable than elsewhere. Watts (1971, 66) notes that in some parts of Northumberland, "unlike most customary tenants in other parts of England [where they had to pay a fine to the landlord], tenants could freely sell all or part of their tenant-right for an outright cash payment."
32. Holford and Stringer (2010).
33. The subsequent century would be one of shifting relations between the two states, depending on the balance at power at the Scottish court between the pro-English and pro-French factions. The rise of Protestantism in Scotland, and the prospect that James VI of Scotland would inherit the English throne, tended to bring the latter group to power, and the second half of the 16th century had many periods of peaceful relations, during which the two sides tended to cooperate in border affairs.
34. Quoted from King and Etty (2015, 161).
35. Quoted in Maxwell (1912, 170).
36. Quoted in Bain (1894, 31).
37. See Robb (2018, 116–24) for arguments supporting this claim and the broader claims made in this paragraph.
38. Quoted in Robb (2018, 117).
39. Quoted in Bain (1898, I:191).
40. MacKenzie (1951).
41. Bain (1894, 3).
42. King and Etty (2015, 162).
43. Neville (1988).
44. King and Etty (2015, 166).
45. King and Etty (2015, 167).
46. Bain (1898, II:396).
47. Fraser (2008).
48. Nicolson et al. (1777, lxxv).
49. British Library, Mss. Cotton Caligula B, VIII, fos. 438–39 Quoted in Boscher (1985, 128).
50. Quoted in O'Sullivan (2016, np).
51. "Instructions to the English Commisioners." Quoted in Bain (1898, II:17). For a more general account of the potential advantages of outsider bureaucrats, see Bhavnani and Lee (2018).
52. Spence (1977, 90).
53. Watts and Watts (1975).
54. Quoted from Watts (1971, 67).

55. Our discussion of this case largely follows Upton (1998).
56. Our account of the Spanish case is based on Storrs (2006); Anderson (1979); Lynch (1989); and Elliott (1984).
57. Storrs (2006, ch. 5).
58. The French monarchy, by contrast, was in its most administratively and militarily expansive period and had little to fear from Spanish encroachment in its border regions.
59. Lynch (1989, 64–66).
60. Our account of the French case follows Beik (1985); Collins (1988); Hickey (2019); and Parker (1986).
61. Beik (1985) and Anderson (1979).
62. These calculations are based on Bonney (1999), file MALM031.
63. Quoted from Kiser and Linton (2002, 903). See also Behrens (1963).
64. See Articles 71–74 of the Treaty of Westphalia.
65. At the Congress of Tropau (1820), the powers jointly declared that "states, which have undergone a change of government due to revolution, the result of which threaten other states, ipso facto cease to be members of the European Alliance. . . . If, owing to such alterations, immediate danger threatens other states the powers bind themselves, by peaceful means, or if need be, by arms, to bring back the guilty state into the bosom of the Great Alliance" (quoted in Middlebush (1933, 40)). See also Ghervas (2015).
66. Our discussion of the Congress of Vienna and the agreements made at the Congress follows the accounts of Schroeder (1994); Chapman (2006); and King (2008).

Chapter 4

1. Fairbank and Chen (1968).
2. For an account of the famous Macartney mission, see Lamb (2013).
3. Ravina (2016).
4. Jansen (2002, 83).
5. Lee and Schultz (2012) and Michalopoulos and Papaioannou (2016).
6. Lindley (1926, 211)
7. Quoted in Lindley (1926, 211–12)
8. Acemoglu, Johnson, and Robinson (2002) and Acemoglu and Robinson (2012).
9. In fact, the institutions of governance that they set up in the colonies often differed in crucial ways from the institutions they set up at home in Europe. For example, as part of the policy of providing government services cheaply, colonial states often delegated administration to local elites, an institution known as indirect rule (Iyer 2010; Mamdani 1996). While this process bore a superficial resemblance to the type of plural and multilayered concepts of political authority found in early modern Europe, in the late colonial period it was merely a matter of administrative convenience. Every effort was made to emphasize, both in practice and in theory, the final supreme authority of the colonial power. African chiefs, for instance, were appointed by the colonial state, dismissed by it, and received salaries from it; see

Acemoglu, Reed, and Robinson (2014) for some examples. Note, however, that some indigenous groups could profit from becoming intermediaries between other groups and the colonial state (Lee 2017).

10. Treaty of Tientsin, 1858, British version, Article V.
11. Treaty of Tientsin, 1858, British version, Article III.
12. Kayaoglu (2010, 66–67).
13. Winichakul (1997).
14. See Perdue (2010). The Qing willingness to make exceptions for the Russians has some similarities to the ways in which the Romans treated other powerful empires such as the Parthians; on this, see Schlude (2009).
15. Farooqi (2004, 61–65).
16. Powell (2018).
17. Davies (1932, 71–98).
18. Quoted in Hamilton (1906, 410).
19. Quoted in Hamilton (1906, 409).
20. Siddique (2014, 34).
21. Omrani (2009, 190).
22. Siddique (2014, 37–40).
23. House of Commons (1901, 130).
24. Tripodi (2016, 192).
25. Davies (1932, 95).
26. Tripodi (2016, 159).
27. Hopkins (2015).
28. Tripodi (2016, 50).
29. Ahmed (1980, 143–64).
30. United Nations Office on Drugs and Crime (2008, 12).
31. Khan (2017).
32. Dawn (2018).
33. Sammon (2008, 9).
34. Committee on Foreign Affairs (2017, 16–21).
35. Rashid (2010).
36. Markey (2007).
37. Siddique (2014, 57–61). When the Taliban were in power in Afghanistan in the late 1990s, they approached the Pakistanis on three occasions to discuss recognition of the Durand line (Siddique 2014, 60).
38. See Herbst (2014); Boone (2003); Mamdani (1996); and Young (1994), among others.
39. Acharya, Harding, and Harris (2020) and Acemoglu, Reed, and Robinson (2014).
40. Lombard (2020).
41. Quoted from Lombard (2020, 27).
42. In fact, Lombard (2020, 9–10) notes that "the only things that French administrators saw as valuable in these lands were the wild animals. . . . What little infrastructural or institutional development occurred was largely concentrated in the southern, riverine area near Bangui. . . . The north-east . . . [was] left largely to its own devices, except for the demarcation of the national parks. . . ."

43. A very similar argument is made by Atzili (2007). See also Herbst (2014).

44. Even in China, though, which we discussed as a case of successful assimilation, the process of incorporating border regions such as the Xinjiang Autonomous Region or Tibet into the state continues; see, e.g., Zhang (2021) and McNamee and Zhang (2019). Border skirmishes with India have persisted as well.

Chapter 5

1. Zacher (2001) and Kocs (1995).

2. Other examples of territorial redistributions include transfers to a rising France from a declining Spain at the Treaty of Nijmegen (1697), from a declining Spain to the emperor at the Treaty of Utrecht (1713–14), from Austria to a rising Prussia at the Treaty of Aix-la-Chapelle (1748), from France to a rising Britain at the Treaty of Paris (1763), from a declining Poland to its neighbors (1772–93), and from a declining France to a rising Germany at Versailles (1871)—all cases in which the territorial transfer confirmed long-term shifts in relative economic and military power. Similarly, the rise and fall of the Ottoman Empire's military capability relative to the Western powers was paralleled by massive gains and losses in territory. See, e.g., Levy (2015) and Kennedy (2010).

3. Huth (2009, 79–80).

4. See Lee and Zhang (2017) and Lee (2019b) for some of the difficulties and how to overcome them.

5. The argument here follows the standard arguments in crisis bargaining theory— e.g., Fearon (1995)—which asserts that wars can occur when rulers have conflicting private information about their capabilities and choose conflict on that basis.

6. On this point, see also Goemans and Schultz (2017).

7. Our account of this case follows Sater (2007) and Farcau (2000).

8. Peru was also moving in this period to develop and control the nitrates in its portion of the Atacama.

9. Sater (2007) also suggests that the ambiguity and poor demarcation of the region's borders—a product of the confused dissolution of the Spanish Empire—contributed to Chile's interest in conquering the region.

10. Farcau (2000, 54).

11. The five states that recognized Biafra were Gabon, Haiti, the Ivory Coast, Tanzania, and Zambia.

12. Hubbard (2000, xi).

13. See for example, "Spain: Independent Scotland would be at the back of the EU queue," *The Guardian*, March 14, 2017. https://www.theguardian.com/uk-news/2017/mar/14/spain-independent-scotland-would-be-at-the-back-of-eu-queue.

14. See Lee and Paine (2019c) on decolonization.

15. It is reasonable to predict this despite the fact that miscoordination could happen with positive probability in a mixed strategy equilibrium when $d < \min\{K_A, K_B\}$.

16. Our account of this case follows that of Pennell (1982).

17. Our discussion of this case follows Tellez (2016); Kaplan (2008); Logan (2000); Acharya, Harding, and Harris (2020), and the references therein.

18. Prunier (1998, 225), for example, writes that "the Somali system of peacemaking, vital in a conflictual nomadic society, remained largely intact."

19. On elections in Somaliland, Kaplan (2008, 255) notes that foreign observers "were fairly unanimous in their views that [the elections] were, on the whole, the freest and most transparent democratic exercises ever staged in the Horn of Africa." For fuller accounts of Somaliland's institutions, see Tellez (2016) and Acharya, Harding, and Harris (2020).

20. Logan (2000, 20).

21. Kaplan (2008, 256).

22. Spears (2003, 96).

23. Somaliland's neighbors have more selfish interests in play. Ethiopia fears that the relatively successful new country could attract the allegiance of their own Somali minorities. Djibouti worries that Somaliland will divert economic activity away from them. The Somali government is concerned about additional separatist claims.

24. Our discussion of this case follows Pirenne (1932) and Lingelbach (1933).

25. Pirenne (1932, 4–5)

26. Lingelbach (1933, 59–60).

27. Quoted in Lingelbach (1933, 50–51).

28. All three of the initial candidates had been French, but were viewed as being unacceptable either to the powers or to the incumbent French regime (Pirenne 1932, 14–28).

29. The Treaty of XXIV Articles, or Treaty of London.

30. Acemoglu and Robinson (2006) and Boix (2003).

31. This is, for instance, the assumption of Meltzer and Richard (1981).

32. See Radio Free Europe. "Pakistan: New Government Announces Major Reforms in Tribal Areas." April 3, 2008. https://www.rferl.org/a/1079732.html.

33. See, e.g., Vengroff (1976) and Dincecco et al. (2019) for closely related arguments, particularly having to do with population density and tax collection.

34. It is also an unsettled one in our opinion, given the myriad of ways in which question framing affects survey responses. However, the findings of Milner and Kubota (2005) suggest that at least for developing countries, democratization makes them more open to free trade as the newly enfranchised working class demands greater trade openness.

35. Gilmour (1985, ch. 11).

36. McIntosh (2018).

37. Marketplace (2017).

38. Lacina (2017).

39. Reiter and Stam (2002).

40. These arguments are summarized by Huth and Allee (2002).

41. Quoted in Pervillé (2008, 18).

42. This view receives some support from recent work by Abramson and Carter (2016a, 2016b) and Carter and Goemans (2011), who show that old boundaries

frequently become focal points for territorial disputes; new boundaries are less stable than old ones; and periods of systemic instability see more disputes.

43. Owsiak (2012) and Schultz (2014) find that mutually agreed borders are more stable, while Libecap and Lueck (2011) find that rectangular systems of division lead to fewer disputes than those with more ambiguous systems.

Chapter 6

1. Fearon and Laitin (2003, 75).
2. Lee and Paine (2019*b*).
3. See Swaan (1988) for a closely related argument.
4. Laitin, Solé, and Kalyvas (1994).
5. Gellner (1983).
6. Anderson (2006). Note that where states do not promote nationalism, other political entrepreneurs could use similar techniques to promote ethnic identities; on this, see Lee (2019*a*) and Miguel (2004).
7. Weber (1976, 98–99). The same was true at Toulon, where true natives seldom mixed with [northerners], "whom they don't yet consider their compatriots." Unsurprisingly, peasants went to great lengths to avoid conscription, "since conscription was seen not as a duty owed to some larger community or nation, but as a heavy tribute exacted by an oppressive and alien state" (295–96).
8. Weber (1976, 111).
9. The relationship between these investments and the costs of governing have been clearly established, both theoretically and empirically. Lee and Zhang (2020), e.g., show that linguistic standardization encourages citizens to abide by the laws, by lowering transaction costs. Miguel (2004) shows that the effective nation-building effort by the Tanzanian government relative to neighboring Kenya had positive consequences for public goods provision. Perhaps most relevant, Konrad and Qari (2012) find that patriotism is correlated with tax compliance cross-nationally.
10. Toft (2005) and Paine (2016).
11. It is also worth noting that our model is pertinent to new questions regarding the relationship between nationalist attachments and the integration of the global economy, which undermines the power of states to exercise full monopoly control of their governance market. Mayda and Rodrik (2005) show that support for protectionist policies is greater among those who are most nationalist. Lan and Li (2015) similarly document a relationship between Chinese nationalism and city level economic openness to trade in China. Michaels and Zhi (2010) and Fisman, Hamao, and Wang (2014) show how negative political sentiments between the citizens of states have adverse effects on commerce between them.
12. See Whelpton (2005) for the Nepal case.
13. Arora (2006).
14. Gupta (1975, 790–95).

15. In 1987 under Operation Poomalai, the Indian Air Force air dropped supplies over Jaffna to aid the Tamil Tigers.
16. Lacina (2017).
17. Violations can be subtle as well, as when one side takes an interest in human rights abuses in another country by appealing to universalist moral principles (Krasner 1999).
18. Quoted in Anastasakis and Madden (2016, 2).
19. The early 19th-century meetings focused on establishing a balance of power through alliances (e.g., the Holy Alliance, the Quadruple and Quintuple Alliances, etc.). Subsequent meetings dealt with the issue of whether regime change within a state represented systemic threats and whether a state that has undergone regime change could still be part of its alliance—e.g., the Congresses of Tropau (1820); Laibach (1821); and Verona (1822). The late 19th-century meetings focused less on preventing regime change and more on preventing territorial disputes—for example, efforts to grant de facto sovereignty to Serbia, Bulgaria, and Romania at the Congress of Berlin (1878), and to resolve conflicting territorial claims in Africa at the Berlin Conference (1884–85), which established many African borders that persist to this day. See Schroeder (1994) and Elrod (1976) for more on the Concert of Europe.
20. We are of course not the first to discuss the coordinating role of international organizations. For prior seminal work, see Finnemore (1993) and Abbott and Snidal (1998).
21. Lee and Paine (2019a).
22. Algeria, e.g., was the subject of four UN General Assembly debates between 1957 and 1959, all of which were highly critical of French rule and helped convince the French that they could not remain in Algeria in the long term (Alistair 1978). UN resolution 1514 (1960) declared that "the process of liberation is irreversible, and . . . in order to avoid serious crises, an end must be put to colonialism and all practices of segregation and discrimination associated therewith" and that the UN "welcom[es] the emergence in recent years of a large number of dependent territories into freedom and independence." The UN Special Committee on Decolonization, established by the resolution, maintains a list of colonies and holds hearings on their status. When nations become independent, they join the UN, marking a symbolic and legal end to their dependent status.
23. Coggins (2014) gives foundations for the basic idea and explores it more fully.
24. The classic dominant firm model is Forchheimer and Kuhn (1983).
25. Kempton and Levine (1995).
26. Alhajji and Huettner (2000).

Chapter 7

1. OECD Economic Outlook (2007).
2. Broadberry and O'Rourke (2010).
3. O'Rourke and Williamson (1999) argue that the first wave of globalization in the 19th century was the result of a series of innovations in transport that reduced

the cost of international transport drastically, especially from 1870 to World War I. These included canal construction on the European continent and in the United States, steamships and steamship-associated technology, the railroad, and mechanical refrigeration.

4. A long line of theoretical work has argued that trade increases welfare, going back to Ricardo (1891), and elaborated in seminal contributions by Dornbusch, Fischer, and Samuelson (1977); Deardorff (1980); and Bhagwati (1993). Recent empirical work has also established that trade increases welfare, e.g., Broda and Weinstein (2006); Ossa (2015); and Melitz and Redding (2014).

5. Krasner (1976) has made a similar argument, suggesting that it was the most powerful, hegemonic states that found that the efficiency gains of trade openness outweigh its risks.

6. Bagwell and Staiger (1999) have also argued that the GATT/WTO created new practices of negotiation, reciprocity, and non-discrimination, which allowed large states to escape a terms-of-trade driven prisoner's dilemma.

7. See, e.g., Goldstein and Gulotty (2014) on how the US carefully geographically targeted its reciprocal reduction of tariffs to prevent the formation of a concentrated import-competing opposition to liberalization.

8. Autor, Dorn, and Hanson (2013) point to the uneven distributional impacts of trade, arguing that even if aggregate welfare increases, some people are made worse off. In addition, Trefler (2004) provides evidence that the North American Free Trade Agreement (NAFTA) resulted in a loss of manufacturing jobs in Canada, while Goldberg and Pavcnik (2004) provide evidence on how trade liberalization has benefited manufacturing in developing countries.

9. In fact, the unwillingness of Europe and the United States to stop protecting their agricultural sectors was one the main factors that ended the WTO Doha round of trade talks in failure after 14 years of negotiation. See, e.g., Hopewell (2020) and, for an an older argument, Ruggie (1982), who argues that Western states limited the GATT/WTO's potential negative effects on vulnerable sectors such as agriculture by encouraging intra-industry trade and discouraging inter-industry trade.

10. In the most rudimentary political economy models of democracy, such as our model in Chapter 5, the principal is traditionally thought of as being the median voter.

11. Grossman and Helpman (1992) capture the influence of powerful special interest groups on policy through a model of lobbying.

12. Rodrik (2018) makes a similar argument, criticizing the prevailing way in which trade agreements are crafted.

13. Even absent such regulation, businesses have incentives to relocate to areas with lower wages and high human capital, but these are still consequences of policies chosen by governments. For prior research on the importance of this kind of competition, see Dean, Lovely, and Wang (2005) and Copeland and Taylor (2004). For evidence that this competition influences domestic tax policy, see Basinger and Hallerberg (2004) and Abbas and Klemm (2013). In addition, Mosley and Uno (2007) show that trade openness (but not FDI flows) is associated with greater race-to-the-bottom policies in workers rights, while Greenhill, Mosley, and Prakash (2009)

argue that increasing trade openness serves to transmit better labor standards across borders. Mosley (2010) adjudicates between these perspectives by arguing that when multinational production is embodied in directly owned FDI, it increases labor rights, but when it is embodied in subcontracting, it decreases labor rights. Malesky and Mosley (2018) also argue for a "trading up" mechanism by which firms in developing countries upgrade their labor standards to be able to export to high-labor-standard countries, and governments who want these increased exports actively encourage such upgrading.

14. The OECD estimates that BEPS practices alone have cost countries up to $240 billion in lost taxes a year. Other economic studies such as Crivelli, De Mooij, and Keen (2015) suggest even higher losses, possibly more than double the OECD estimates. On top of this, a recent study by a team of economists (Guyton et al. 2021) found that even random auditing of wealthy individuals underestimated the degree of tax avoidance that is taking place, as random audits generally do not uncover two important strategies for tax evasion: evasion through foreign intermediaries and pass-through businesses. The study estimated that these strategies have enabled the top 1% of richest individuals to avoid paying $175 billion in taxes annually, which is just over one-third of taxes that are evaded.

15. See https://www.oecd.org/sdd/na/Irish-GDP-up-in-2015-OECD.pdf.

16. Li (2006) argues that countries often offer tax breaks to multi-national companies (MNCs) to compensate for weak rule of law and property rights. Jensen (2013) shows that democracy and electoral competition lead governments to enact higher taxes on MNCs, restricting the tax competition incentive. Baccini, Li, and Mirkina (2014) show that tax competition by Russian regions resulted in increased FDI inflows and Rixen (2011) argues that reforming the global corporate tax regime is difficult because of the challenge in getting states to make binding commitments.

17. Cerullo (2019).

18. Hainmueller and Hiscox (2006).

19. Bhagwati and MacMillan (2004) and Wolf (2004).

20. Buckman (2004).

21. Sanders (2017) and Warren (2019).

22. The IMF's recommendations include, as an example, digitizing tax collection and fiscal reporting standards in order to reduce tax avoidance and fraud (Kitsios, Jalles, and Verdier 2020). In addition, the IMF's Financial Action Task Force (FATF) has since 2000 identified countries that encourage money laundering by placing them on a pair of lists called the blacklist and greylist. The OECD, in addition, has identified countries that meet its own criteria of being tax havens and has put them on a "List of Uncooperative Tax Havens" until they reform their tax policies (OECD 2000). The OECD reports are available at https://www.oecd.org/tax/beps/ and a description of the IMF's recommendations to fight tax evasion created by firms taking advantage of competition in the international governance market is available at https://www.imf.org/en/Publications.

23. OECD (2021).

24. Of course, not all powerful people benefit from competition in governance. Many businesses for example benefit from protectionism—subsidies or favorable regulatory treatment by their home governments. The Japanese steel industry and French agriculture, for instance, have both benefited from high tariff and non-tariff barriers to entry and extensive government subsidies. For industries such as these, the managed features of the current international trade regime are important, enabling sectors with sufficient domestic political clout to win exceptions from broad movements towards free trade.

25. Richter, Samphantharak, and Timmons (2009) find that firms that lobby more receive favorable tax rates and Fairfield (2010) argue that Argentina and Chile have different corporate tax policies due to different levels of firm political power.

26. Though this figure is original, the link between destination GDP per capita (which is highly correlated with governance quality) and immigrant inflow is well documented; see, e.g., Mayda (2010). In addition, Docquier, Rapoport, and Salomone (2012); Bergh, Mirkina, and Nilsson (2015); Ariu, Docquier, and Squicciarini (2016), and Poprawe (2015) have all pointed out that destination quality of government and institutions is an independent pull-factor in the migration decision.

27. See La Porta et al. (1999); Besley and Persson (2009); Lee and Zhang (2017); and Garfias (2018), among many others on the variation in governance quality across states.

28. The extent to which an autocratic state will prevent its citizens from leaving depends on a host of factors. On the one hand, there are certainly examples of states where the government has gone to great lengths to restrict the ability of its citizens to move to another country. East Germany's system of walls, barbed wire, and minefields are well known. On the other hand, weak and non-functional states may find it costly or impossible to build the bureaucratic structures needed to keep their citizens in. In general, formal restrictions on citizen exit are now very rare: North Korea is the only country that we are aware of that requires an exit visa for all citizens. And, moreover, weak states may find that the benefits of emigration outweigh the costs. Not only can exit remove people who would otherwise attempt to overthrow the regime, but the remittances they send back might be valuable for the economy and easier for a primitive bureaucracy to tax than economic production within the country itself (Ahmed 2012).

29. Peters (2014) shows that firms are generally in favor of opening borders to immigrants, and Hainmueller and Hiscox (2010) show in a survey experiment that highly skilled immigration is favored most by highly educated respondents. (This finding is justified by a model in which highly skilled citizens might also favor the immigration of highly skilled immigrants if the economic complementaries created by their productivity outweigh any of the competition effects.) On the other hand, Scheve and Slaughter (2001) have found that lower-skilled workers are more likely to support immigration restrictions; see also Monras (2020) and Dustmann, Schönberg, and Stuhler (2017). In addition, Hainmueller and Hiscox (2007) show that high-skill Europeans support immigration more than lower-skill Europeans regardless of migrant skill level, suggesting that cultural values rather

than labor market competition may be an important factor in determining individual preferences over immigration policy.

30. Geddes and Scholten (2016).

31. Williams (2020) and Skaperdas (2001).

32. Fearon and Laitin (2003; 2004) and Bates (2008).

33. Eizenstat, Porter, and Weinstein (2005).

34. Lessing (2017).

35. Mantzikos (2011).

36. Walter (1997) and Gilligan and Sergenti (2008).

37. Fearon and Laitin (2004) propose a system of "neotrusteeship" along these lines.

38. Such asymmetries have existed in the past and have not led to problems when they are minor. For example, Germany has been the largest economy in Europe, and the leader of the European integration project, but does not have a permanent seat in the Security Council, while Britain and France do. The same argument could have been made about Japan in the 1980s, when the Japanese economy was already the second largest in the world and growing rapidly with no signs of slowing down. China, however, is a different story, with its economy already larger than that of the United States and continuing to grow faster.

39. See also Christensen (1999) and Mearsheimer (2005; 2001). More generally, international relations theory points to the commitment problem faced by rising powers vis-à-vis the hegemon, leading the hegemon to initiate a preventive war (Gilpin 1981). In addition to this, Debs and Monteiro (2014) emphasize an informational problem where the hegemon is uncertain that the rising power will become more powerful in the future. They argue that it is this uncertainty that generates war.

40. Shifrinson (2020) and Schweller (2018) argue that the US and China have both economic and geopolitical reasons to accommodate China's rise peacefully.

41. Manufacturing workers in developed countries were displaced mainly by robots and to some extent overseas workers. See Autor, Dorn, and Hanson (2013) and Trefler (2004) for some recent work on jobs lost to foreign competition and Acemoglu and Restrepo (2019) for a survey of recent work on jobs lost to automation.

42. Acemoglu et al. (2020), Frey and Osborne (2017), and Webb (2019) all look at the impact of artificial intelligence taking newer, high-skill jobs, many in the service sector. See also "The Quiet Ways Automation Is Remaking Service Work," *The Atlantic*, Jan. 11, 2019 (https://www.theatlantic.com/technology/archive/2019/01/automation-hotel-strike-ai-jobs/579433/).

43. See, e.g., Chatterjee (2005). In addition, Chaudhuri, Goldberg, and Jia (2006) estimate welfare impact of Trade-Related Aspects of Intellectual Property Rights (TRIPS) in India and report significantly negative welfare effects; see Duggan, Garthwaite, and Goyal (2016) for a counterpoint.

44. Matthews (2003).

45. "China theft of technology is biggest law enforcement threat to US, FBI says," *The Guardian*, Feb. 6, 2020.
46. See, e.g., Fajgelbaum et al. (2020).
47. Delaware, with just under 1 million people, is home to more than a million businesses and more than two-thirds of Fortune 500 companies. See Dyreng, Lindsey, and Thornock (2013) for more.
48. Osiander (2001).

Bibliography

Abbas, S. M. Ali and Alexander Klemm. 2013. "A partial race to the bottom: corporate tax developments in emerging and developing economies." *International Tax and Public Finance* 20(4):596–617.

Abbott, Kenneth W. and Duncan Snidal. 1998. "Why states act through formal international organizations." *Journal of Conflict Resolution* 42(1):3–32.

Abramson, Scott F. and David B. Carter. 2016a. "The historical origins of territorial disputes." *American Political Science Review* 110(4):675–98.

Abramson, Scott F. and David B. Carter. 2016b. "Systemic uncertainty and the emergence of border disputes." *American Political Science Review* 10(4):675–98.

Acemoglu, Daron, David Autor, Jonathon Hazell, and Pascual Restrepo. 2020. "AI and jobs: evidence from online vacancies." Technical report National Bureau of Economic Research.

Acemoglu, Daron and James A. Robinson. 2006. *Economic Origins of Dictatorship and Democracy*. Cambridge University Press.

Acemoglu, Daron and James A. Robinson. 2012. *Why Nations Fail: The Origins of Power, Prosperity, and Poverty*. Currency.

Acemoglu, Daron and Pascual Restrepo. 2019. "Automation and new tasks: how technology displaces and reinstates labor." *Journal of Economic Perspectives* 33(2): 3–30.

Acemoglu, Daron, Simon Johnson, and James A. Robinson. 2002. "Reversal of fortune: geography and institutions in the making of the modern world income distribution." *Quarterly Journal of Economics* 107:1231–94

Acemoglu, Daron, Simon Johnson, and James A. Robinson. 2005. "Institutions as a fundamental cause of long-run growth." *Handbook of Economic Growth* 1:385–472.

Acemoglu, Daron, Tristan Reed, and James A. Robinson. 2014. "Chiefs: economic development and elite control of civil society in Sierra Leone." *Journal of Political Economy* 122(2):319–68.

Acharya, Avidit and Alexander Lee. 2018. "Economic foundations of the territorial state system." *American Journal of Political Science* 62(4):954–66.

Acharya, Avidit, Robin Harding, and J. Andrew Harris. 2020. "Security in the absence of a state: traditional authority, livestock trading, and maritime piracy in northern Somalia." *Journal of Theoretical Politics* 32(4):497–537.

Agnew, John. 2009. *Globalization and Sovereignty*. Rowman & Littlefield.

Ahmed, Akbar S. 1980. *Pukhtun Economy and Society: Traditional Structure and Economic Development in a Tribal Society*. Routledge and Kegan Paul.

Ahmed, Faisal Z. 2012. "The perils of unearned foreign income: aid, remittances, and government survival." *American Political Science Review* 106(1):146–65.

Alesina, Alberto and Enrico Spolaore. 1997. "On the number and size of nations." *Quarterly Journal of Economics* 112(4):127–56.

Alhajji, A. Fayçal and David Huettner. 2000. "OPEC and other commodity cartels: a comparison." *Energy Policy* 28(15):1151–64.

Alistair, Horne. 1978. *A Savage War of Peace: Algeria 1954–1962*. Viking.

Allison, Graham. 2017. *Destined for War: Can America and China Escape Thucydides's Trap?* Houghton Mifflin Harcourt.

Anastasakis, Othon and David Madden. 2016. *Balkan Legacies of the Great War: The Past Is Never Dead*. Springer.

Anderson, Benedict. 2006. *Imagined Communities*. Verso Books.

Anderson, Matthew Smith. 2014. *The Rise of Modern Diplomacy 1450–1919*. Routledge.

Anderson, Perry. 1979. *Lineages of the Absolutist State*. Verso.

Ariu, Andrea, Frédéric Docquier, and Mara P. Squicciarini. 2016. "Governance quality and net migration flows." *Regional Science and Urban Economics* 60:238–48.

Arora, Vibha. 2006. "Roots and the route of secularism in Sikkim." *Economic and Political Weekly* 41:4063–71

Atzili, Boaz. 2007. "When good fences make bad neighbors: fixed borders, state weakness, and international conflict." *International Security* 31(3):139–73.

Autor, David, David Dorn, and Gordon Hanson. 2013. "The China syndrome: local labor market effects of import competition in the United States." *American Economic Review* 103(6):2121–68.

Baccini, Leonardo, Quan Li, and Irina Mirkina. 2014. "Corporate tax cuts and foreign direct investment." *Journal of Policy Analysis and Management* 33(4):977–1006.

Bagwell, Kyle and Robert W. Staiger. 1999. "An economic theory of GATT." *American Economic Review* 89(1):215–48.

Bain, Joseph. 1894. *Calendar of Border Papers*. Vol. I. Edinburgh: HM General Register House.

Bain, Joseph. 1898. *Calendar of the State Papers Relating to Scotland and Mary, Queen of Scots, 1547–1603: Preserved in the Public Record Office, the British Museum and Elsewhere in England*. HM Stationery Office.

Bairoch, Paul. 1988. *Cities and Economic Development: From the Dawn of History to the Present*. University of Chicago Press.

Barkin, J. Samuel. 2021. *The Sovereignty Cartel*. Cambridge University Press.

Basinger, Scott J. and Mark Hallerberg. 2004. "Remodeling the competition for capital: how domestic politics erases the race to the bottom." *American Political Science Review* 98(2):261–76.

Bates, Robert H. 2001. *Prosperity and Violence*. W. W. Norton.

Bates, Robert H. 2008. "State failure." *Annual Review of Political Science* 11:1–12.

Bayer, Reşat. 2006. "Diplomatic exchange dataset." http://correlatesofwar.org.

Behrens, Betty. 1963. "Nobles, privileges and taxes in France at the end of the *Ancien Regime*." *Economic History Review* 15(3):451–75.

Beik, William. 1985. *Absolutism and Society in Seventeenth-Century France*. Cambridge University Press.

Beniger, James. 2009. *The Control Revolution*. Harvard University Press.

Bergh, Andreas, Irina Mirkina, and Therese Nilsson. 2015. "Pushed by poverty or by institutions? Determinants of global migration flows." IFN Working Paper No. 1077.

Bertrand, Joseph. 1883. "Review of Cournot's Rechercher sur la theoric mathematique de la richesse?" *Journal des Savants* 499:508.

Besley, Timothy and Torsten Persson. 2009. "The origins of state capacity: property rights, taxation, and politics." *American Economic Review* 99(4):1218–44.

Bhagwati, Jagdish. 1993. "The case for free trade." *Scientific American* 269(5):42–49.

Bhagwati, Jagdish and Margaret MacMillan. 2004. *In Praise of Globalization*. Oxford University Press.

Bhavnani, Rikhil R. and Alexander Lee. 2018. "Local embeddedness and bureaucratic performance: evidence from India." *The Journal of Politics* 80(1):71–87.

Biggs, Michael. 1999. "Putting the state on the map." *Comparative Studies in Society and History* 41(2):374–405.

Bloch, Marc. 1939. *Feudal Society*. Routledge.

Boix, Carles. 2003. *Democracy and Redistribution*. Cambridge University Press.

Bonney, Richard. 1999. *The Rise of the Fiscal State in Europe c.1200–1815*. Oxford University Press.

Boone, Catherine. 2003. *Political Topographies of the African State: Territorial Authority and Institutional Choice*. Cambridge University Press.

Boscher, Paul Gerard. 1985. "Politics, administration and diplomacy: the Anglo-Scottish border 1550–1560." PhD thesis. Durham University.

Boulding, Kenneth Ewart. 1962. *Conflict and Defense: A General Theory*. University of Michigan Press.

Bradbury, Jim. 2015. *Philip Augustus*. Routledge.

Branch, Jordan. 2011. "Mapping the sovereign state." *International Organization* 65(1): 1–36.

Branch, Jordan. 2013. *The Cartographic State: Maps, Territory, and the Origins of Sovereignty*. Cambridge University Press.

Brewer, John. 1990. *The Sinews of Power*. Harvard University Press.

Broadberry, Stephen and Kevin H. O'Rourke. 2010. *The Cambridge Economic History of Modern Europe*. Vol. 2: *1870 to the Present*. Cambridge University Press.

Broda, Christian and David E. Weinstein. 2006. "Globalization and the gains from variety." *The Quarterly Journal of Economics* 121(2):541–85.

Buckman, Greg. 2004. *Globalization: Tame It or Scrap It?: Mapping the Alternatives of the Anti-globalization Movement*. Zed Books.

Bueno De Mesquita, Bruce. 2013. *Principles of International Politics*. Sage.

Bull, Hedley. 2012. *The Anarchical Society: A Study of Order in World Politics*. Macmillan.

Burton, John. 1877. *Register of the privy council of Scotland*. Vol. I. Edinburgh: HMRO.

Carr, Edward Hallett. 1946. *The Twenty Years' Crisis, 1919–1939: An Introduction to the Study of International Relations*. Macmillan.

Carter, David B. and Hein E. Goemans. 2011. "The making of the territorial order: new borders and the emergence of interstate conflict." *International Organization* 65(2):275–309.

Cerullo, Megan. 2019. "60 of America's biggest companies paid no federal income tax in 2018." https://www.cbsnews.com/news/2018-taxes-some-of-americas-biggest-companies-paid-little-to-no-federal-income-tax-last-year/.

Chapman, Tim. 2006. *The Congress of Vienna 1814–1815*. Routledge.

Chatterjee, Patralekha. 2005. "India's new patent laws may still hurt generic drug supplies." *The Lancet* 365(9468):1378.

Chaudhuri, Shubham, Pinelopi K. Goldberg, and Panle Jia. 2006. "Estimating the effects of global patent protection in pharmaceuticals: a case study of quinolones in India." *American Economic Review* 96(5):1477–1514.

Christensen, Thomas J. 1999. "China, the US-Japan alliance, and the security dilemma in East Asia." *International Security* 23(4):49–80.

Coggins, Bridget. 2014. *Power Politics and State Formation in the Twentieth Century: The Dynamics of Recognition*. Cambridge University Press.

Collins, James B. 1988. *Fiscal Limits of Absolutism: Direct Taxation in Early Seventeenth-Century France*. University of California Press.

Committee on Foreign Affairs. 2017. "US policy towards Pakistan." Technical report [United States House of Representatives].

Copeland, Brian R. and M. Scott Taylor. 2004. "Trade, growth, and the environment." *Journal of Economic Literature* 42(1):7–71.

Cox, Eugene L. 2015. *The Green Count of Savoy*. Princeton University Press.

Crivelli, Ernesto, Ruud A. De Mooij and Michael Keen. 2015. *Base Erosion, Profit Shifting and Developing Countries*. International Monetary Fund.

Davies, C. Collin. 1932. *The Problem of the North-West Frontier, 1890–1908*. Cambridge University Press.

Dawn (Staff Reporter). 2018. "Govt to restore tax exemptions enjoyed by Fata, Pata." *Dawn*, Sept. 27.

Dean, Judith M., Mary E. Lovely, and Hua Wang. 2005. *Are Foreign Investors Attracted to Weak Environmental Regulations? Evaluating the Evidence from China*. The World Bank.

Deardorff, Alan V. 1980. "The general validity of the law of comparative advantage." *The Journal of Political Economy* 88(5):941–57.

Debs, Alexandre and Nuno P. Monteiro. 2014. "Known unknowns: power shifts, uncertainty, and war." *International Organization* 68(1):1–31.

Deudney, Daniel and G. John Ikenberry. 1999. "The nature and sources of liberal international order." *Review of International Studies* 25(2):179–96.

Dincecco, Mark, James Fenske, Anil Menon, and Shivaji Mukherjee. 2019. "Pre-colonial warfare and long-run development in India." Centre for Competitive Advantage in the Global Economy (CAGE) Working Paper 426.

Dixon, Philip. 2016. "Mota, Aula et Turris: the manor-houses of the Anglo-Scottish border." In *Late Medieval Castles*. Boydell & Brewer, pp. 127–56.

Docquier, Frédéric, Hillel Rapoport, and Sara Salomone. 2012. "Remittances, migrants' education and immigration policy: theory and evidence from bilateral data." *Regional Science and Urban Economics* 42(5):817–28.

Dornbusch, Rudiger, Stanley Fischer, and Paul Anthony Samuelson. 1977. "Comparative advantage, trade, and payments in a Ricardian model with a continuum of goods." *The American Economic Review* 67(5):823–39.

Duggan, Mark, Craig Garthwaite, and Aparajita Goyal. 2016. "The market impacts of pharmaceutical product patents in developing countries: evidence from India." *American Economic Review* 106(1):99–135.

Dumont, Jean, Baron de Carlscroon, and Bernard Picart. 1726. *Corps Universel Diplomatique du Droit des Gens*. Brunel, Pierre.

Dustmann, Christian, Uta Schönberg, and Jan Stuhler. 2017. "Labor supply shocks, native wages, and the adjustment of local employment." *The Quarterly Journal of Economics* 132(1):435–83.

Dyreng, Scott D., Bradley P. Lindsey, and Jacob R. Thornock. 2013. "Exploring the role Delaware plays as a domestic tax haven." *Journal of Financial Economics* 108(3): 751–72.

Edelstein, David M. 2017. *Over the Horizon: Time, Uncertainty, and the Rise of Great Powers*. Cornell University Press.

Eizenstat, Stuart E., John Edward Porter, and Jeremy M. Weinstein. 2005. "Rebuilding weak states." *Foreign Affairs* 84:134–46.

Elden, Stuart. 2013. *The Birth of Territory*. University of Chicago Press.

Elliott, John Huxtable. 1984. *The Revolt of the Catalans*. Cambridge University Press.

Elliott, John Huxtable. 2002. *Imperial Spain 1469-1716*. Penguin.

Elrod, Richard B. 1976. "The concert of Europe: a fresh look at an international system." *World Politics* 28(2):159–74.

Fairbank, John King and Tatuan Chen. 1968. *The Chinese World Order: Traditional China's Foreign Relations*. Harvard University Press.

Fairfield, Tasha. 2010. "Business power and tax reform: taxing income and profits in Chile and Argentina." *Latin American Politics and Society* 52(2):37–71.

Fajgelbaum, Pablo D., Pinelopi K. Goldberg, Patrick J. Kennedy, and Amit K. Khandelwal. 2020. "The return to protectionism." *The Quarterly Journal of Economics* 135(1):1–55.

Farcau, Bruce W. 2000. *The Ten Cents War: Chile, Peru, and Bolivia in the War of the Pacific, 1879-1884*. Greenwood Publishing Group.

Farooqi, Naimur Rahman. 2004. "Diplomacy and diplomatic procedure under the Mughals." *The Medieval History Journal* 7(1):59–86.

Fearon, James D. 1995. "Rationalist explanations for war." *International Organization* 49(3):379–414.

Fearon, James D. and David D. Laitin. 2003. "Ethnicity, insurgency, and civil war." *American Political Science Review* 97(1):75–90.

Fearon, James D. and David D. Laitin. 2004. "Neotrusteeship and the problem of weak states." *International Security* 28(4):5–43.

Federal Trade Commission. 1948. *Report on International Electrical Equipment Cartels*. US Government Printing Office.

Fernandez, Raquel and Dani Rodrik. 1991. "Resistance to reform: status quo bias in the presence of individual-specific uncertainty." *The American Economic Review* 81: 1146–55.

Finnemore, Martha. 1993. "International organizations as teachers of norms: the United Nations Educational, Scientific, and Cutural Organization and science policy." *International Organization* 47(4):565–97.

Fisman, Raymond, Yasushi Hamao, and Yongxiang Wang. 2014. "Nationalism and economic exchange: evidence from shocks to Sino-Japanese relations." *The Review of Financial Studies* 27(9):2626–60.

Forchheimer, Karl and W. E. Kuhn. 1983. "Imperfect monopoly: some theoretical considerations." *Nebraska Journal of Economics and Business* 22(2):65–77.

Fraser, George. 2008. *The Steel Bonnets*. Skyhorse Publishing Inc.

Frey, Carl Benedikt and Michael A. Osborne. 2017. "The future of employment: how susceptible are jobs to computerisation?" *Technological Forecasting and Social Change* 114:254–80.

Friedman, David. 1977. "A theory of the size and shape of nations." *Journal of Political Economy* 85(1):59–77.

Gambetta, Diego. 1996. *The Sicilian Mafia: The Business of Private Protection*. Harvard University Press.

Garfias, Francisco. 2018. "Elite competition and state capacity development: theory and evidence from post-revolutionary Mexico." *American Political Science Review* 112(2):339–57.

Geddes, Andrew and Peter Scholten. 2016. *The Politics of Migration and Immigration in Europe*. Sage.

Gellner, Ernest. 1983. *Nations and Nationalism*. Cornell University Press.

Gennaioli, Nicola and Hans-Joachim Voth. 2015. "State capacity and military conflict." *The Review of Economic Studies* 82(4):1409–48.

Ghervas, Stella. 2015. "The long shadow of the Congress of Vienna: from international peace to domestic disorders." *Journal of Modern European History* 13(4):458–63.

Gilligan, Michael J. and Ernest J. Sergenti. 2008. "Do UN interventions cause peace? Using matching to improve causal inference." *Quarterly Journal of Political Science* 3(2): 89–122.

Gilmour, David. 1985. *The Transformation of Spain: From Franco to the Constitutional Monarchy*. Quartet Books Ltd.

Gilpin, Robert. 1981. *War and Change in World Politics*. Cambridge University Press.

Goemans, Hein E. and Kenneth A. Schultz. 2017. "The politics of territorial claims: a geospatial approach applied to Africa." *International Organization* 71(1):31–64.

Goldberg, Pinelopi K. and Nina Pavcnik. 2004. "Trade, inequality, and poverty: what do we know? Evidence from recent trade liberalization episodes in developing countries." In *Globalization, Poverty, and Inequality*. Brookings Institution, pp. 223–69.

Goldstein, Judith and Robert Gulotty. 2014. "America and trade liberalization: the limits of institutional reform." *International Organization* 68(2):263–95.

Gommans, Jos J. L. 2002. *Mughal Warfare: Indian Frontiers and Highroads to Empire 1500 1700*. Routledge.

Goodare, Julian. 1989. "Parliamentary taxation in Scotland, 1560–1603." *The Scottish Historical Review* 68(185):23–52.

Greenhill, Brian, Layna Mosley, and Aseem Prakash. 2009. "Trade-based diffusion of labor rights: a panel study, 1986–2002." *American Political Science Review* 103(4): 669–90.

Greif, Avner. 1993. "Contract enforceability and economic institutions in early trade." *American Economic Review* 83(3): 525–48.

Gross, Leo. 1948. "The Peace of Westphalia, 1648–1948." *American Journal of International Law* 42(1):20–41.

Grossman, Gene M. and Elhanan Helpman. 1992. "Protection for sale." NBER Working Paper No. w4149.

Gupta, Ranjan. 1975. "Sikkim: the merger with India." *Asian Survey* 15(9):786–98.

Guyton, John, Patrick Langetieg, Daniel Reck, Max Risch, and Gabriel Zucman. 2021. "Tax evasion at the top of the income distribution: theory and evidence." Technical report National Bureau of Economic Research.

Hadley, Erik J. 2006. "Privilege and reciprocity in early modern Belgium: provincial elites, state power and the Franco-Belgian frontier, 1667–1794." PhD thesis. State University of New York at Buffalo.

Hainmueller, Jens and Michael J. Hiscox. 2006. "Learning to love globalization: education and individual attitudes toward international trade." *International Organization* 60(2):469–98.

Hainmueller, Jens and Michael J. Hiscox. 2007. "Educated preferences: explaining attitudes toward immigration in Europe." *International Organization* 61(2):399–442.

Hainmueller, Jens and Michael J. Hiscox. 2010. "Attitudes toward highly skilled and low-skilled immigration: evidence from a survey experiment." *American Political Science Review* 104(1):61–84.

Hamilton, Angus. 1906. *Afghanistan*. Heinemann.

Herbst, Jeffrey. 2014. *States and Power in Africa*. Princeton University Press.

Hickey, Daniel. 2019. *The Coming of French Absolutism*. University of Toronto Press.

Hobbes, Thomas. 1651. *Leviathan*. Vol. 21. Yale University Press.

Hobson, John M. and Jason C. Sharman. 2005. "The enduring place of hierarchy in world politics: tracing the social logics of hierarchy and political change." *European Journal of International Relations* 11(1):63–98.

Holford, Matthew and Keith Stringer. 2010. *Border Liberties and Loyalties*. Edinburgh University Press.

Holzgrefe, J. L. 1989. "The origins of modern international relations theory." *Review of International Studies* 15(1):11–26.

Hopewell, Kristen. 2020. *Breaking the WTO*. Stanford University Press.

Hopkins, Benjamin D. 2015. "The frontier crimes regulation and frontier governmentality." *The Journal of Asian Studies* 74(2):369–89.

House of Commons. 1901. *Parliamentary Papers, House of Commons*. Vol. 49. HM Stationery Office.

Hubbard, Charles M. 2000. *The Burden of Confederate Diplomacy*. University of Tennessee Press.

Huth, Paul K. 2009. *Standing your Ground: Territorial Disputes and International Conflict*. University of Michigan Press.

Huth, Paul K. and Todd L. Allee. 2002. *The Democratic Peace and Territorial Conflict in the Twentieth Century*. Vol. 82. Cambridge University Press.

Iyer, Lakshmi. 2010. "Direct versus indirect colonial rule in India: long-term consequences." *The Review of Economics and Statistics* 92(4):693–713.

Jacobs, James B., Coleen Friel, and Robert Raddick. 2001. *Gotham Unbound: How New York City Was Liberated from the Grip of Organized Crime*. NYU Press.

Jansen, Marius B. 2002. *The Making of Modern Japan*. Harvard University Press.

Jensen, Nathan M. 2013. "Domestic institutions and the taxing of multinational corporations." *International Studies Quarterly* 57(3):440–48.

Jervis, Robert. 1978. "Cooperation under the security dilemma." *World Politics* 30(2): 167–214.

Jervis, W. Henley. 1872. *A History of the Church of France, from the Concordat of Bologna, AD 1516, to the Revolution: (The Gallican Church). With an introduction. With portraits*. Vol. 1. J. Murraÿ.

Kadercan, Burak. 2015. "Triangulating territory." *International Theory* 7(1):125–61.

Kang, David C. 2010. *East Asia before the West: Five Centuries of Trade and Tribute*. Columbia University Press.

Kaplan, Seth. 2008. "The remarkable story of Somaliland." *Journal of Democracy* 19(3):143–57.

Kayaoglu, Turan. 2010. *Legal Imperialism: Sovereignty and Extraterritoriality in Japan, the Ottoman Empire, and China*. Cambridge University Press.

Kempton, Daniel R. and Richard M. Levine. 1995. "Soviet and Russian relations with foreign corporations: the case of gold and diamonds." *Slavic Review* 54(1):80–110.

Kennedy, Paul. 2010. *The Rise and Fall of the Great Powers*. Vintage.

Keohane, Robert. 2005. *After Hegemony*. Princeton University Press.

Khan, Javed. 2017. "KP govt asked to close 600 arms manufacturing factories." *Pakistan Times*. March 31.

King, Andy and Claire Etty. 2015. *England and Scotland, 1286–1603*. Palgrave Macmillan.

King, David. 2008. *Vienna, 1814: How the Conquerors of Napoleon Made Love, War, and Peace at the Congress of Vienna*. Broadway Books.

Kiser, Edgar and April Linton. 2002. "The hinges of history: state-making and revolt in early modern France." *American Sociological Review* 67(6):889–910

Kitsios, Emmanouil, João Tovar Jalles, and Genevieve Verdier. 2020. "Tax evasion from cross-border fraud: does digitalization make a difference?" Nov. 1. IMF Research Paper Series.

Kocs, Stephen A. 1995. "Territorial disputes and interstate war, 1945–1987." *The Journal of Politics* 57(1):159–75.

Konrad, Kai A. and Salmai Qari. 2012. "The last refuge of a scoundrel? Patriotism and tax compliance." *Economica* 79(315):516–33.

Konrad, Kai and Stergios Skaperdas. 2012. "The market for protection and the origin of the state." *Economic Theory* 50(2):417–43.

Krasner, Stephen. 1993. "Westphalia and all that." In *Ideas and Foreign Policy*. Ithaca: Cornell University Press pp. 235–64.

Krasner, Stephen. 1999. *Sovereignty*. Princeton University Press.

Krasner, Stephen D. 1976. "State power and the structure of international trade." *World Politics* 28(3):317–47.

Krugman, Paul. 1979. "A model of innovation, technology transfer, and the world distribution of income." *Journal of Political Economy* 87(2):253–66.

La Porta, Rafael, Florencio Lopez-de Silanes, Andrei Shleifer, and Robert Vishny. 1999. "The quality of government." *The Journal of Law, Economics, and Organization* 15(1):222–79.

Lacina, Bethany. 2017. *Rival Claims: Ethnic Violence and Territorial Autonomy under Indian Federalism*. University of Michigan Press.

Laitin, David, Carlota Solé, and Stathis Kalyvas. 1994. "Language and the construction of states." *Politics & Society* 22(1):5–29.

Lamb, Hubert Horace. 2013. *Climate: Present, Past and Future*. Vol. 1. Routledge.

Lan, Xiaohuan and Ben G. Li. 2015. "The economics of nationalism." *American Economic Journal: Economic Policy* 7(2):294–325.

Lane, Frederick C. 1979. *Profits from Power*. SUNY Press.

Lapsley, Gaillard Thomas. 1900. *The County Palatine of Durham: A Study in Constitutional History*. Vol. 8. Longmans, Green and Company.

Larkins, Jeremy. 2009. *From Hierarchy to Anarchy*. Springer.

Leake, Elisabeth. 2016. *The Defiant Border: The Afghan-Pakistan Borderlands in the Era of Decolonization, 1936–65*. Cambridge University Press.

Lee, Alexander. 2017. "Redistributive colonialism: caste, conflict and development in India." *Politics & Society* 45(2):173–224.

Lee, Alexander. 2019a. *From Hierarchy to Ethnicity: The Politics of Caste in Twentieth-Century India*. Cambridge University Press.

Lee, Alexander. 2019b. "Land, state capacity, and colonialism: evidence from India." *Comparative Political Studies* 52(3):412–44.

Lee, Alexander and Jack Paine. 2019a. *Colonialism and Democracy: The Origins of Pluralism and Authoritarianism in the Non-European World*. Unpublished MS.

Lee, Alexander and Jack Paine. 2019b. "The great revenue divergence." Working Paper.

Lee, Alexander and Jack Paine. 2019c. "What were the consequences of decolonization?" *International Studies Quarterly* 63(2):406–16.

Lee, Alexander and Kenneth Schultz. 2012. "Comparing British and French colonial legacies." *Quarterly Journal of Political Science* 7(4):365–410.

Lee, Melissa M. and Nan Zhang. 2017. "Legibility and the informational foundations of state capacity." *The Journal of Politics* 79(1):118–32.

Lee, Melissa M. and Nan Zhang. 2020. "Literacy and State-Society Interactions in Nineteenth Century France." *American Journal of Political Science* 64(4):1001–16.

Lee, Stephen J. 2005. *Aspects of European History 1494–1789*. Routledge.

Lessing, Benjamin. 2017. *Making Peace in Drug Wars: Crackdowns and Cartels in Latin America*. Cambridge University Press.

Levi, Margaret. 1989. *Of Rule and Revenue*. University of California Press.

Levy, Jack S. 2015. *War in the Modern Great Power System: 1495–1975*. University Press of Kentucky.

Li, Quan. 2006. "Democracy, autocracy, and tax incentives to foreign direct investors: a cross-national analysis." *The Journal of Politics* 68(1):62–74.

Libecap, Gary D. and Dean Lueck. 2011. "The demarcation of land and the role of coordinating property institutions." *Journal of Political Economy* 119(3):426–67.

Lindley, Mark F. 1926. *The Acquisition and Government of Backward Territory in International Law*. Longmans, Green, and Company.

Lingelbach, William E. 1933. "Belgian neutrality: its origin and interpretation." *The American Historical Review* 39(1):48–72.

Logan, Carolyn. 2000. "Overcoming the state-society disconnect in the former Somalia: putting Somali political and economic resources at the root of reconstruction." USAID/REDSO.

Lombard, Louisa. 2020. *Hunting Game: Raiding Politics in the Central African Republic*. Cambridge University Press.

Lopez, Robert Sabatino. 1976. *The Commercial Revolution of the Middle Ages, 950–1350*. Cambridge University Press.

Lynch, John. 1989. *Bourbon Spain, 1700–1808*. Blackwell.

MacKenzie, W. 1951. "The Debateable Land." *Scottish Historical Review* 30(110):109–25.

Maddison, Angus. 2007. *The World Economy*. Academic Foundation.

Malesky, Edmund J. and Layna Mosley. 2018. "Chains of love? Global production and the firm-level diffusion of labor standards." *American Journal of Political Science* 62(3):712–28.

Mallet, Jean-Roland. 1789. *Comptes rendus de l'administration des finances du royaume de France*. chez Buisson.

Mamdani, Mahmood. 1996. *Citizen and Subject: Contemporary Africa and the Legacy of Late Colonialism*. Princeton University Press.

Mantzikos, Ioannis. 2011. "Somalia and Yemen: the links between terrorism and state failure." *Digest of Middle East Studies* 20(2):242–60.

Marketplace. 2017. "The big reason Catalonia wants to secede may be economic: it's one of the richest regions in Spain." *Marketplace* Sept. 29.

Markey, Daniel. 2007. "A false choice in Pakistan." *Foreign Affairs* July/Aug., pp. 85–102.

Marshall, Monty G., Keith Jaggers, and Ted Robert Gurr. 2002. "Polity IV dataset." Computer file.

Matthews, Duncan. 2003. *Globalising Intellectual Property Rights: The TRIPS Agreement*. Routledge.

Mattingly, Garrett. 1955. *Renaissance Diplomacy*. Courier Corporation.

Maxwell, Herbert. 1896. *A History of Dumfries and Galloway*. Blackwood.

Maxwell, Herbert. 1912. "Chronicle of Lanercost." *Scottish Historical Review* 9: 159–71.

Mayda, Anna Maria. 2010. "International migration: a panel data analysis of the determinants of bilateral flows." *Journal of Population Economics* 23(4):1249–74.

Mayda, Anna Maria and Dani Rodrik. 2005. "Why are some people (and countries) more protectionist than others?" *European Economic Review* 49(6):1393–1430.

McIntosh, Matthew A. 2018. "A fiscal history of Catalonia from 1714 to the present." https://brewminate.com/a-fiscal-history-of-catalonia-from-1714-to-the-present/.

McNamee, Lachlan and Anna Zhang. 2019. "Demographic engineering and international conflict: evidence from China and the Former USSR." *International Organization* 73(2):291–327.

McNeill, William. 1989. *The Age of Gunpowder Empires, 1450–1800*. Amer Historical Assn.

Mearsheimer, John J. 2001. *The Tragedy of Great Power Politics*. W. W. Norton & Company.

Mearsheimer, John J. 2005. "The rise of China will not be peaceful at all." *The New Republic*, Aug. 9, p. 4.

Melitz, Marc J. and Stephen J. Redding. 2014. "Missing gains from trade?" *American Economic Review* 104(5):317–21.

Meltzer, Allan H. and Scott F. Richard. 1981. "A rational theory of the size of government." *Journal of Political Economy* 89(5):914–27.

Michaels, Guy and Xiaojia Zhi. 2010. "Freedom fries." *American Economic Journal: Applied Economics* 2(3):256–81.

Michalopoulos, Stelios and Elias Papaioannou. 2016. "The long-run effects of the scramble for Africa." *American Economic Review* 106(7):1802–48.

Middlebush, Frederick Arnold. 1933. "Non-recognition as a sanction of international law." In *Proceedings of the American Society of International Law at its Annual Meeting (1921–1969)*. Vol. 27, pp. 40–55.

Migdal, Joel S. 1988. *Strong Societies and Weak States: State-Society Relations and State Capabilities in the Third World*. Princeton University Press.

Miguel, Edward. 2004. "Tribe or nation? Nation building and public goods in Kenya versus Tanzania." *World Politics* 56(3):327–62.

Milgrom, Paul, Douglass North, and Barry Weingast. 1990. "The role of institutions in the revival of trade." *Economics & Politics* 2(1):1–23.

Milner, Helen V. and Keiko Kubota. 2005. "Why the move to free trade? Democracy and trade policy in the developing countries." *International Organization* 59(1): 107–43.

Monras, Joan. 2020. "Immigration and wage dynamics: evidence from the Mexican peso crisis." *Journal of Political Economy* 128(8):3017–89.

Mosley, Layna. 2010. *Labor Rights and Multinational Production*. Cambridge University Press.

Mosley, Layna and Saika Uno. 2007. "Racing to the bottom or climbing to the top? Economic globalization and collective labor rights." *Comparative Political Studies* 40(8):923–48.

Nelson, Ronald Roy. 1969. *The Home Office, 1782–1801*. Duke University Press.

Neville, Cynthia. 1988. "Border law in late medieval england." *Journal of Legal History* 9(3):335–56.

Nexon, Daniel. 2009. *The Struggle for Power in Early Modern Europe*. Princeton University Press.

Nicolson, Joseph, Richard Burn, William Nicolson, Daniel Scott, and Henry Hornyold-Strickland. 1777. *The History and Antiquities of the Counties of Westmorland and Cumberland*. Vol. 2. Printed for W. Strahan.

North, Douglass C. 1990. "Institutions, institutional change and economic performance." Cambridge University Press.

North, Douglass Cecil. 1981. *Structure and Change in Economic History*. W. W. Norton.

OECD. 2000. "Towards global tax co-operation: progress in identifying and eliminating harmful tax practices." Progress report.

OECD. 2021. "Statement on a two-pillar solution to address the tax challenges arising from the digitalisation of the economy." Oct. 8.

Olson, Mancur. 1993. "Dictatorship, democracy, and development." *American Political Science Review* 87(3):567–76.

Olson, Mancur. 2000. *Power and Prosperity: Outgrowing Communist and Capitalist Dictatorships*. HeinOnline.

Oman, Charles. 1968. *The Art of War in the Middle Ages, AD 378–1515*. Cornell University Press.

Omrani, Bijan. 2009. "The Durand line: history and problems of the Afghan-Pakistan border." *Asian Affairs* 40(2):177–95.

O'Rourke, Kevin H. and Jeffrey G. Williamson. 1999. *Globalization and History: The Evolution of a Nineteenth-Century Atlantic Economy*. MIT Press.

Osiander, Andreas. 1994. *The States System of Europe, 1640–1990*. Clarendon Press.

Osiander, Andreas. 2001. "Sovereignty, international relations, and the Westphalian myth." *International Organization* 55(2):251–87.

Ossa, Ralph. 2015. "Why trade matters after all." *Journal of International Economics* 97(2):266–77.

O'Sullivan, Dan. 2016. *The Reluctant Ambassador*. Amberley Publishing.

Outlook, OECD Economic. 2007. "OECD economic outlook." OECD, vol. 2007(1).

Owsiak, Andrew P. 2012. "Signing up for peace: international boundary agreements, democracy, and militarized interstate conflict." *International Studies Quarterly* 56(1):51–66.

Page, Scott E. 2006. "Path dependence." *Quarterly Journal of Political Science* 1(1):87–115.

Paine, Jack. 2016. "Rethinking the conflict "resource curse": how oil wealth prevents center-seeking civil wars." *International Organization* 70(4):727–61.

Parker, David. 1986. *The Making of French Absolutism*. Arnold.

Parker, Geoffrey. 1996. *The Military Revolution*. Cambridge University Press.

Parker, Geoffrey. 2000. *The Grand Strategy of Philip II*. Yale University Press.

Pennell, C. R. 1982. "Ideology and practical politics: a case study of the Rif War in Morocco, 1921–1926." *International Journal of Middle East Studies* 14(1):19–33.

Perdue, Peter C. 2010. "Boundaries and trade in the early modern world: negotiations at Nerchinsk and Beijing." *Eighteenth-Century Studies* 43(3): 341–56.

Pervillé, Guy. 2008. "De Gaulle et le problème algérien en 1958." *Outre-Mers. Revue d'histoire* 95(358):15–27.

Peters, Margaret E. 2014. "Trade, foreign direct investment, and immigration policy making in the United States." *International Organization* 68(4):811–44.

Peters, Margaret E. 2017. *Trading Barriers*. Princeton University Press.

Phillips, Andrew. 2010. *War, Religion and Empire: The Transformation of International Orders*. Cambridge University Press.

Philpott, Daniel. 2001. *Revolutions in Sovereignty*. Princeton University Press.

Pickles, John. 2004. *A History of Spaces: Cartographic Reason, Mapping, and the Geo-Coded World*. Routledge.

Pierson, Paul. 2000. "Increasing returns, path dependence, and the study of politics." *American Political Science Review* 94(2):251–67.

Piketty, Thomas. 2018. *Capital in the Twenty-First Century*. Harvard University Press.

Pirenne, Henri. 1932. *Histoire de Belgique*. Vol. VI. Maurice Lamertin.

Poprawe, Marie. 2015. "On the relationship between corruption and migration: empirical evidence from a gravity model of migration." *Public Choice* 163(3):337–54.

Powell, Robert. 2018. "Endogenous intractability: why some persistent problems persist." Working paper.

Prunier, Gérard. 1998. "Somaliland goes it alone." *Current History* 97(619):225–28.

Rae, Thomas I. 1966. *The Administration of the Scottish Frontier, 1513–1603*. Edinburgh University Press.

Rashid, Ahmed. 2010. *Taliban*. Yale University Press.

Ravina, Mark. 2016. "Japan in the Chinese tribute system." In *Sea Rovers, Silver, and Samurai: Maritime East Asia in Global History, 1550–1700*, ed. Tonio Andrade, Xing Hang, Anand A Yang, and Kieko Matteson. University of Hawai'i Press.

Reeves, Jesse S. 1944. "International Boundaries." *American Journal of International Literature* 38:533.

Reiter, Dan and Allan C. Stam. 2002. *Democracies at War*. Princeton University Press.

Rendall, Matthew. 2006. "Defensive realism and the Concert of Europe." *Review of International Studies* 32(3):523–40.

Ricardo, David. 1891. *Principles of Political Economy and Taxation*. G. Bell and sons.

Richter, Brian Kelleher, Krislert Samphantharak, and Jeffrey F. Timmons. 2009. "Lobbying and taxes." *American Journal of Political Science* 53(4):893–909.

Rixen, Thomas. 2011. "From double tax avoidance to tax competition: explaining the institutional trajectory of international tax governance." *Review of International Political Economy* 18(2):197–227.

Robb, Graham. 2018. *The Debatable Land: The Lost World between Scotland and England*. Picador.

Rodrik, Dani. 1997. *Has Globalization Gone Too Far?* The Institute for International Economics.

Rodrik, Dani. 2018. "What do trade agreements really do?" *Journal of Economic Perspectives* 32(2):73–90.

Rodrik, Dani, Arvind Subramanian, and Francesco Trebbi. 2004. "Institutions rule: the primacy of institutions over geography and integration in economic development." *Journal of Economic Growth* 9(2):131–65.

Rokkan, Stein. 1975. "Dimensions of state formation and nation building." In *The Formation of National States in Western Europe*. Princeton University Press, pp. 562–600.

Roosen, William James. 1976. *Age of Louis XIV: The Rise of Modern Diplomacy*. Routledge.

Rostow, Walt Whitman. 1959. "The stages of economic growth." *Economic History Review* 12(1):1–16.

Rousseau, Jean-Jacques. 1762. *The Social Contract: And, the First and Second Discourses*. Yale University Press.

Ruggie, John. 1993. "Territoriality and beyond." *International Organization* 47(1):139–74.

Ruggie, John Gerard. 1982. "International regimes, transactions, and change: embedded liberalism in the postwar economic order." *International Organization* 36(2): 379–415.

Sammon, Robert Lane. 2008. "Mullas and maliks: understanding the roots of conflict in Pakistan's federally administrated tribal areas." Master's thesis University of Pennsylvania.

Sanders, Bernie. 2017. "Sanders and colleagues call on Trump to crack down on offshoring." https://www.sanders.senate.gov/newsroom/press-releases/sanders-and-colleagues-call-on-trump-to-crack-down-on-offshoring.

Sater, William F. 2007. *Andean Tragedy: Fighting the War of the Pacific, 1879–1884*. University of Nebraska Press.

Schelling, Thomas C. 1960. *The Strategy of Conflict*. Harvard University Press.

Scheve, Kenneth and David Stasavage. 2010. "The conscription of wealth: mass warfare and the demand for progressive taxation." *International Organization* 64(4):529–61.

Scheve, Kenneth F and Matthew J. Slaughter. 2001. "Labor market competition and individual preferences over immigration policy." *Review of Economics and Statistics* 83(1):133–45.

Schlude, Jason Michael. 2009. "Rome, Parthia, and empire: the first century of Roman-Parthian relations." PhD thesis. University of California, Berkeley.

Schroeder, Paul W. 1994. *The Transformation of European Politics, 1763–1848*. Oxford University Press.

Schultz, Kenneth. 2015. "Mapping interstate territorial conflict." *Journal of Conflict Resolution* 61:1565–90.

Schultz, Kenneth A. 2014. "What's in a claim? De jure versus de facto borders in interstate territorial disputes." *Journal of Conflict Resolution* 58(6):1059–84.

Schultz, Kenneth and H. E. Goemans. 2014. "Aims, claims and the bargaining model of war." Stanford University, mimeo. 56(1):17–31.

Schweller, Randall. 2018. "Opposite but compatible nationalisms: a neoclassical realist approach to the future of US–China relations." *The Chinese Journal of International Politics* 11(1):23–48.

Scott, James. 2014. *The Art of Not Being Governed*. Yale University Press.

Scott, James C. 1998. *Seeing like a State: How Certain Schemes to Improve the Human Condition Have Failed*. Yale University Press.

Shifrinson, Joshua. 2020. "The rise of China, balance of power theory and US national security: reasons for optimism?" *Journal of Strategic Studies* 43(2):175–216.

Siddique, Abubakar. 2014. *The Pashtun Question: The Unresolved Key to the Future of Pakistan and Afghanistan*. Hurst & Company Ltd.

Skaperdas, Stergios. 2001. "The political economy of organized crime: providing protection when the state does not." *Economics of Governance* 2(3):173–202.

Social Security Administration. 2015. "Social security programs throughout the world: the Americas, 2015." https://www.ssa.gov/policy/docs/progdesc/ssptw/2014-2015/americas/mexico.html.

Spears, Ian. 2003. "Somaliland and Africa's territorial order." *Review of African Political Economy* 30(95):89–98.

Spence, Richard T. 1977. "The pacification of the Cumberland borders, 1593–1628." *Northern History* 13(1):59–160.

Spruyt, Hendrik. 1996. *The Sovereign State and its Competitors*. Princeton University Press.

Stiglitz, Joseph. 2002. *Globalization and its Discontents*. W. W. Norton.

Storrs, Christopher. 2006. *The Resilience of the Spanish Monarchy, 1665–1700*. Oxford University Press.

Strayer, Joseph R. 1970. *On the Medieval Origins of the Modern State*. Princeton University Press.

Sumption, Jonathan. 2009. *The Hundred Years War, Volumes I–III*. Vol. 3. University of Pennsylvania Press.

Swaan, Abram de. 1988. *In Care of the State: Health Care, Education and Welfare in Europe and the USA in the Modern Era*. Oxford University Press.

Tellez, Jorge Campos. 2016. "Collecting taxes in Somaliland: how bureaucrats create fiscal revenue in an unrecognised state." DIIS working paper.

Tilly, Charles. 1985. "War making and state making as organized crime." In *Bringing the State Back In*, ed. Peter Evans. Cambridge University Press, pp. 169–85.

Toft, Monica Duffy. 2005. *The Geography of Ethnic Violence: Identity, Interests, and the Indivisibility of Territory*. Princeton University Press.

Tough, Douglas Leonard Walton. 1928. *The Last Years of a Frontier: A History of the Borders during the Reign of Elizabeth*. Clarendon Press.

Trefler, Daniel. 2004. "The long and short of the Canada-US free trade agreement." *American Economic Review* 94(4):870–95.

Tripodi, Christian. 2016. *Edge of Empire: The British Political Officer and Tribal Administration on the North-West Frontier 1877–1947*. Routledge.

United Nations Office on Drugs and Crime. 2008. "Illicit drug trends in Pakistan." Technical report United Nations.

Upton, Anthony F. 1998. *Charles XI and Swedish Absolutism, 1660–1697*. Cambridge University Press.

Vaughan, Richard. 1965. *The Valois Dukes of Burgundy*. Lane, Allen.

Vengroff, Richard. 1976. "Population density and state formation in Africa." *African Studies Review* 19(1):67–74.

Vries, Oebele. 2015. "Frisonica libertas: Frisian freedom as an instance of medieval liberty." *Journal of Medieval History* 41:1–20.

Wagner, R. Harrison. 2010. *War and the State: The Theory of International Politics*. University of Michigan Press.

Waldron, Arthur. 1990. *The Great Wall of China: From History to Myth*. Cambridge University Press.

Wallerstein, Immanuel. 1984. *The Politics of the World-Economy: The States, the Movements and the Civilizations*. Cambridge University Press.

Walter, Barbara F. 1997. "The critical barrier to civil war settlement." *International Organization* 51(3):335–64.

Warren, Elizabeth. 2019. "A new approach to trade." Medium.

Watts, Sheldon J. 1971. "Tenant-right in early seventeenth-century Northumberland." *Northern History* 6(1):64–87.

Watts, Sheldon J. and Susan J. Watts. 1975. *From Border to Middle Shire: Northumberland, 1586–1625*. Leicester University Press.

Webb, Michael. 2019. "The impact of artificial intelligence on the labor market." Available at SSRN 3482150.

Weber, Eugen. 1976. *Peasants into Frenchmen*. Stanford University Press.

Whelpton, John. 2005. *A History of Nepal*. Cambridge University Press.

Williams, Phil. 2020. "Here be dragons: dangerous spaces and international security." In *Ungoverned Spaces*. Stanford University Press, pp. 34–54.

Winichakul, Thongchai. 1997. *Siam Mapped: A History of the Geo-body of a Nation*. University of Hawaii Press.

Wolf, Martin. 2004. *Why Globalization Works*. Vol. 3. Yale University Press.

Young, Crawford. 1994. *The African Colonial State in Comparative Perspective*. Yale University Press.

Zacher, Mark W. 2001. "The territorial integrity norm: international boundaries and the use of force." *International Organization* 55(2):215–50.

Zhang, Anna. 2021. "Go west young Han: internal migration as a strategy of counterinsurgency." Stanford University Press.

Index

Note: Italicized page numbers indicate material in photographs or illustrations.